PRAISE FOR *THE COMPLEAT MONARCHIST*

"Enhanced by Coulombe's literary, philosophical, and theological scholarship, *The Compleat Monarchist* is a powerful book that will persuade any rational person of the merits of monarchy. Its author has earned his reputation as a voice of sanity amid the madding crowd."

—**MARK DOOLEY**, author of *Moral Matters: A Philosophy of Homecoming*

"Charles Coulombe is one of the most erudite and eloquent of Catholic writers. His deep understanding of history, theology, and political philosophy and his vivid literary imagination are woven together in this thoughtful and thought-provoking defence of monarchy. It might be said, were the pun to be permitted, that it is his crowning achievement!"

—**JOSEPH SHAW**, editor of *A Defence of Monarchy*

"Why would monarchy—a civilisational principle that emerges directly out of nature and which has been consecrated by supernatural religion for millennia—need an American historian to explain it to us? Following centuries of violent revolution and civilisational repudiation in what has been a succession of egalitarian, democratic, and utopian experiments, most of us are so uprooted from our own tradition that we stand in desperate need of an authoritative guide. We are all in Coulombe's debt as we seek to find our way home."

—**SEBASTIAN MORELLO**, author of *Conservatism and Grace*

"'For every monarchy overthrown, the sky becomes less brilliant because it loses a star.' In a world that appears to be increasingly suffering from an acute case of cultural drought and crisis of identity, time and time again we see that the further the West strays from its Christian foundations, including sacral monarchy, the more severe this cultural drought and amnesia becomes. In *The Compleat Monarchist*, Charles Coulombe truly outdoes himself by capturing the essence of what monarchy was and can be again, taking the reader on a masterful exploration of how Christian kingship embodies immortal principles that served our civilization for centuries. Whether you are a devoted monarchist, a convicted republican, or a skeptic of all political programs, this book will inform, enlighten, and challenge you."

—**ROSS M. MCEWEN**, The Royal Stuart Society

THE COMPLEAT MONARCHIST

The Compleat Monarchist

❖

CHARLES A. COULOMBE

Foreword by Fr. Aidan Nichols, OP

Os Justi
Press

Os Justi Press
P.O. Box 21814
Lincoln, NE 68542
www.osjustipress.com

Send inquiries to
info@osjustipress.com

ISBN 978-1-965303-20-7 (paperback)
ISBN 978-1-965303-21-4 (hardcover)
ISBN 978-1-965303-22-1 (ebook)

Layout by Michael Schrauzer
Cover by Julian Kwasniewski
Cover image: Ignác Roskovics,
The Coronation of Saint Stephen (1900)

To their late Majesties
OTTO,
de jure Emperor of Austria,
Apostolic King of Hungary,
King of Bohemia, etc.;
and
KIGELI,
King of Rwanda.
God rest them both.

The glories of our blood and state
Are shadows, not substantial things;
There is no armour against Fate;
Death lays his icy hand on kings:
Sceptre and Crown
Must tumble down,
And in the dust be equal made
With the poor crooked scythe and spade.

James Shirley

❧ CONTENTS ❧

❖ F O R E W O R D ❖

CHARLES COULOMBE'S *THE COMPLEAT MONARCHIST* might easily be dismissed as "tongue in cheek." Latinists among the readership of Os Justi Press would no doubt prefer to call it *lingua in maxillam*, but the outcome is much the same. In the representative democracies of modern Europe, justifications of such monarchical forms as remain are rarely offered on any basis more ambitious than the one contained in the old saw, "If it ain't broke, don't fix it." Once the advent of the welfare state turned kings and queens into adjuncts of civic benevolence, and the celebrity culture completed the job by vulgarizing their photographs, making a case for their theological role became hard indeed. And as for the suggestion that Uncle Sam might exchange his white top hat for a crown and his blue tailcoat and red-and-white striped trousers for an ermine mantle, the effort must seem entirely quixotic.

But the ermine mantle was not in fact the bespoke clothing of sacred monarchy, though in post-medieval Europe *couturiers* eventually persuaded monarchs to ape the aristocracy. As anyone who watched the coronation of Charles III could notice, the candidate was vested in the *colobium*, the plain white shift used by ancient Christians as a sign of nakedness before God (the symbolism is baptismal). Over that was put the *super-tunica*, a variant of the dalmatic worn by deacons. That told viewers how the king is an ecclesiastical person, even though his department of the Church is *regnum*, not *sacerdotium*. His concern is with the fate of the temporal city in its relation to the heavenly City of which the Church is the provisional presence and the dominically founded instrument. That gives the king or queen a duty of care for the Church-body. Not a duty that is all-defining of their role, but co-defining of it nonetheless. "Kings shall be your foster fathers and their queens your nursing mothers," prophesied Isaiah (49:23). In Christian monarchies, accordingly, kings have been expected to succour, and queens to suckle (not of course literally), the membership of holy Church.

That raises two questions. The first is whether it is desirable for the state to confess God, and more specifically God as made known in Judaeo-Christian revelation. Until that first question is answered, the second, which follows it, is hardly worth raising. The second question runs, if the state should confess the true religion, does the symbolism of sacred monarchy help or hinder that confession?

The prior question is largely avoided in modern Catholicism, though the Prologue to the Second Vatican Council's Declaration on Religious Liberty answers it in the affirmative plainly enough. In the post-Ascension regime of salvation history, when the risen Christ is reigning, all principalities and powers are to be placed under his feet. In a pluralist society where, in once homogenously Christian lands Catholic Christians — or any Christians — have become or are becoming minoritarian, that confession is only spoken *sotto voce*. But its mediation in norms and values can still be expressed in policy and law, though leaving in shadow completeness in theological underpinning.

Granted, then, that the state should (in the words of a modern British politician) "do God," how might a sacred monarchy assist the state in this respect? The answer is found in *colobium* and *super-tunica*, which here represent the inherent symbolism of the royal office. As a member of the Church, re-donning the baptismal garment, the king stands before the God from whom all being derives, stands as one who is nothing before the one who is all. The utter simplicity of the *colobium* points to the total contrast with God of the one who bears the *persona* of the state. It is a standing reminder of the due limits of power. Nevertheless, by a grace that the prayers and anointing implore, the candidate goes on to became, in clothing with the *super-tunica*, a living icon of Christ the Servant-King, the original deacon: "I am among you as one who serves" (Lk 22:27). The beauty and richness of the fabric point to the extraordinary privilege that entails. In heaven, to serve is to reign and vice versa, in sharp contradiction to the Luciferians with their hellish motto, *non serviam*. By iconizing Jesus Christ, the prince undertakes to serve his people by guarding, though his words and deeds, the norms and values that belong with Christified humanity — whether non-Christified humanity is aware of the fact or not.

In any civil society, below the level of state sovereignty lie provinces and cities. More modest in their claims on us, they are the appropriate locus for republican polity. Their leadership is not asked to render manifest the ultimate nature of the state. Its task is, instead, to draw out of the private concerns of individuals the shared public good, the *res publica*, of local communities, whether singly or in association. The desire to convert monarchies into republics is based on a failure to distinguish between these two constituent orders of civic reality.

The arguments for monarchy are basically of three kinds: providentialist — monarchy has been the state form most used by the providence of God to further the Christianization of peoples; sacramental — monarchy permits the symbolic clothing of civil authority with the mantle of Christ the Servant-King, thus setting in a most desirable way the ethos of the state; pragmatic — monarchy transcends factions (no one has voted either for or against the king) as well as the ravages of time (the royal institution necessarily considers both conservation of heritage and provision for future generations).

In this humorous yet serious book, Charles Coulombe interweaves such arguments with a great stock of monarchist lore, covering an impressively wide range of historical, geographical, and religious instantiations. The overall message emerges clearly enough: royalism, or supporting the *Reichsidee*, is not so much a sign of political immaturity as a dawning of wisdom. The question remains: are ideologically saturated societies with religiously illiterate cultures capable of seeing the point?

Aidan Nichols, OP

◄ INTRODUCTION ►

Whereas it has pleased Almighty God to call to His Mercy our late Sovereign Lady Queen Elizabeth the Second of Blessed and Glorious Memory, by whose Decease the Crown of the United Kingdom of Great Britain and Northern Ireland is solely and rightfully come to The Prince Charles Philip Arthur George: We, therefore, the Lords Spiritual and Temporal of this Realm and Members of the House of Commons, together with other members of Her late Majesty's Privy Council and representatives of the Realms and Territories, Aldermen and Citizens of London, and others, do now hereby with one voice and Consent of Tongue and Heart publish and proclaim that The Prince Charles Philip Arthur George is now, by the Death of our late Sovereign of Happy Memory, become our only lawful and rightful Liege Lord Charles the Third, by the Grace of God of the United Kingdom of Great Britain and Northern Ireland and of His other Realms and Territories, King, Head of the Commonwealth, Defender of the Faith, to whom we do acknowledge all Faith and Obedience with humble Affection; beseeching God by whom Kings and Queens do reign to bless His Majesty with long and happy Years to reign over us.

Given at St James's Palace this Tenth day of September in the year of Our Lord two thousand and twenty-two.

GOD SAVE THE KING[1]

THE ACCESSION OF KING CHARLES III TO THE throne of his fathers was one of the biggest stories of 2022—and the attendant ceremonies and rituals kept people's attention through His Majesty's coronation the following year. All across the British Isles and the Commonwealth, various public officials and politicians made the above or similar proclamations in sonorous tones, appearing to radiate at once belief in God and true loyalty to the king. Despite the great number of them that are atheists or republicans (or both), for the most part they played their roles well, little though it actually meant.

The British (and the Dutch and Scandinavians) are masters at maintaining outward appearances whilst changing the interior utterly. If one relied only upon British and Commonwealth

---

[1] "The Principal Proclamation," The Royal Household, September 10, 2022, https://www.royal.uk/principal-proclamation.

official linguistic formulae, one would think that the new king is indeed master in his new realms. Every bill passed through Lords and Commons begins: "Be it enacted by the King's most Excellent Majesty, by and with the advice and consent of the Lords Spiritual and Temporal, and Commons, in this present Parliament assembled, and by the authority of the same, as follows . . . "

Lovely as the ceremonies are, the monarch has no more control over the affairs of Britain and the other Commonwealth Realms than he does over the American government and congress. For reasons that will become apparent as one looks over the essays in this book, historical events have stripped him of much of his ancestors' powers.[2] He can no longer protect his people from their politicians, which, as Franz Joseph once famously remarked to Teddy Roosevelt, was that veteran emperor's conception of his role as a modern monarch.[3] So sadly true is this that Charles III's new first minister, Sir Keir Starmer, Knight Bachelor, has announced that he will abolish the remaining hereditary lords in Britain's upper house. The king can do nothing to defend the constitution, because his own right to the throne is based upon a previous successful attack on the British constitution, way back in 1688. Then, as now, this further snatching of power by the oligarchy-of-the-moment is presented to the masses as an advance in liberty, when it is yet another chain.

But such usurpation is well-nigh universal today, when just a few years ago the world's real rulers put their subjects back into their toy-boxes to wait out the pandemic — releasing them only in accordance with arbitrary and often contradictory standards. We live in a world run by relentless power, with little or no notion of either authority or legitimacy, two forgotten qualities without which power cannot be wielded rightly by its owners. They can compel obedience, but not loyalty. So it is that they have busied themselves for the past few decades — and never more than since the fall of the Soviet Union — attacking all that is good, true, or beautiful. That is

[2] See also Joseph Shaw, ed., *A Defence of Monarchy: Catholics under a Protestant King* (Angelico Press, 2023).
[3] Igor Lukes, *On the Edge of the Cold War: American Diplomats and Spies in Postwar Prague* (Oxford University Press, 2012), 17.

not the job of any sort of government; but today there seems no alternative to these so-called democratic governments.

Needless to say, none of these regimes is monarchical, in the sense of the Christian monarchy that was attempted from the 300s until 1918, although a few crowned republics remain, their sovereigns along for the roller-coaster ride with their bemused peoples. But neither are they democracies, in the sense that oligarchs have used the word to disguise their rule since 1688, 1776, or 1793. The desires or even the well-being of the majority of people matters as little to the majority of their elected rulers as that of His Majesty the King means to the Right Honourable Sir Keir Starmer, KB.

Nevertheless, there really is, or has been, *something else* on offer: the Christian monarchy just mentioned. In this volume we shall explore various aspects of it and attempt to show where it might well prove a better alternative to what we have now—damning with faint praise though that may be. For the past two and a half centuries (longer in the British Isles), its proponents fought a long and losing battle with the fathers of what we have now—a situation that with 20/20 hindsight we can see in somewhat clearer terms than many of them could. It may be said that the last of them were defeated by the mid-twentieth century. So what relevance do they have for us now?

It is this author's contention that they retain a great deal of relevance, in terms of both Church and state. Our ancestors saw Christian kingship as just that—a participation in the kingship of Christ. Whatever may have happened over the past two centuries, God is eternal and so is His kingship. Principles do not die, and right remains right. In response, psychologically and historically, monarchy is the government most natural to man. If one believes, as I do, that man's last end is to be united eternally with his maker, it does make sense that he should conform himself to an order God has blessed since first describing what kind of king he wanted for the children of Israel in the book of Deuteronomy.

But before there can be any kind of action on this issue, there needs to be a body of principles; if we do not know what we want—unless we are already in power and can pull it out of our people regardless of rhyme or reason—we need to know what we are shooting for. A good deal of my adult life has been devoted to trying to figure these things out: the nature of Christian monarchy and what its proponents have had in common. The results you see before you. Before anything benevolent can really develop, a great many of these ideas need to be looked at and thought about by a great many.

I do not expect to see a vast counterrevolution in my life-time — although, to be fair, I did not expect to see the fall of the Soviet Bloc either. Of course, it would be a dream come true to see a Habsburg crowned successively at Budapest, Prague, Krakow, Aachen, Milan, and Rome, as it would be to see the same ceremony for a Bourbon at Reims. I'd settle for Charles III dissolving all of his parliaments on his own recognisance, appointing prime ministers from the local political pool whose competence he believed in, and, in the Commonwealth Realms and British Overseas Territories, selecting governors-general, governors, and lieutenant governors of his own to keep an eye on them. I'll not hold my breath.

Nevertheless, I am also aware that beyond human politics lies Divine Providence. The Russian Orthodox canonised Nicholas II and his family and servants (including a Catholic) as martyrs; the Catholic Church has beatified his co-combatant of World War I, Bl. Karl of Austria-Hungary. In this time when the friction between Russia and the West raises once more the spectre of nuclear war, I can well see an unofficial *cultus* arising across denominational lines, asking their intercession for peace. This would be all the more poignant, given Nicholas's failed attempts to prevent war in 1905 and 1914, and Karl's equally frustrated attempts to end it.

In any case, it has been interesting to see the causes of canonisation for a number of royals begun in recent years. Bl. Maria Cristina of Savoy, Queen of the Two Sicilies, was beatified a few years ago, and her son Francis II, last ruler of that realm thus far, has just been made a Servant of God. Ironically, so, too, have Karl's Empress-Queen Zita, and Queen Elena of Italy, wife of Victor Emmanuel III, another of Karl's wartime foes. Looking further back, Madame Élisabeth of France, martyred sister of Louis XVI, has recently achieved the same rank — which has brought further consideration upon her brother and her sister-in-law, Marie Antoinette; both were described as martyrs by the pope of the time, Pius VI. The formation of the Anglican Ordinariates within the Catholic Church has renewed some interest in a clutch of British royal Servants of God: Henry VI, Mary Queen of Scots, and James II and VII, as well as the great proponent of Anglican-Roman reconciliation, Charles I. As their *culti* develop—and especially if any of them are canonised—it will be impossible for there not to be political repercussions of some kind.

All of that, of course, stands against the background of decaying governmental systems across the planet. If God does not permit a nuclear conflict to devastate us, then perhaps the oft-predicted "Triumph of the Immaculate Heart," "Reign of the Sacred Heart," and the like shall coincide with a restoration of Christian monarchy. In any case, it is hard to believe that we shall not see some kind of regime change over the next few decades. It is important, when that happens, that enough people have positive ideas regarding what should follow. As I say, I doubt I shall live to see it. But if my poor labours contribute, however slightly, to a more humane and less blasphemous future, I shall be deeply grateful. Please God, I shall then be in a position in which my prayers may avail to help the young of those times accomplish whatever God asks of them.

❧OUTLINE OF THE ARGUMENT❧
of This Book

I. THE FUNDAMENTALS OF MONARCHY
Chapter 1, "Are You a Monarchist?," *explains the different kinds of monarchy and the five points of traditional Catholic monarchy.*

Chapter 2, "The Varieties of Monarchist Experience," *dispels myths surrounding monarchy and describes its various manifestations in archetypal figures, political roles for monarchs, and contemporary royalty around the world.*

Chapter 3, "One Cheer for Constitutional Monarchy!," *describes how various twentieth-century constitutional monarchies have trended toward democratic ruin, even as some monarchs have stood up for their people.*

Chapter 4, "The Limits of Power," *underlines the importance of properly distinguishing between power and legitimate authority, as well as identifying their abuses.*

II. CHURCH, STATE, AND THE HOLY ROMAN EMPIRE
Chapter 5, "What Is Christendom?," *distinguishes between four different eras of Christendom, culminating in the one that reigns in the hearts of all the baptised.*

Chapter 6, "Sacrum Imperium," *reflects on the idea of the Holy Empire: its origin, fruits, and influence on contemporary institutions.*

Chapter 7, "Europe and the Empire," *delves into the European inheritance of the HRE, including how it has fallen apart in the past two centuries and prospects for restoration.*

Chapter 8, "Disembodied Church and Zombie State," *explains how the Church has effectively been separated from states, which have substituted a secular religion for it — with devastating consequences. The reaction to Covid-19 particularly demonstrated this reality.*

Chapter 9, "The Quest for a Catholic State," *surveys efforts to institute corporate governments throughout the world according to Catholic social teaching.*

Chapter 10, "Bl. Karl, Clericalism, and Lay Church Governance," *ties the phenomenon of clericalism to the papacy's loss of temporal power and explains how lay governance in the Church traditionally operated, with a focus on Franz Joseph and Bl. Karl of Austria.*

Chapter 11, "Guelphs and Ghibellines Revisited," expounds the distinction between papal and imperial power in both abstract and practical terms, including how it has played out in history.

III. RECENT INTELLECTUAL ENGAGEMENT WITH MONARCHY

Chapter 12, "Romantic Conservatives: The Inklings in Their Political Context," *reviews the monarchical and distributist leanings of Lewis, Tolkien, and Williams; also includes historical overviews of romanticism in Europe and its relation to conservatism throughout the West.*

Chapter 13, "Kingship in the Work of the Inklings," *further develops the themes and content of the preceding chapter.*

Chapter 14, "The Counterrevolution Revisited," *summarizes counterrevolutionaries and the benefits of studying their works and efforts.*

Chapter 15, "Postliberalism, Integralism — What Does It All Mean?," *recounts the origin of integralism, what unites its various branches, and the negative consequences of prevailing divisions among them.*

IV. MONARCHY TODAY

Chapter 16, "Confessions of an American Monarchist," *chronicles the author's personal monarchist journey, culminating in a summary of five conservative principles and a look at the state of monarchy in the last century and today.*

Chapter 17, "The Only Love That Dare Not Speak Its Name," *briefly summarizes the current state of the various European monarchies.*

Chapter 18, "What Is Legitimism?," *presents an overview of leading legitimist attempts to promote and preserve monarchical lines of inheritance across the globe, concluding with a review of the five points of traditional Catholic monarchy and their application for Americans.*

Chapter 19, "The Aragorn Option," *raises the prospects of restoring monarchical heirs to their thrones, and the self-sacrifice of the people that is a necessary prerequisite.*

Chapter 20, "After the Crowning," *compares the coronation of Charles III to that of Bl. Karl, and laments how far modern monarchy and society have fallen.*

Chapter 21, "Hailing the Chiefs," *compares the religious and ceremonial functions of the United States president with the all-but-nominal powers of modern monarchs.*

Chapter 22, "Wanted: Real Leadership," *dilates upon the evil, insanity, and stupidity of bad leadership and the goodness, sanity, and intelligence of its opposite.*

Chapter 23, "A New Charter for the Nobility," *relates the mechanics of noble titles and roles in the Middle Ages and beyond, ending with a reflection on the current dearth of functional nobility and what it means for nobles and commoners alike.*

Chapter 24, "Nostalgia, Revival, and Restoration," *catalogs movements both ancient and modern that strive to return to a golden age, and proposes what they reveal about our desire for the supernatural.*

PART I

The Fundamentals
of Monarchy

CHAPTER 1

Are You a Monarchist?

MOST PEOPLE ASKED THE TITLE QUESTION today would doubtless contemptuously answer "no!" Some few—very few in these United States— might answer in the affirmative. But how well do either really understand what they are denying or assenting to? Just what is a monarchy? For that matter, what is a republic? Just as our federal union, Hitler's Germany, and North Korea are all called republics, so too are Austria-Hungary, Canada, and Imperial China called monarchies. But in both cases, what a world of difference! About the only thing you can say that most monarchies have in common is the hereditary principle in choosing the sovereign—but that is not the case today with either the Holy See, the Sovereign Military Order of Malta (SMOM), or the Co-Principality of Andorra; nor, for long stretches of history, was it true for either the Holy Roman Empire or the Polish-Lithuanian Commonwealth.

There is, of course, as with republics, a great difference between types of monarchy. This diversity is reflected in those that survive today. Of these, Great Britain and the Commonwealth Realms (sharing the British king but in all ways independent from HM's UK government—Canada, Australia, New Zealand, Jamaica, and twelve others), Denmark, Norway, Sweden, the Netherlands, Belgium, Luxembourg, Andorra, Samoa, and Spain are Christian constitutional monarchies—that is, the monarch reigns but does not rule, and the politicians do so in Their Majesties' names. The Holy See, SMOM, Liechtenstein, Tonga, Lesotho, Swaziland, and Monaco are—to a greater or lesser degree—Christian absolute monarchies; this means that the sovereign has the preponderance of political power subject to law and/or tradition (this seems like a lot, but it leaves them unable to bring in abortion or same-sex marriage—the ability to change reality belongs only to absolute "democracies"). There are Islamic monarchies—Jordan (the closest to Western in style), Morocco, Malaysia (which is, as a federal constitutional monarchy, a case apart), Brunei, Kuwait, the United Arab Emirates, Qatar, Bahrain, Oman, and Saudi Arabia — in these the will of the ruler is tempered only by Sharia law or whatever other codes he chooses to bind himself with. There are three Buddhist monarchies — Bhutan (where the King recently divested himself of absolute power), Thailand, and Cambodia, in all of which the king's authority is as much or more religious than political. Then there is the Empire of Japan, where under the American-imposed 1947 constitution the emperor has no power but remains an important symbol in national life. There are, in addition, throughout the Third World an army of sultans, rajas, hereditary kings and tribal chiefs, and various other "traditional rulers" (as they are called in United Nations-speak) ruling or reigning over select areas within ostensible republics.

Speaking of which, republics too come in several varieties, knowledge of which will help us focus in on the question at hand. As with monarchy, we generally suppose that republics do not rely on the hereditary principle for choosing their head of state, though that is not always the case, as with North Korea, Cuba, and the Duvalier dynasty in Haiti. There are four major types of republics in the world today. The first is the executive republic, where the elected president has many of, most of, or more than the powers of such as Louis XIV, Henry VIII, or Alexander III; such are the United States, Russia, France, and most of Latin America. There are parliamentary republics, where the president — generally elected by parliament and not by the populace as a whole — is a ceremonial figurehead with all the weakness and none of the prestige of a constitutional monarch (this is why their palaces are generally retirement homes for used-up politicians). Most European republics are of this variety. There are Islamic republics, which claim to incarnate both Sharia and the will of the people; and then there is a wide variety of failed states — all of which claim to be republics.

A true red herring that cuts across all of these lines is what media, government, and academia — the unholy trinity of opinion manufacture — are pleased to call democracy. Supposedly, all republics and constitutional monarchies are democracies by definition — although a certain strand of American

conservatism insists upon the difference between a constitutional republic such as the United States once was, and a
democracy. But what is democracy? One might define it as
majority rule, but since the great majority of countries that
now have abortion and same-sex marriage had them imposed
by judicial or legislative fiat when a great majority of their
populations did not want them, this definition does not hold
water. Indeed, democracy can be defined as whatever those
really ruling a given country wish it to be—hence the old
joke that the United States has a representative democracy,
the pre-1989 Soviet Bloc featured "people's democracy," and
cannibalism, as Idi Amin defined it, is "nutritional democracy." In reality, democracy functions as a smokescreen for
those in power.

But to call oneself a monarchist—even before we define our
terms further—is to claim heirship to a record of failure in the
last century or so. Since I was born in 1960, a lot of monarchies
have been overthrown: Nepal, Laos, Iran, Afghanistan, South
Arabia, Yemen, Ethiopia (the last Christian empire), Rwanda,
Burundi, Libya, Zanzibar, and Greece—all of which did far
worse afterwards, however badly they might have been doing
before. The same is true of those Commonwealth republics that
more or less peacefully overthrew the Queen: Mauritius, Fiji,
Trinidad and Tobago, Malta, Ceylon, Sierra Leone, Rhodesia, The
Gambia, Kenya, Malawi, Tanganyika (Tanzania after merging
with Zanzibar), Uganda, Nigeria, Ghana—and most disastrous
of all, the Union of South Africa. My brother was born a mere
seven years before me, but in that time monarchical attrition
was rife: Vietnam, Tibet, Egypt and Sudan, Iraq, Pakistan, and
Tunisia all bit the dust. Our father was born in 1926; before
my brother came, he saw the overthrow of the kings of Italy,
Romania, Bulgaria, Albania, Yugoslavia, and the regent of
Hungary—and India and Ireland switched from Dominions
to republics. Grandpa hit the jackpot, however! After his birth
in 1890, Madagascar, Korea, Portugal, China, Germany (and its
constituent monarchies), Austria-Hungary, Russia, Turkey, and
Mongolia all fell—as had Brazil the year before he was born.
Certainly the Wars of the Three Kingdoms and the American,
French, and Latin American Revolutions—to say nothing of
the sad ends of Iturbide and Maximilian in Mexico—did not

end well for monarchists. Bear in mind, of course, that all of
these fallen thrones were as different from one another as the
surviving ones are.

Even so, if you google "Why I am a monarchist," you shall get
about 10,900 results — and that includes only English-speakers.
John Médaille,[1] Michael Warren Davis,[2] and Ryan Hunter,[3]
Americans all, appear on the first page and give different
cogent answers to the question. Mr. Davis asks a very important
question: "But perhaps you might ask yourself—you who grew
up on tales of King Arthur, and Cinderella, and *The Chronicles
of Narnia*—when did you *stop* being a Monarchist?" Indeed,
indeed. One might well make the argument that, just as the
soul is naturally Christian, it is also naturally monarchist. In
any case, each gentleman's response to the stated question is
worth reading.

But we still want to find out a bit more about the varieties
of monarchy before we can discover the answer to the title
question—as to whether you, dear reader, really are a monarchist yourself. Now, I must here admit an open bias. I am
not really interested that much in non-Christian monarchies.
I would not have wanted to live under the Ottomans or the
Qing. That said, however, such sovereigns were almost always
better than the freedom-talking tyrants who succeeded them.
Nevertheless, I shall leave them out of the discussion.

Before I move on to more contemporary matters, however,
I want to bring up for your delectation the views of Aristotle
and St. Thomas Aquinas on the matter of governance. They
held that there were three kinds of good government — monarchy, aristocracy, and what they called "polity"—that is to
say, rule by an educated, landholding, and military-serving
citizenry. Opposed to these three were their corresponding bad
governments: tyranny, oligarchy, and what they called "democracy"—mob-rule. As far as they were concerned, however,

---

[1] John Médaille, "Why I am a Monarchist," *Front Porch Republic*, November 29,
2010, https://www.frontporchrepublic.com/2010/11/why-i-am-a-monarchist/.
[2] Michael Warren Davis, "Why I'm a Monarchist," *The Imaginative Conservative*,
March 13, 2014, https://theimaginativeconservative.org/2014/03/im-monar-
chist.html.
[3] Ryan Hunter, "Why I am a Monarchist," *Orthodox in the District*, November
3, 2015, https://ryanphunter.wordpress.com/2015/11/03/why-i-am-a-mon-
archist/.

the best form of government was "mixed," featuring king, nobility, and landholding, service-minded commoners. This was the medieval form of government—and it survives in a desiccated mummified form in the current British system, which resembles its origins in the same way and degree that the Church of England resembles medieval Catholicism. Of course, neither sage spoke of a mixed regime such as that which prevails throughout the West today, seamlessly combining tyranny, oligarchy, and the mob! But one other feature of medieval governance that must be touched upon is the dichotomy between authority and power. Authority—which is the right to say what ought to be done—came from God and was mediated to the sovereign through the Church, hence the coronation rite; power, the ability to make things happen, was diffused throughout the estates of the realm. The king had some, but so too did the Church, the nobility, the guilds, the towns—even the peasantry. A good king was like an orchestra leader, while a bad one brought not despotism but anarchy, as contending power-holders fought for more. With us, it is the opposite—power is concentrated in our ruling elites, while authority is dispersed among a largely amorphous electorate.

Regardless of when they were deposed or lost their powers, the monarchs of Europe have left a strong mark upon every aspect of life, both in the mother continent and in the daughter nations across the seas—including our United States. This includes law, the arts, the military, hunting, literature, and even much of the built heritage. Certainly, the first impulses toward government support of historical preservation, conservation, education, agriculture, and anything else came from them, and we all benefit from that rich if forgotten legacy. But one supposes that gratitude is not a modern virtue.

In any case, this brings us to another monarchical division; from the seventeenth to the nineteenth centuries, the royal houses of the British Isles, France, Spain, and Portugal divided; the last-named century also saw the royal houses of Savoy and Hohenzollern annex or dominate all the other sovereign houses in Italy and Germany, with the influence of the Habsburgs being confined to their own domains. But these struggles were as much over ideology—the nature of the monarchy in the given country—as genealogy. Within the context of the modern world, the senior lines wished to retain the traditional sort of monarchy as developed in their respective countries, while the junior became the creatures of the new national oligarchies, who wished to conceal their dominance with royal trappings. In the Three Kingdoms, the supporters of the older line were first called Cavaliers during the first round of civil wars, and then Jacobites; their equivalents in France were called Legitimists (a name that came also to be applied to all such groups in Europe generically), in Spain the Carlists, and in Portugal the Miguelists. All lost; with the exception of the Stuarts, who became extinct in the male line, they all eventually sought refuge (alongside the deposed German and Italian houses) in Habsburg Austria.

Although the Russian tsars continued as champions of Orthodoxy, the new monarchies of the Netherlands and Belgium were founded on more or less liberal principles, while those of Romania, Serbia, Bulgaria, and Greece were erected on a strange mix of liberalism and Orthodoxy. The Scandinavian kings, on the other hand, like the British, accommodated themselves to oligarchical "democracy." Thus, they survived alongside the British and the Benelux sovereigns when the World Wars swept away most of Europe's monarchs.

All of that having been said, as I am not much interested in the non-Christian monarchies, neither am I really that interested in the liberal or constitutional monarchies — save to maintain the existing ones, which do have certain benefits, and in any case would be replaced with something worse. Nor am I unaware that from time to time some of their monarchs (or in the case of Canada, Australia, and South Africa, their governors-general) come into salutary constitutional conflict with "their" governments. But it is legitimist monarchy that interests me.

To be sure, the proponents of traditional monarchy in the British Isles, France, Iberia, and Central Europe all had very different national mores. But ironically, as an American, it is easier for someone like me to see their commonalities than it might be for them. There are, roughly, five points in common, and it is upon these five points that a monarchism for the twenty-first century can be developed. They may be summed up as Altar, Throne, subsidiarity, solidarity, and — for want of a better word — occidentalism. Let us deal with each in turn.

THE FIVE POINTS OF TRADITIONAL CATHOLIC MONARCHY

1. *The Altar*

The Altar symbolises the place of the Church in society. Mediator of divine authority to the monarch, the Church crowns and anoints him. But it also is the animating philosophy, the arbiter of morals. Accompanying public and private life, its ceremonial enriches everything from openings of the legislature and judiciary to school graduations. These not only sanctify but symbolise the Church's proper role in education, social work, and every aspect of life.

2. *The Throne*

The Throne deals with the place of the monarch himself. Deriving his authority from God and national tradition, in the modern world he must have sufficient power to protect his people from their politicians, in the pithy phrase of Franz Joseph.[4] No Christian monarch, as we have mentioned, has ever been absolute over society in the way that—say—the Supreme Court of the United States is. But it seems to me that powers vested in the presidency by the Constitution, as opposed to the ones usurped by subsequent presidents and the judiciary— would be sufficient. Moreover, where subjects, enamoured as they are with the supposed power given them by voting, are content to allow presidents to usurp power, one can imagine how watchful they would be for any such actions on the part of a monarch—precisely because he was hereditary.

3. *Subsidiarity*

All of the groups referred to earlier included provincial or local liberties—what we call today subsidiarity—among their rallying cries. This means that, politically, as much power as can be wielded effectively is devolved to the lowest possible level. In other words, while the king and his ministers preside over foreign and military affairs, whatever can be best done by the provinces is left to them. They in turn leave to the counties what is best for them, and they to the towns and villages. But in, with, and under these levels of governance are what Leo XIII called "mediating bodies," which modern commentators call "civil society"—churches, unions, societies, guilds, schools,

---

[4] Lukes, *On the Edge*, 17.

and organisations of all kinds that are neither government nor business — all the way down to the family, each with the autonomy proper to it. Moreover, the autonomy of mediating bodies is not a gift or a grant, but a *right*, as confirmed in numerous coronation oaths throughout European history.

4. Solidarity

Solidarity or class cooperation has gone by many names through the past few centuries: solidarism, social monarchy, distributism, guild socialism, corporatism, and a number of others. What these various systems have in common is the idea that economics must be for the common good, and the first component of the common good is material provision sufficient to allow the inhabitants of a place to concentrate on the salvation of their souls rather than just avoiding starvation. Ideas of how to achieve this vary considerably; but at the end of the day, the sovereign is the guardian of all of the economic interests among his subjects and does his level best to secure them both sufficient harmony and sufficient freedom to pursue their welfare in this world and the next.

5. Occidentalism

The last is the most difficult to define, but basically it is this: from the time that Christianity became the established church of Armenia, Ethiopia, Georgia, Nubia, and the Roman Empire, there has always existed the notion of Christendom, of the *res publica Christiana* — the idea that in a vague and loose way, all Christian realms were part of the same entity, despite whatever disputes they might have among themselves. It is the idea of the Holy Empire, whether Byzantine or Holy Roman; the *Reichsidee*, as the Germans put it. Used as we are to identifying empires with despotism, it is difficult for us to understand what that meant originally: an organic but free union. As Viscount Bryce describes it,

> The territories over which Frederick would have declared his jurisdiction to extend may be classed under four heads: —
>
> First, the German lands, in which, and in which alone, the Emperor was, up till the death of Frederick the Second (A. D. 1250), effective ruler.

Second, the non-German districts of the Holy Empire, where the Emperor was acknowledged as sole monarch, but in practice little regarded.

Third, certain outlying countries, owing allegiance to the Empire, but governed by kings of their own.

Fourth, the other states of Europe, whose rulers, while admitting the superior rank of the Emperor, were virtually independent of him.[5]

This idea would be carried on in different ways down to 1806. This underlying unity was not merely imperial; the Muslim invasion underscored the fact that Christian lands were really one—*Abendland* in German, *l'Occident* in French. Despite the disruption brought about between East and West in 1054 and then with the Protestant Revolt, the survival of this idea is indicated by the Crusades and the various holy and Catholic leagues against the Muslim menace, down to the eighteenth century. Much the same might be said about the various coalitions poised against the French Revolution, culminating in the Holy Alliance. A touch or two of this same spirit might be detected in the foundation of the European Union and the United Nations, far as those bodies may have strayed from any resemblance to this ideal.

All of which having been said, what does this mean for the monarchist of the twenty-first century? Obviously, if one lives in a country with such a tradition, it is a matter of either increasing the position of the existing monarchy to something approaching its days of greatness or restoring it where it has been overthrown. But what of the United States? Surely monarchy is an impossible notion for our country—irrelevant at best, ridiculous at worst? By no means.

It is certainly true that monarchism as an organised force in our country departed with the Loyalists in 1783. There have been a few—mostly literary figures—who have claimed the title since: Fitz-Greene Halleck, Ralph Adams Cram, and T. S. Eliot, to name a few, as well as ethnic figures who have had connexions to foreign monarchist groups, such as Wilfrid Beaulieu, Pedro Villaseñor, and Alcée Fortier. There have been and are philosophical monarchists, who, without loyalty to a particular dynasty, believe it in one or more of its various

---

[5] James Bryce, *The Holy Roman Empire* (Macmillan Company, 1913), 182–83.

forms to be a better form of government. There are religious
monarchists, who—whether Catholic, Orthodox, Anglican,
Lutheran, Muslim, Buddhist, or Hindu—consider monarchy
to be the form of government most favourable to their faith.
Ever since 1789, foreign revolutions have sent thousands of
emigres to our shores, and often they or their descendants
retain some loyalty to their ancestral dynasty. Lastly, there
are the Anglophiles, who to a greater or lesser degree wish
that our country was still connected somehow to Great Britain.

But such monarchism is a sentiment to indulge, not a cause
to fight for. Still less is there a dynasty or even a unified "crown
of America" to rally around. There were attempts to offer that
crown to Bonnie Prince Charlie, Prince Henry of Prussia, and
Washington himself—all of whom refused it. San Francisco's
beloved Norton I claimed to be "Emperor of the United States
and Protector of Mexico"—but it was the major symptom of
his madness. For all that, his adopted city accepted his scrip as
legal tender. Harry Turtledove and Richard Dreyfuss imagined
a world where the American Revolution had never occurred in
The Two Georges (Tor Books, 1996). Walter Miller's *A Canticle for
Leibowitz*, which chronicles the history of the Church in a future
post-atomic-war North America also shows the successive
rise of the Harq-Hannegan dynasty from barbarian warlords
to Tudor-style emperors of Texarkana to constitutional monarchs of the Atlantic Confederacy. When the latter power is
faced with an atomic war even worse than the one that almost
wiped out mankind before, the defence minister refers to "His
Supremacy's government." In response, a lady reporter shoots
back: "His Supremacy is an eleven-year-old boy, and to call it
his government is not only archaic, but a highly dishonorable—
even cheap!—attempt to shift the responsibility. . . ."[6] My own
Star-Spangled Crown (Tumblar House, 2016) was an attempt to
imagine a future where a truly American monarchy was able
to tie up the many loose ends in our national life.

But does any of this have any relevance to these United
States outside the realm of fiction? Yes, I believe it does. Let
us look again at those five points of Traditional Catholic Monarchy and see where they might bring us. At first glance, the

---

[6] Walter M. Miller Jr., *A Canticle for Leibowitz* (J. B. Lippincott Company, 1960), 254.

most opposed to the American ethos and impossible to bring to fruition would be the first—the Altar. This country has always prided itself on its religious diversity; surely, then, the adoption of Catholicism as the religion of the nation is not worth considering? Put in those terms, yes. But let us look at reality. *Every society has an animating philosophy that functions as its state church.* In the Soviet Union, it was communism. With us, it was a combination of a synthetic religion of the country that basically deified the American experience and could be indulged in alongside any other faith, and a shared moral consensus. But the latter was destroyed during the 1960s, and the former is dying before our very eyes. Something must replace it, if the country is to survive. Why not Catholicism? Orestes Brownson foresaw its necessity for national liberty as early as the 1840s. Seen in this fashion, evangelising our native land becomes as much a patriotic as a religious duty. If ever we accomplish it, the national institutions will adjust to it—even as did those of Rome and the barbarians, from which adjustment came Christendom. Obviously, we are speaking of a long-term project; but one has to start somewhere—and this is something any Catholic American monarchist would join in on as a *sine qua non*.

The second is even harder—the Throne! But again, not as hard as one might think, given the quasi-regal status of the American presidency. As Eric Nelson wrote, "On one side of the Atlantic, there would be kings without monarchy; on the other, monarchy without kings."[7] Of course, as we have seen during the Obama and Trump administrations, the current system makes the head of state president not of everyone, but only of those who voted for him—while those who did not despise him. The personal staff of the president at the White House incorporates all the functions of both the Royal Household and Downing Street. In my novel I proposed a fictionalised version of the House of Liechtenstein as our prospective dynasty, because the youngest heir will inherit the claims to the British Isles of the Stuarts (under whom twelve of the thirteen colonies were founded) and so descends from

---

[7] Eric Nelson, *The Royalist Revolution: Monarchy and the American Founding* (Harvard University Press, 2014), 232.

the French and Spanish Bourbons—thus encompassing within himself all three of our foundational monarchical traditions. But, in truth, it would be extremely difficult to simply install a monarch in this country—although it would probably be wise to use a European dynast rather than draw from an American family, as sectional neutrality alone would call for it. In any case, there is little to be done in this area as things stand at the moment, save to speculate—and to vote for presidential candidates who might execute the office with a touch of style and dignity, as did Franklin D. Roosevelt (FDR) and John F. Kennedy (JFK) (whose policies I definitely did not agree with) and Ronald Reagan (with whom I did!).

Subsidiarity, however, is another thing entirely. This country was built on state sovereignty—anything that would encourage states' rights is important. But more important still is the need for healthy communities: county and city, town and country. Intelligent participation in local politics, local historical societies, historical preservation, conservation, cultural activities, and stimulating local businesses are all things that should attract monarchists—not only because the ends are worthwhile in themselves, but also because of the training one will get in doing things and the opportunities that will emerge to share one's beliefs. Above all, as the aforementioned American religion dies, it is taking with it American patriotism. A new patriotism must be constructed from the bottom up: love of town leading to love of county, to love of state, to region, and then to the totality of the states—a love of country based not upon some abstract ideology, but upon what is actually *here*. Evangelisation requires love of those to be evangelised—this we cannot do without exploring our area thoroughly. We must regain a sense of the commonweal, of our country as a proper realm, filled with things that go together to make up a worthy focus of loyalty and love.

That sense of commonweal must bleed over into our economic life where it can. Solidarity means not only looking after the poor, the sick, and the elderly—it also means trying to reconcile the various competing economic claims according to our state in life. If we are in management, we should try to accommodate labour; if are with the union, we ought to try to see what we do in common with management. Shopping at local businesses and farmer's markets is also something we can do in attempting to build a community worthy of a monarch. We need to learn, and, where we can, employ, the social teachings of the Church. All of these are possible sources of monarchist action.

So too with forming our views regarding that Europe from whence we or our fathers came. We must remember that Europe, and many of Europe's sovereigns — from Ferdinand and Isabel, who bankrolled Columbus, to King Christian X of Denmark, from whom we bought the Virgin Islands — erected the solid foundations upon which our national life has been built. When Europe is healthy, so are we; when not, not. Today, as we know, Europe is in bad shape. The mother continent needs the five principles more now than ever before. The Austrian Paneuropa movement, headed by the Archduke Karl von Habsburg, has some insights into just what Europe is:

> Christian motivated thinking and acting is the only alternative to the inhumane ideologies of Marxism, consumerism, Islamic fundamentalism, nationalism, and other sectarian doctrines of salvation. It is rooted in the realization that there is an absolutely valid order of values that extends beyond all times and forms and is anchored in the transcendental. Anyone who violates them does not merely damage the community; it also becomes a plaything for uncontrolled and uncontrollable forces. That is why we also want to know and shape politics in accordance with these values. Christianity has shaped Europe for almost two millennia. That's why Europe will be Christian, or it will not be Europe anymore.[8]

They go on to explain:

> Europe is not just a geographical term for us, encompassing the area between the Atlantic and the Urals. Because of their centuries of common destiny, the peoples of our continent form a spiritual unity, which should now finally be accompanied by political unity, so that Europe can exist in peace and freedom as an equal partner of the great powers. The soul of this continent is Christianity. Whoever takes it out of political action makes Europe a soulless body, a fragile construction that is exposed to all the influences and currents of the Zeitgeist.

---

[8] "Grundsätze," Paneuropa, accessed February 6, 2025, https://www.paneuropa.at/philosophie/grundsaetze/, my translation.

But in addition to the Altar, the Throne, too, is important for
Europe. Fr. Aidan Nichols, OP, in his *Christendom Awake* would
call the Holy Roman Empire back into being:

> Catholicism, as Orthodoxy, has, historically, regarded
> the monarchical institution in this light: raised up by
> Providence to safeguard the content of the natural law in
> its transmission through history as that norm for human
> co-existence which, founded as it is on the Creator, and
> renewed by him as the Redeemer, cannot be made subject
> to the positive law, or administrative fiat, or the dictates
> of cultural fashion. Let us dare to exercise a Christian
> political imagination on an as yet unspecifiable future.
> The articulation of the foundational natural and Judaeo-
> Christian norms of a *really* united Europe, for instance,
> would most appropriately be made by such a crown, whose
> legal and customary relations with the national peoples
> would be modelled on the best aspects of historic practice
> in the (Western) Holy Roman Empire and the Byzantine
> "Commonwealth"—to use the term popularised by Pro-
> fessor Dimtri Obolensky.
>
> Such a crown, as the integrating factor of an inter-
> national European Christendom, would leave intact the
> functioning of parliamentary government in the repub-
> lican or monarchical polities of its constituent nations
> and analogues in city and village in other representative
> and participatory forms. As the Spanish political theorist
> Alvaro D'Ors defines the concepts, power—that is, gov-
> ernment—as raised up by the people can and should be
> distinguished from authority. Power in this sense puts
> questions to those in authority as to what ought to be
> done. It asks whether technically possible acts of govern-
> ment, for coordinating the goals of individuals and groups
> in society, chime, or do not chime, with the foundational
> norms of society, deemed as these are to rest on the will
> of God as the ultimate giver of the shared human goal.
> Authority, itself bereft of such power, answers out of a
> wisdom which society can recognise.[9]

But even if we do as the good Dominican suggests, and "dare
to exercise a Christian political imagination on an as yet
unspecifiable future," what relevance would a loosely connected Christian European Empire made up of constituent
monarchies have for our American homeland—even if that

---

[9] Aidan Nichols, OP, *Christendom Awake: On Re-Energizing the Church in Culture*
(William B. Eerdmans, 1999), 84–85.

same unimaginable future saw our states recast as a similar monarchy of their own? Well, as the manifesto of another organisation, Identità Europea, puts it:

> By encouraging a EUROPEAN IDENTITY we do not intend to promote a "western culture" which absorbs and dissolves all diversities in a leveling attempt. On the contrary, our aim is to enlarge this identity beyond the European boundaries, thus recovering that large part of our continent "outside Europe"—from Argentina to Canada and from South Africa to Australia—which looks at the old continent not as a distant ancestor but as a real homeland.[10]

We owe it to ourselves to encourage the attempts of Europeans to revive their continent—which, in a very real way, is ours too.

All of this having been said, it is time now to answer the question posed by our title.

1. If you believe in bringing this country to Christ in His Church, both for the salvation of souls and for its corporate survival;
2. If you want a nonpartisan, dignified head of government who shall endeavour to rule with equity regardless of faction or region;
3. If you want to love and be proud of an harmonious country made up of revitalised and prosperous states, counties, and municipalities;
4. If you would like to see all classes and conditions of your countrymen working together for the common good; and
5. If you would like to see the lands from whence came our religion and culture prosper in tandem with us and the other Christian nations;

then you may well indeed be a monarchist yourself. If nothing else, it is something worth deeply thinking about.

---

[10] "Manifesto of European Identity," Identità Europea, April 19, 1997, https://web.archive.org/web/20230512023113/http://www.identitaeuropea.it/?page_id=862.

CHAPTER 2

The Varieties of Monarchist Experience

Regardless of his personal imperfections, a monarch represents the majesty of history. He is an heir—a link in a
chain that leads to the Middle Ages that in turn connects
to antiquity and beyond, to the beginning of measured
time when the first hero slew the dragon of disorder and
established the rule of law.

—Charles Fenyvesi[1]

MONARCHICAL MYTHS AND ARCHETYPES

As one may have gleaned from the last chapter, there is a
wide variety of monarchies past and present; so too of monarchists. Indeed, we might almost speak of "monarchisms,"
rather than monarchism as some sort of coherent political
doctrine. And yet, like "conservatism"—a word that describes
any number of beliefs, some of which are utterly contradictory
to one another—it is not without some value. Nevertheless, it
would probably be helpful to give some idea of monarchism
as it exists in the year 2025.

To begin with, we should probably say what it is not. Monarchism is not, of itself, "conservative," although, to be sure,
many monarchists would call themselves that in terms of
retaining their national traditions. It all depends, you see,
upon what the individual is trying to "conserve." There are
certainly a great many republicans in the world who would
call themselves "conservative," by which they mean they are
trying to preserve the supposed victories of the revolutions of
1688, 1776, 1789, 1911, or 1917—that is, whenever the rightful
sovereigns were ejected in the British Isles, these United States,
France, China, or Russia by the national oligarchy or bourgeoisie. There are others who wish to preserve or restore an utterly
unfettered market as an undoubted absolute good. For obvious

---

[1] Charles Fenyvesi, *Splendor in Exile: The Ex-Majesties of Europe* (New Republic
Books, 1979), 278–79.

reasons, most who call themselves monarchists would view the ideological heirs of those who started the problem with some suspicion. Given the paternalistic nature of monarchy, they would rather see some controls on the economy and culture. But these they would be consider on an issue-by-issue basis, rather than the socialists' endorsement for government controls of every kind as their version of absolute good. In this, the monarchist looks to the will of God, the honour of the king, and the good of the subject, a triad that allows for very few sweeping and absolute formulae in this area.

Nor can monarchism be called "authoritarian," still less "totalitarian," in the sense of granting complete power over the lives of the people to those in government. Monarchs are inevitably bound by traditions — many of them religious, others not — which have the effect of limiting how far monarchs can go. That doesn't mean they never made life miserable for those around them. But even Henry VIII could not alter the nature of marriage; he could only take control of the Church in his country for the purpose of securing an annulment and then execute two of his six wives for infidelity. He could not, however, simply alter the nature of marriage on a whim, as one of our Supreme Court justices was able to do in *Obergefell v. Hodges*. It is the mark of dictators, strong men, or oligarchies that — unfettered by faith or custom — they are able to alter reality to fit their own image of the world, or at least to satisfy their lust for power. Modern monarchists inevitably support existing monarchies and restorations, because they love liberty and see the king as the best bulwark against either dictatorship or a political class so in love with itself that it is cut off from reality.

Another anti-monarchical canard peculiar to those Commonwealth countries that retain the king as sovereign (Canada, Australia, New Zealand, and a number of smaller states in the West Indies and Pacific) is the notion that the monarchy is "foreign" or a "colonial relic." Now, this is true only in the sense that everything the British brought to those countries — the English language, Christianity, common law, indeed every element of civilisation — is subject to the same criticism. The stark reality is that the king, his governors-general, and his Australian state and Canadian provincial viceroys operate only on the advice of the local government, without reference to the

British government. The truth is that republican politicians look
to the United States and see a country where the political class
are supreme, untrammeled by even the shadow of the monarchy (whose representatives still retain the "reserve powers,"
allowing them to, among other things, dismiss a prime minister
who tries to govern illegally, as happened in Australia in 1975).

Now, one charge that can be made against many monarchists
is that they are nostalgics or romantics. As the elderly Maude
tells her young lover Harold in *Harold and Maude,*

> I don't regret the kingdoms—what sense in borders and
> nations and patriotism—but I do miss the kings. When
> I was a little girl in Vienna, I was taken to the palace
> for a garden party. I can still see the sunshine on the
> fountains, the parasols, and the flashing uniforms of the
> young officers.[2]

And, indeed, decades ago, Charles Fenyvesi wrote quite
perceptively:

> Nostalgia for royalty is not a potent political force; it
> cannot send people out into the street to demonstrate.
> Monarchism has become a mood rather than a move-
> ment—a longing for another century, a way of expressing
> a sense of loss, an argument with time.[3]

But however true that might have been in 1980, when there
were still many White Russians running about and innumerable former subjects of the Habsburgs and Hohenzollerns, it
is far less so now.

Nevertheless, it must be admitted that several of the archetypes of kingship retain their hold upon the imagination in a
way no president can—save to the degree that he resembles
them. When sovereigns like Franz Joseph of Austria, George III
of Great Britain, Louis XIV of France, or Victoria and Elizabeth
II are around so long that they eventually seem to become the
national grandparent, having been on the throne before most
of their subjects were born, life without them seems unimaginable—until they die. The martyr-king who knowingly sheds
his blood, like Charles I, Louis XVI, Nicholas II, or Karl I, is a
Christlike sacrifice for his people. There is also the lost prince,

---

[2] Colin Higgins, *Harold and Maude* (Avon Books, 1971), 67.
[3] Fenyvesi, *Splendor in Exile,* 277.

whose very disappearance inspires a host of charlatans; examples include Sebastian of Portugal, the Lost Dauphin of France, and Dmitri and Grand Duchess Anastasia of Russia. There is the dispossessed prince, such as Bonnie Prince Charlie in the eighteenth century, Henri, Comte de Chambord in the nineteenth, or Michael of Romania in the twentieth. Another is the king who returns to set things right, like Charlemagne, Justinian, or Henri IV of France. And finally, there is the sleeping king, like Arthur, Frederick Barbarossa, or Constantine XI, who *will* return one day to save his people. The fact that these archetypes are still powerful — and by no means only among monarchists — is shown by the skillful use of all of them by Tolkien in *The Lord of the Rings*. "The hands of the king are the hands of a healer" is an old saying in Gondor;[4] but the kings of England and France cured scrofula by their touch, as the kings of Spain cast out demons, and those of Denmark, epilepsy. Of course, there are also scores of royal saints of various kinds.

All this being true, it is no surprise that one basic source of monarchism today — or at least of a disposition toward it — as found in Christian circles comes from devotion to a given martyr-king. In France (and in a few places in Belgium and Italy), the days around January 21 see a number of requiem Masses offered for Louis XVI and a torchlight procession in his honour, for this king whom Pope Pius VI called a martyr. On and around January 30, Anglo-Catholic churches throughout the world offer Masses revering Charles I as a saint (the only man whom the Church of England canonised); the high point of these festivities is the placing of wreaths at the statute of the White King in London's Trafalgar Square by the Society of King Charles the Martyr, the Royal Martyr Church Union, and the Royal Stuart Society. The latter organisation also organises requiems for Mary Queen of Scots, James II (both of whose causes for canonisation, while stalled, have not been officially closed), and the other members of the House of Stuart. Nicholas II and his murdered family are venerated as saints by the Orthodox Churches — and indeed, the Russian, Serbian, Romanian, Bulgarian, and Georgian Orthodox hierarchies have all urged restoration of the monarchy in

---

[4] J. R. R. Tolkien, *The Lord of the Rings: The Return of the King* (Ballantine Books, 1965), 169. On the Inklings, see chapters 12 and 13 below.

their respective countries. The Ethiopian Orthodox Church practically revere Haile Selassie, the last reigning Christian emperor, as a martyr, due to his brutal death at the hands of revolutionaries in 1975. On October 21, the date of the marriage of Austria's last monarch, Karl, to his Empress Zita (who is up for beatification), the former is honoured as a blessed with a proper Mass. The Emperor Karl League of Prayers works for his canonisation, and his *cultus* and shrines continue to expand in number — not only in the countries he formerly ruled, but in Germany, France, Belgium, England, Italy, Spain, Switzerland, Lebanon, the Philippines, Australia, Brazil, Chile, Canada, and the United States. Obviously, any church or abbey blessed with royal tombs continues to pray for the repose of their souls. Not all devotees of these saints are monarchists in any practical way; but they certainly are not blind to the benefits of a system that produced such men.

But do not think that the religious underpinnings of kingship mean that monarchists are uniformly devout or wish for their national faith to regain a dominant role in their country's life — though of course, many are and do. As early as the eighteenth century, there was Bolingbroke, a zealous Jacobite who was not a religious believer in any real sense. Until he was quite elderly, the leading French royalist thinker Charles Maurras had no personal faith but merely valued Catholicism for its key role in the formation of the French identity. One of our most famous American monarchists, H. P. Lovecraft, was an avowed atheist. Nevertheless, he famously wrote in "A Description of the Town of Quebeck in New-France, Lately Added to His Britannick Majesty's Dominions,"

> There now broke out — in 1775 — that unhappy warfare betwixt His Maj[ty]'s thirteen more southerly colonies and the home government; which culminated in the loss of those colonies to the Empire, and which may in times to come bring about their tragicall ingulphment in a new and alien barbarism of mongrel and autochthonous origin, in which all the standards of civilisation will be lost in a brainless worship of size, speed, wealth, success, and luxury, sad chapter to record![5]

---

[5] H. P. Lovecraft, *Collected Essays*, ed. S. T. Joshi (Hippocampus Press, 2005), vol. 4, "Travel," 157.

For some monarchists, the pro forma ritual backing that Anglicanism gives to the monarchies of the Commonwealth and Lutheranism to those of Scandinavia (and, for that matter, the generic American civil religion that supports our institutions) is quite sufficient. Indeed, as we shall see, together with local liberties this is one of the big fault lines across monarchism.

TWO MODELS FOR THE MONARCH'S POLITICAL ROLE

But what of the political role of the monarch? There are at least two schools of thought in this regard. All monarchists, however, would agree with the following preparatory observations. An emperor or king (unless he is self-made, like Bonaparte) is trained all his life for the role he will one day play. Obviously, he brings to that role his own strengths and weaknesses. But as everyday life shows us, a trained plodder usually does a more dependable job than a brilliant amateur—and few elected heads of state are brilliant. Moreover (despite recent trends, from Pope Benedict to the sovereigns of Spain, Belgium, and the Netherlands), a monarch is usually in the job for life. Where he has executive power, this allows him to set long-term policy; where he does not, his consultations with, warnings to, and advice for "his" successive prime ministers is based upon a wealth of background and experience they cannot hope to match in their relatively short time in office. As has often been said, an elected official spends half his term learning his job and the other half trying to get himself (or at least his party) re-elected. Needless to say, he commands the loyalty solely of the portion of the population that elected him.

With those realities in the background, we may now examine the two most prevalent models of monarchy. The surviving western monarchies (Great Britain and the Commonwealth, the Netherlands, Belgium, Luxembourg, Spain, Sweden, Norway, and Denmark) as well as—for the moment, anyway—Japan, are constitutional; that is, the sovereign reigns but does not rule. Outside the spectrum of everyday politics, he serves as a trans-party focus of loyalty. As noted earlier, his functions are ceremonial and often quasi-religious in nature. He makes visits all over his realm, opening bridges, receiving deputations, and generally acting as national cheerleader. Ambassadors present their letters of credence to him, and he opens and closes parliament. Oaths are sworn to him by soldiers, judges, bureaucrats, and even elected government officials to symbolise their allegiance to the country rather than the party. But "his" ministers are responsible to the majority of the politicians who inhabit parliament, and to the collection of dominant interests that engineer and finance their election thereto. While the reserve powers may confer upon him a limited ability to correct things if the system stumbles in terms of pure legality, his ability to protect his people from their politicians (as Emperor Franz Joseph described his role to Theodore Roosevelt) is severely limited. This is pointed up by the clashes between the sovereigns and the governments of Belgium and Luxembourg over abortion and euthanasia, wherein the attempts by those rulers to defend the most helpless of their subjects from death were easily brushed aside by the political leadership. While the legitimacy of this system depends upon the political class being truly the voice of the majority (a highly debatable proposition in itself), many monarchists favour its retention where present and its adoption as the desired programme of restoration. Certainly, whatever its defects, it would be better than the status quo in parliamentary republics like Portugal, Germany, Austria, and Italy. There, the former royal (now presidential) palace becomes a sort of retirement home for washed-up politicians; surrounded by remnants of monarchical pomp, they do not have even the personal strengths and historical ties to the people over whom they nominally preside that constitutional monarchs enjoy.

The other model for Western monarchists is that of chief executive (often wrongly called "absolute" — wrongly because, as just noted, no monarch can utterly violate tradition the way a president or judiciary can in republics). In such a system, the government ministers are responsible to the sovereign for their tenure, and he sets political policy — all in addition to carrying out the ceremonial duties his constitutional brethren are also obliged to perform. As with the presidents of the United States, France, and Latin America (when the latter are elected rather than coming to power in a coup), he must secure the passage of budgets and other matters through the national legislature. Unlike a constitutional monarchy, where all the king's official actions must normally be countersigned by a "responsible" minister, in this system, the emperor or king is responsible to God alone for his actions — although, as sovereigns have found from at least the time of Magna Carta, they must also be aware of immediate realities. In the existing Christian monarchies — and in Japan, where they appear to be becoming dominant — some monarchists would like to see emulated the experience of Liechtenstein, where the reigning prince regained his power after a showdown with the politicians. This is the sort of monarchy many would like to see restored in various places. Again, it does come down to whether one believes the democratic myth — that the politicians really speak for the people as a whole, rather than being mere mouthpieces for the dominant oligarchy.

CONTEMPORARY ROYALTY AROUND THE WORLD

The struggle between these two visions of monarchy and the debate over the role of Christianity in the state, as a source of legitimacy or mere ritual background, have been the major impulses for much of modern European history. They also contribute to ongoing division between monarchists today. The great dynastic divisions that have plagued Western European royal families from 1688 to the present owe their existence as much to this ideological divide as to obscure genealogical issues. The Jacobites in the British Isles and colonies, the Carlists in Spain, the Miguelists in Portugal, and the Legtimists in France stood for an executive monarchy, provincial liberties, and the predominance of the Church in the nation's social life, while their respective opponents held the opposite. Proof that this division was more than genealogical lies in the fact that Jacobitism and Carlism outlasted their own branches of their royal families and sought other branches for leadership to accomplish their goals. In France, the Legitimist line died out, and the Orleanists adopted many of their beliefs for a new French monarchy; this change was in great part the work of Charles Maurras and his Action Français. But when the Orleans heir became increasingly liberal in the latter twentieth century, the Legitimist side roared into new life around a Spanish Bourbon who dedicated himself to the restoration of a traditional French monarchy. To confuse matters further, there is also an heir to the Bonapartes — whose mother, however, is a Bourbon princess, albeit of an Italian branch. Meanwhile, in Portugal the liberal line died out, and the Miguelists — banished from their homeland for almost a century — became the recognised heirs and returned home, where the current heir lives. In Spain, then, there are Carlists as well as defenders of the status quo; in France there are Legitimists, Orleanists, and Bonapartists. The remaining Jacobites are mostly reconciled to the current house but would like to see more power given it. Certainly, for those who bother to read King Charles's writings and acquaint themselves with his numerous philanthropies (as opposed to having their negative views of the king manufactured for them by the media), there may be some hope for a more positive activist monarchy yet. Irish monarchists divide into those who would like to reenter the Commonwealth, albeit as a republic; Jacobites; and adherents of one or another of the many Gaelic royal families — after all, under the high kings at Tara, Ireland featured five provincial kings and numerous sub-kings.

Central Europe was dominated by the Holy Roman Empire (the emperor of which had nominally been the suzerain of all Western Christendom), latterly ruled by the Habsburgs — who were forced to abdicate that imperial throne for the one substituted and newly created in Austria by Napoleon in 1806. Subsequent to his fall, Austria dominated the Italian and German states until the wars of Italian and German Unification, which left the kings of Prussia as German emperors and the kings of Sardinia as kings of Italy (the latter, of a constitutional variety). To the Habsburgs were left their other realms, including Hungary, the Czech lands, Croatia, Slovenia, a chunk of Poland, and so on. World War I deposed the Hohenzollerns and the remain German princes (Bavaria, Saxony, etc.) and the Habsburgs — whose saintly last Emperor Karl did not abdicate but tried to regain his Hungarian throne twice before his untimely death. The Habsburg lands were partitioned into unstable ethnic nations, leaving, as Churchill observed, a power vacuum for Hitler and Stalin to fill. Karl's son, Archduke Otto, eventually turned his attention from regaining his father's thrones to uniting Europe according to the Christian vision of Charlemagne; he threw his weight behind the European Union. Italy's last king (thus far) was deposed in a rigged election in 1946 — personally pious and a member of an ancient dynasty, he nevertheless represented a very liberal constitutional monarchy. The result of all of this history is that Central Europe offers a true crazy quilt of monarchist movements: adherents of Otto's European vision and/or a restored Habsburg monarchy encompassing some or all of its former people; devotees of the various Italian and German kingdoms, principalities, grand duchies, and duchies on the one side, and of the Hohenzollerns and Savoys (now divided into two warring branches along ideological lines to some degree) on the other; and varying groups wishing the restoration of the Kingdom of Poland in one form or another.

In contrast to these — ironically considering their history — the monarchist scene in the Balkans has been quite stable. Kings Michael of Romania and Simeon II of Bulgaria, crown princes Alexander of Serbia, Nicholas of Montenegro, and Leka of Albania, and King Constantine II of Greece (who died in 2023) all returned to their homelands, and, save the latter (who, for many years, still received difficulty from the various incompetent Greek governments) and King Michael (who died in 2017), currently live in one or more of their royal palaces and, in a reduced way, act as constitutional monarchs in all but name and specifically governmental ceremonial (although Simeon actually *was* Bulgaria's prime minister for a while). As noted, the Serbian, Bulgarian, and Romanian Orthodox Churches have officially endorsed restoration, and monarchists in those countries work toward that day. In addition, in a vague way for all Orthodox and a very specific one for a particular branch of Greek nationalism, there is hope for recovering Constantinople one day, and with it, the Byzantine Empire.

What of Russia, the third Rome? Despite the cavils of certain Romanoff descendants, the Grand Duchess Maria Vladimirovna and her son, the Grand Duke George, act more and ever more as heirs to the throne — going about the world (including Russia) from their base in Spain, scattering decorations among émigrés and current governmental officials alike; rumour has it that as part of his attempts at renewing his motherland, Putin supports a restoration in much the same way as Franco did in Spain; here too, the Russian Orthodox Church endorses the idea. As a side note, when Ethiopia's Marxist revolutionaries deposed and murdered Emperor Haile Selassie, the then Soviet

Union reversed itself, backing the new regime against long-time Soviet client Somalia. This was an act with disastrous results for both the Soviet Union and Somalia, and it could only have been motivated by a weird communist romanticism. At any rate, Russian monarchists (and they, too, come in varying stripes, but the grand duchess's adherents are dominant) are riding high — as they are in neighbouring Georgia, where a recently-born prince unites the bloodlines of the two feuding branches of the age-old Bagrationi dynasty, the restoration of which the local Orthodox Church also endorses — as does the Ethiopian Orthodox Church to some degree.

In Scandinavia and the Benelux countries, the monarchy remains — despite its powerlessness — a strong symbol of nationality, both at home and for descendants of their peoples abroad. Indeed, in Belgium the monarchy is the only glue remaining to keep Walloons and Flemish together. Belgian King Albert II went even further, when he kept appointing caretaker prime ministers for over a year as the deeply divided parliament kept failing to produce a majority. The reserve powers are like a fire extinguisher — rarely used, but essential when needed.

Outside the United States, the Americas offer several monarchist varieties of their own. In Spanish-speaking America, the division since independence into liberal and conservative offers one strand that upholds each nation's connexion with the mother country — Hispanidad. Adherents of this belief hope one day to see the king of Spain as, at very least, the head of an Hispanic commonwealth. Mexico had two ill-starred emperors of her own: Iturbide and Maximilian; the latter, being childless, adopted the former's grandson as his heir, and that family subsists until today. Brazil broke away from Portugal as an independent empire in 1822 under Pedro I, a prince of the Royal House of Braganza; while Emperor Pedro II was deposed by the oligarchy in 1889 as punishment for freeing the slaves, his descendants are still around today. There is also a large and divided monarchist movement in Brazil, which is growing in strength in response to the republic's increasing enfeeblement. Canada has a trifurcated monarchist movement of its own: those who are intent on preserving the current constitution; the "High Tories," philosophical Anglophone monarchists (such as John Farthing, George Grant, and Ron Dart) inspired by the Jacobites and Tories of Britain and the loyalist tradition, which brought American refugees to the nation after the American Revolution; and the French royalist/ nationalist tradition expressed by such luminaries as Marcel Trudel, Fr. Lionel Groulx, and Maurice Duplessis. Although shattered during the Quiet Revolution of the 1960s, this last tradition is making a small comeback. Together with the High Tories, it represents the partnership upon which Canada was originally based.

So much for Christendom. Islamic monarchies and monarchists are generally of three kinds. The first is almost tribal; the Saudis and the Yemenites (deposed in 1963, after which a long civil war with republicans ended in their defeat six years later) fit that bill. As quasi-religious leaders of Islam, they are — to put it mildly — unfriendly to Christians, though they may cooperate with Western governments for certain ends. Their adherents are deeply Muslim. Second, there is the Westernized variety, who often ruled or rule a restive Muslim majority through a network of minority peoples in Iran, Iraq, Afghanistan, Egypt, Libya, Tunisia, and the Ottoman Empire in its final years (the overthrow of each of these countries has been disastrous for us all in the long run); the network also includes Jordan, Morocco, Oman, the United Arab Emirates, Qatar, the Malaysian sultanates, Brunei, and Bahrain. Although these monarchies' most loyal followers are often non-Muslims or secularised Muslims, they are also supported by various Sufi sects, most notably the Naqsbandi. Last, and most daunting, are our foes in the Islamic State in Iraq and Syria (ISIS), who would see a universal caliphate engulf the whole world. Monarchists to be sure, but none whom I would like to see accomplish their goals.

Of the great Confucian monarchies, China, Korea, and Vietnam are long gone; only Japan remains. Politically, of course, they have been obliterated in the first three lands; but the philosophy behind them remains — and so does the culture they generated in terms of court ceremonial, dance, music, religion, and cuisine. Each of these are preserved carefully, and members of their former ruling families (and descendants of their courtiers) are foremost in their preservation. They are supported in this work by the governments of communist China and Vietnam, as well as über-capitalist South Korea. Thus, today the tourist can take in an imperial sacrifice ritual at Beijing's Temple of Earth, the changing of the Royal Guard at one of the palaces in Seoul, or a court dance in the Forbidden City in Hue. Who knows where this may lead? In Japan, where the postwar constitution imposed by the victorious allies limited the position of the emperor in many ways, the current prime minister, Shigeru Ishiba, and many of the ruling Liberal Democratic Party are members of the monarchist group Nippon Kaigi. Under Prime Minister Abe, there was a great deal of discussion about amending the constitution to extend the emperor's powers and revive the nation's right to wage war. In response, Emperor Akihito spoke in an oblique way about abdicating, and the crown prince of the necessity to learn from the past. Whether this constituted agreement with or opposition to the suggested moves was not entirely clear.

In Buddhist monarchies, such as those of Bhutan, Thailand, and Cambodia today, and Laos, Burma, and Sri Lanka in times past, the king is head of the "Sangha," the whole community of Buddhists in the nation. This has allowed the king of the first-mentioned country to guide it through a series of coups and elections, but his course has been stable compared to that of Cambodia's long-time ruler, King-turned-Prince-turned-King Sihanouk, whose adventures were amazing but resulted in his son occupying what seems to be a currently secure throne. Laos's king was murdered by the communists sometime after their takeover in 1975, but the royal family continues to lead the Laotian community in exile. A similarly revered status allowed the long-deposed Burmese dynasty to survive under the military regime that ended in 2011. Hindu monarchy was very similar in many respects, for which reason devout Hindus in Nepal support the restoration of King Gyanendra, who was deposed in 2008.

As the Europeans colonised the Americas, Africa, Asia, and Oceania, they came in contact with a great number of small sultanates, kingdoms, and other monarchies. Those who cooperated with the Europeans generally retained their positions until independence. In Latin America, most of these were obliterated by the new republican authorities. In the rest of the

world, only Tonga, Swaziland, Lesotho, Burundi, and Rwanda
became independent national monarchies; the latter two suffered revolutions and then endless rounds of mind-numbing
ethnic slaughter between Hutus and Tutsis at the behest of
various presidents (I had the honour of knowing Kigeli V
of Rwanda; what a blessing it would have been for his poor
realm had this kind gentleman been able to retain his throne).
Elsewhere in the postcolonial world, countless traditional
sovereignties continue to play a strong local role under more
or less rickety republican regimes, where they often exert a
stabilising influence in their own territories while the dreary
series of military coups and rigged elections continues to play
out in the capital. The sultans and rajas of Indonesia and the
maharajas and nawabs of India, Pakistan, and Bangladesh still
receive the respect of their erstwhile subjects. The tribal kings
of Uganda, having been dispossessed by Milton Obote and Idi
Amin, were restored to their thrones in 1993, and many African and Pacific countries have "Houses of Chiefs" at either the
national or state level. Hawaiian nationalists long to restore
their country's kingdom, unjustly annexed (according to a
congressional apology issued in 1993) by the United States. Yet
even in these United States, there are traces of such traditional
rulerships: the governors of the New Mexico Pueblos stand in
a feudal relationship to the presidency, as once they did to
the king of Spain. This relationship is symbolised by the two
sets of *bastones de mando* or "canes" each pueblo possess — one
from the king and the other from President Lincoln. At the
same time, the Senate of American Samoa is elected not by
the general populace but by the heads of the chiefly families.

This brings us at last to these United States. Unlike any other
nation on earth, we do not have a monarchical tradition; but
we did and do have monarchists. Some Loyalists did not leave,
but like St. Elizabeth Ann Seton and her husband, and the first
Episcopal Bishop Samuel Seabury, stayed behind to do what
good they could under the new regime. In time, individuals
such as Ralph Adams Cram and Isabella Stewart Gardner took
up the Jacobite cause. T. S. Eliot, an exile in London, famously
declared himself a "royalist in politics." Some, such as H. P.
Lovecraft, felt compelled to reexamine the American Revolution
in the light of its results. Later, in the 1930s, various American

monarchists (including Cram) as well as other writers with alternative viewpoints could be found in the *American Review* of Seward Collins. Nor were two regional monarchical traditions lacking in adherents. The French-Canadian version mentioned earlier was publicised in the *Sentinelle* and *Travailleur* newspapers of Woonsocket, Rhode Island and Worcester, Massachusetts. In Mexico after the Cristero wars of the 1920s, the Sinarquistas preached the gospel of Catholic government and Hispanidad; for a while they were present in Latino communities throughout the Southwest and allegedly made a showing in the Los Angeles Zoot Suit Riots of 1944 — as a result, they even make a cameo appearance in James Ellroy's novel *The Big Nowhere* (Mysterious Press, 1988). In the 1960s, Catholic monarchists emerged from the pages of *Triumph* magazine, which featured Carlist Frederick Wilhelmsen and French royalist supporter Gary Potter, among others. Over at *National Review*, despite the republicanism of most conservatives of the time, Erik von Kuehnelt-Leddihn never ceased to praise the institution. Add to those tenuous traditions of monarchist intellectualism our colonial heritage, our governmental structure, and the fact that members of literally every monarchist movement, cause, or sentiment that we have touched upon in this chapter have made their home in this country, and it will become apparent that monarchism of one sort or another is deeply rooted in our soil. It is diverse to the point of incoherence, not unlike the nation itself — it is as American as apple pie.

There only remains to wonder if, as the strength of our founding myths and their ability to animate our institutions continue to wane, America's "other" set of traditions could be called in to maintain our body politic. Certainly, the three most memorable presidents of the twentieth century were also the most faux-regal: FDR, JFK, and Ronald Reagan. The first-named was the most successful in achieving his goals — but it took him three and a quarter terms in office to so. For all the glamour of Camelot, Kennedy's blip on the time screen was more show than substance, and despite the immense reassurance Reagan gave the country that it was still "morning in America," were he to come back today, he might doubt whether he had really accomplished anything. Nevertheless, the trio's respective senses of style and most un-republican interest in the arts and sciences have guaranteed them some place in the nation's memory. Without a doubt, in some future crisis another president will invoke their legacies and Lincoln's to justify whatever illegal acts he feels compelled to enact to restore order.

But what about explicit interest in monarchy in some form in these United States? There has been a minor boomlet of interest since the appearance of Hans Hermann Hoppe's *Democracy — The God That Failed: The Economics and Politics of Monarchy, Democracy, and Natural Order* (Transaction, 2001). Diverse academics such as John Médaille, Lee Walter Congdon, and William S. Lind have declared themselves monarchists. The rise of the internet alongside the ongoing collapse of the national consensus has unleashed a new generation of young American monarchists of innumerable varieties — blogging away and in touch with the likeminded here and overseas. Will anything like a coherent body of American monarchist political thought emerge? Who knows? Still, as H. P. Lovecraft himself observed, "with strange aeons even death may die."[6]

One thing is certain. If this country — and indeed the other countries that make up what was once Christendom — are to survive, they shall require both a new animating principle and a new myth of governance. In this book, I nominate those that built the West in the first place: Altar and Throne. Regardless of whether that happens, and regardless of whether this or any other country survives, those two ideas shall endure, until the great king of all, *Christus Rex, Kristos Pantokrator*, shall draw this world's drama to a close. Until that day, these words of archmonarchist J. R. R. Tolkien shall, at least somewhere, remain absolutely true:

> All that is gold does not glitter,
> Not all those who wander are lost;
> The old that is strong does not wither,
> Deep roots are not reached by the frost.
> From the ashes a fire shall be woken,
> A light from the shadows shall spring;
> Renewed shall be blade that was broken,
> The crownless again shall be king.[7]

---

[6] H. P. Lovecraft, *The Dreams in the Witch House and Other Weird Stories*, ed. S. T. Joshi (Penguin Books, 2004), 30.
[7] J. R. R. Tolkien, *The Lord of the Rings: The Fellowship of the Ring* (Ballantine Books, 1965), 231.

CHAPTER 3

One Cheer for Constitutional Monarchy!

For every monarchy overthrown the sky becomes less brilliant because it loses a star. A republic is ugliness set free.
—Anatole France

O N NOVEMBER 30, 2021, BARBADOS JETTI-
soned Queen Elizabeth II as sovereign, ending the
country's almost 395-year-old monarchy and joining the ranks of the banana republics within the Commonwealth, alongside such partners as Fiji, Trinidad, and South
Africa. The country's governor-general, Dame Sandra Mason,
became the country's first president, joining the roll of shame
of final viceroys who metamorphose into their nation's first
chief consumer at the public trough. As is usually the case in
such affairs (South Africa and Australia being notable exceptions), there was not even a perfunctory referendum, signaling
the ruling party's lack of confidence in their subjects' voting
the "correct" way.

Nevertheless, why should we care about yet another small
Caribbean country's ruling clique taking even the shadow of
authority unto their lovely selves?

As per usual when this ritual is gone through, the local
politicos trumpet the idea that ending the only form of government the nation has ever known is somehow "breaking
with the colonial past," which in itself is supposed to be a
reason to celebrate. Were that in fact the case, there is much
more that Barbados must shed—its legal system, language,
religion, culture, folklore, indeed, its very population, since
the island was uninhabited when the English under Charles I
settled the then-empty paradise. Above all, the Westminster
system and the parasitical political class itself should be thrown
on the colonial ash heap. But of course, that is not what it is

about — or ever is, in Commonwealth Realms with politicos who wish to break their oaths to the king and perjure themselves in pursuit of the top of the brass ring. Nothing infuriates the darlings more than that there is one government job that even theoretically is not theirs for the asking.

The tragic truth is that while political pigs in their blankets may indeed aspire to wielding every scrap of power practically available — and even be appointed governor-general on the prime minister's advice in countries such as Canada, Australia, New Zealand, and Jamaica — the top job is beyond them. The king is still the king, and as long as he or his heirs remain monarchs over their lands, the top job remains unavailable, no matter how powerless it may appear.

In the Commonwealth Realms, as in the United Kingdom, on paper the king (or the governor-general who nominally represents him) wields the predominance of power. The reality, of course, is that the supposed elected representatives of the people who hold a majority in the local parliament put their party leader in as prime minister or premier, and he heads the management team called the cabinet for so long as they can hold on to that majority. Normally the monarch or viceroy acts on the prime minister's advice, the royal prerogative being exercised at the politicos' behest however they choose. The royals and viceroys leave to them the actual business of governing, while they get on with the business of promoting national unity, ceremonially and otherwise. Obviously, this is a chore to which politicians are not well suited. That is why in Britain and the Crown Commonwealth all oaths — those taken by the members of the Armed Forces, for example — are made not to the politicians-in-charge but to His Majesty the King. He and his viceroys represent the non- or apolitical ultimate nature of the state; he is in a sense a living flag.

Leading politicians being what they are, however, in such a system they occasionally overstep the admittedly wide latitude they are given to play with. So it is that in very rare cases — as in Canada in 1926 and Australia in 1975 — the sovereign or his representative must step in and use what are called the "reserve powers." Where normally the king, queen, or governor-general would call for or refuse new elections only on the advice of the prime minister, sometimes particularly dodgy tactics on

the part of the senior politician require independent action
in order to protect the constitution. For any viceregal figure
who does so, this is of course the nuclear option, because it
is always political suicide. As with a fire extinguisher, no one
who has the ability to use the reserve powers wants to. Even
so, they can act as the ultimate restraint on the hubris of the
highest politicians in a given country.

But where such a system becomes a republic, the wielder
of the reserve powers becomes part of the very clique he is
supposed to oversee — it is like putting the head of General
Motors in charge of regulating automobile production and
practise. The results are plain to see in the political histories of
every single Commonwealth nation that has made the change.
From India to Fiji to Guyana to Malta, they generally lurch
from one governmental crisis to another; bereft of an apolitical, nonpartisan centre of loyalty — no matter how nominal —
which additionally bears the underlying threat of intervening
if playtime becomes too madcap among the oligarchic set, they
are all increasingly divided in many different ways. Barbados
will no doubt follow in their train.

What is true of the British and Commonwealth Realms is
also true of most of the surviving European monarchies: Spain,
Scandinavia, and Benelux all boast monarchies in which the
nominal ruler is as dependent upon the particular political
class as is His Majesty and his governors-general. As with them,
too, the current systems are the result of several centuries
of political history in which power was taken — at greater or
lesser speed — from the monarch and invested in the politicians. The basic superstition behind this is that, because they
are voted for by the people, these well-placed nabobs speak
on their behalf. Were this true, every power stripped from the
sovereign and thrown to the pols would be another exercise
in expanding democracy.

Enchanting picture though this vision may be, as with so
many mirages, it is not really true. In truth, elected politicians
and their judicial appointees represent secondarily their own
personal interests and desires and primarily those of the interests or factions who fund their campaigns. This is endemic to
what we call democracy; nor is it by itself necessarily an evil,
because — as with actors, artists, and sports figures — politicians

have skills and personality traits that most of us lack. Governance is an intricate skill, to be sure, and most of us are not suited to it. The problems arise when the politicians are allowed all power in heaven and earth and there is nothing or no one to check their endless greed and ambition.

In 1910, after leaving office, ex-president Theodore Roosevelt visited Vienna and met with Emperor Franz Joseph, who two years before had celebrated his Diamond Jubilee of accession. The president asked His Imperial Majesty what he conceived his role as a modern monarch to be; the old Habsburg's response was "to protect my people from their politicians."[1] This was quite true, and he was very successful at it for a long time. But World War I ended that.

It is also an unfortunate truth that as modern constitutional monarchs have crossed swords with their governments over important issues, a strange pattern has emerged: ultimately — as with Sweden's Gustav V in the 1914 Courtyard Speech affair; Denmark's Christian X in the 1920 Easter Crisis; Victor Emmanuel III's dismissal of Mussolini in 1943; and Constantine II of Greece's attempt to dislodge the colonels in 1966 — the sovereigns usually turn out to have been right. But that never seems to do them any good in the immediate, and as with those examples, they usually seem to lose — all in the name of "democracy."

That sort of track record has not escaped more recent royals; in modern times they are extremely loath to get into a fight with the "people's" spokescreatures. So it was that in 1990, after decades of fending off infanticide from Belgium by dint of refusing to sign any measure legalizing it into law, King Baudouin finally abdicated for a day — allowing "Christian" Democratic (CD) Prime Minister Wilfried Martens to get the baby-killing going in Belgium. Time marches on, of course, and abortion having become part of the Christian Democratic gospel, in 2008 the CD Party in Luxembourg wished to bring in legal euthanasia into the Grand Duchy. As with Baudouin, Grand Duke Henri was a believing Catholic and could not assent to legalizing murder. So it was that the Christian Democrats under Prime Minister Jean-Claude Juncker simply altered the constitution, thereby stripping the Grand Duke of that power.

---

[1] Lukes, *On the Edge*, 17.

Slimy politicians are not confined to constitutional monarchies, of course; they are the principal beneficiaries of any
republic. But it is the myth that they speak for the people that
has ultimately paralysed any popular support for the remaining monarchs of the West; even to consider resisting would be
suicidal. Nor can there be any doubt that republics of Scotland,
England, Wales, Northern Ireland (the Union would certainly
break), Denmark, Sweden, Norway, Belgium, the Netherlands,
Spain, and Luxembourg would be far drearier and shoddier
places than they already are. Their royal palaces would be
occupied by the same breed of elderly retired politician seen
in most European parliamentary republics.

Nevertheless, the sad truth remains — and has been underlined in the past two years — that constitutional monarchies are
generally no longer any safer from the politician's vagaries than
are the majority of semi-functioning republics. One wishes
that the current crop of royals would be far more assertive
in their defence of their subjects' rights against the political
establishment. But many of them have been trained to believe
that the pols — no matter how loathsome — somehow really do
represent the will of the people. Others know full well that
doing so might result in a republic, and even worse to follow.

Certainly, many are scandalized by the lifestyle choices of
some royals — both reigning and out-of-power. But apart from
the 84 percent of Liechtensteiners who supported their prince
against their Parliament in the 2003 referendum, there have
been in the twentieth and twenty-first centuries no mass
risings in support of those rulers who have risked everything
to protect their people. Indeed, Manuel II of Portugal, Bl. Karl
of Austria-Hungary, Alfonso XIII of Spain, Umberto II of Italy,
and Michael of Romania voluntarily went into exile to spare
their peoples the horrors of civil war and — in the case of the
last-named — promised mass executions of his supporters.
As far as the moral behaviour of certain royals goes, a populace with standards that have fallen as low as ours is not in
a position to complain if the heir to the throne behaves as
poorly as the majority of its putative subjects. After all, is
that not democratic? Perhaps we ourselves might think of
becoming the kind of subjects who would merit the kind of
royals we admire.

Still, no human situation lasts forever. With their acceptance of lockdowns, enforcement of masking, and coercion to vaccinate, recent leadership has quite effectively revealed the true and arbitrary nature of modern rule—something that may be exacerbated in the future. As Charles Fenyvesi put it, "Regardless of his personal imperfections, a monarch represents the majesty of history. He is an heir—a link in a chain that leads to the Middle Ages that in turn connects to antiquity and beyond, to the beginning of measured time when the first hero slew the dragon of disorder and established the rule of law."[2] Reigning or not, it is far from beyond the realm of possibility that one or more royals may one day find the situation forcing or inviting them to mobilise precisely those traditions they embody in order to save their people from whatever dire fate otherwise awaits them.

---

[2] Fenyvesi, *Splendor in Exile*, 278–79.

❧ CHAPTER 4 ❧
The Limits of Power

We have a King, and yet no King,
For he hath lost his power;
For 'gainst his will his subjects are
Imprison'd in the Tower.
We had some laws (but now no laws)
By which he held his crown;
And we had estates and liberties,
But now they're voted down.
We had religion, but of late
That's beaten down with clubs;
Whilst that profaneness authorized
Is belched forth in tubs.
We were free subjects born, but now
We are by force made slaves,
By some whom we did count our friends,
But in the end proved knaves.
          —Anonymous, "A Mad World, My Masters"[1]

THIS ANONYMOUS BALLAD WAS PENNED around 1642. At that time, the Puritan Parliament was beginning its hostilities against not only King Charles I (whom, in the end, it would murder) and his Cavalier supporters, but all that was left of Merry—indeed, Catholic—England. So, too, did it make war on all that was truest and best in His Majesty's other kingdoms of Scotland and Ireland, to say nothing of Wales, Cornwall, and the American plantations.

Indeed, the last battle of that sorry conflict was fought a decade later in Maryland: the Battle of the Severn on March 25, 1655. The king's older son would return as a compromise in 1660, reign more or less peacefully for a quarter century, and be succeeded by his Catholic younger brother, James II. Having two Protestant daughters to succeed him, he could be tolerated by the heirs of those who had murdered his father. But the birth of his son in 1688 caused the oligarchs who controlled Parliament

---

[1] Charles MacKay, *The Cavalier Songs and Ballads of England from 1642 to 1684* (London, 1863), 14.

to depose him. He and his family went into exile; their Jacobite (from the Latin *Jacobus*, for "James") supporters attempted to restore them militarily in 1715, 1719, and 1745 — the last effort led initially by James's grandson, "Bonnie Prince Charlie."

After that attempt ended with the tragedy of Culloden, Jacobitism survived as a sort of sentiment, sometimes stronger, sometimes weaker — but along the way affecting such things as the Oxford movement and various Celtic nationalisms. As with similar folk around the European continent from 1789 until today, the Cavaliers and Jacobites of song and story were motivated by questions regarding three features of human life: legitimacy, authority, and power. Their defeat certainly resulted in the current situation in the entire Anglosphere (not only in the British Empire; in many ways, the American Revolution and Civil War were repercussions of that earlier conflict).

Today, from the Covid lockdowns to *Traditionis Custodes* to the Chinese population policies, the entire planet is enmeshed in varieties of tyranny, all of which may be traced back to errors regarding legitimacy, authority, and power. Just what are they? Let us look at each in turn.

Power is the ability to make things happen — to be able to convince or to force oneself or others to do something or other, to have the resources to do or make others do what one wishes. Today, one often hears a distinction made between "soft" power, which is the sort of influence exerted by churches, artists, associations of varying kinds, and so on, and "hard" power. The latter means, essentially, brute force as used by individuals, crime families, judiciaries, police, armed forces, and ecclesiastical authorities, wielded against those who cannot resist their might. In and of itself, power is an instrument — a tool, and so, by definition, morally neutral in and of itself. In medieval times, power was diffuse — the king, the nobility, the Church, the gentry, the merchant and craft guilds, and even the peasants and serfs all had some. Today, as the Covid lockdown showed, it is concentrated.

Authority is the right to say what ought to be done. Thus, the doctor has the authority to tell the patient what to do. In Church, state, and private life, authority has traditionally been used to regulate the use of power toward a specific end: the common good. Equally opposed to this is the indiscriminate use of power — all-against-all, which is anarchy; or the use of power for purely private and personal ends, without regard to authority or its law. This is always criminal; but when it is done by rulers with authority, it is despotism. In the Middle Ages, authority was concentrated in the monarch; today, it is conferred by either or both the electorate and the judiciary.

In order to rightfully command obedience, authority requires legitimacy. This is usually conferred upon the rulers by a religion of some sort (it need not be one with a God; communism and modern liberalism function similarly to the established churches of yore). The faith's dogmas determine the rules whereby the society is governed; they also define the common good and the last end of governance.

In the Middle Ages, both Church and state believed that the last end of man was his salvation and that both institutions existed to help him attain that blessed state: the Church by direct application of the grace of Christ to believers via the sacraments, and the state by assisting the Church financially and in other ways, and by creating a state of affairs whereby the individual was sufficiently secure in his safety and his livelihood that he could direct his attention to his soul's good. The Church conferred legitimacy — and so political authority — upon the monarch via the coronation; he, in turn — ideally — used his authority to coordinate, like an orchestra leader, the various powers in the state to operate based on this view of the common good.

With the Protestant Revolt, subsequent revolutions (such as those resisted by the Cavaliers and Jacobites and their continental equivalents), the World Wars, and the technological transformation of society, over the centuries the situation we face now arose. The dominant animating philosophies of today's world have replaced man's voyage to heaven as the final end of governance, and the common good has been redefined as the greatest pleasure for the greatest number.

In a sense, modern leaders have two faces. One is very egalitarian, because the wish to shove their snouts into the common trough, in the same pursuits they declare to be the proper end of their subjects, is quite sincere. At the same time, however, they are extremely despotic, doing their best to suppress alternative views or honest answers to the questions besetting us.

While talking about freedom on the one hand, they are zealous in suppressing what they consider heresy on the other — albeit with kinder, gentler means like cancel culture or "doxxing."

In the meantime, their educational and media industries do their best to reduce the subjects' aspirations to those of their masters — the same trough. Anything higher — most certainly what was considered the common good in days of yore — is seen as a fantasy or illusion to many, if not most, of those currently in charge, from which they must struggle to free those whom they rule.

None of this has left the Catholic Church unscathed. What has happened in the state and culture has certainly affected her leaders to a very great degree — this was the net effect of "opening up to the world." What Benedict XVI denounced in 2016 as the nearly general universalism of Catholics[2] is simply an adoption of the point of view of the world around us. Certainly, if salvation is assured to all, then the Church must point out to her children that they may partake in the moral pig trough offered by the world — the Church exists to say grace over it, so to speak. But those hierarchs who hold this point of view, like their equivalents in the state and culture, immediately find any subjects who will not accept this revision to be threats, deserving of repression and punishment.

In both cases, then, all the power available to the modern rulership shall be used to repress those who dissent from their view of the common good. What makes this problematic, however, is that it is not merely a question of conflict between two points of view. The one espoused by the vast majority of our fathers and many of us today is objectively true; the one that opposes it is objectively false. Now, this is not just a question of good versus evil, although that does explain why the Cavaliers, Jacobites, etc. carried on their seemingly doomed and endless struggle constantly. It is also a question of what is objectively true, of what actually works. Man's final end beyond this world of sin and shadows is no dream — although our fallen natures and the depredations of the devil make it no certainty. God bestows legitimacy upon authority for no other reason than

---

[2] See "Full text of Benedict XVI's recent, rare, and lengthy interview," *Catholic News Agency*, March 17, 2016, https://www.catholicnewsagency.com/news/33591/full-text-of-benedict-xvis-recent-rare-and-lengthy-interview.

that last end; to be legitimate, authority must direct power only toward bringing man to his proper last end. Power, in turn, has no right to be exercised save for that goal. As usual, Dom Guéranger expresses this reality quite forcefully:

> How great, then, is the dignity of human law! It makes the legislator a representative of God, and, at the same time, spares the subject the humiliation of feeling himself debased before a fellow-man! But, in order that the law oblige, that is, be truly a law, it is evident that it must be, first and foremost, conformable to the commands and the prohibitions of God, whose will alone can give it a sacred character by making it enter into the domain of man's conscience. It is for this reason that there cannot be a law against God, or His Christ, or His Church. When God is not with Him who governs, the power he exercises is nothing better than brute force. The sovereign, or the parliament, that pretends to govern a country in opposition to the laws of God, has no right to aught but revolt and contempt from every upright man; to give the sacred name of law to tyrannical enactments of that kind is a profanation unworthy, not only of a Christian, but of every man who is not a slave.[3]

Regardless of whether such usurpation faces opposition or not, there are inherent limitations to the illegitimate application of authority and use of power. When exercised over a long period of time against the authentic common good, in the service of which they were instituted, they tend to break in the hands of their misusers. The subjects do their best to evade the pronouncements of their masters, unconsciously contemptuous of them. Midlevel functionaries shirk their duty, often frustrating the wills of those in charge for mere amusement, if not on account of ideology. The machinery of governance becomes ever more inefficient and begins to totter. Give it a good external push and it collapses. History is replete with such examples.

Unfortunately, all of this does a great deal of damage, initially to the legitimate and God-given exercise of authority on the part of whomever rises to the top in the ecclesiastical and temporal spheres. However long this period in which we

---

[3] Prosper Guéranger, OSB, *The Liturgical Year*, trans. Laurence Shepherd (Newman Press, 1949), vol. 11, "Time After Pentecost: Book 2," 465.

are living through shall last, we must try to keep whatever legitimate exercises of authority there are around us in view. If we live to see it end, it shall fall to us to assist whomever God raises up to rebuild the reputation and strength of the various institutions of Church and state. Just as all the adulteries in history do not change the ideal of matrimony in the slightest, all the abuses of law and power that have ever been do not negate the God-given importance of legitimate and duly exercised authority, nor our obligation to be obedient to it — however obscured by abuse and misapplication it may be.

Above all, let us remember that even in those periods when Church and state had saintly popes and monarchs, life was far from ideal, and neither authority nor power were exercised perfectly. That can be done only in the hereafter, when — should we save our souls — we, too, shall be part of that heavenly kingdom, which has always been and ever shall be the acme of perfection.

PART II

Church, State, and the Holy Roman Empire

CHAPTER 5

What Is Christendom?

T HE IMMEDIACY OF THE QUESTION POSED BY the title of this chapter is reinforced by the season of Christmas—which, despite being under sporadic attack by "holiday" partisans, centers on the one holy day still observed by the majority of the world. Despite the anti-Christian moral tone of many of "her" governments around the world, Queen Elizabeth II received a sprig of the Glastonbury thorn, very publicly attended church on Christmas, sponsored a notable annual Epiphany service, and delivered a generally inspiring Christmas message. Most heads of state in countries with large numbers of self-proclaimed Christians do the same—even our own president follows suit, subject of course to the modern "holiday" caveat. For a short but blessed time, we are universally reminded of Longfellow's poem:

> I heard the bells on Christmas Day
> Their old, familiar carols play,
> And mild and sweet
> The words repeat
> Of peace on earth, good will to men!
> And thought how, as the day had come,
> The belfries of all Christendom
> Had rolled along
> The unbroken song
> Of peace on earth, good will to men![1]

But once the Christmas trees are tossed out, public life throughout the world returns to its accustomed downward course. That Christendom, with belfries that rang out unanimously their joy at the birth of the Prince of Peace, vanishes once more like Brigadoon—only to revive slowly as holiday advertising commences the day before Hallowe'en.

---

[1] C. Merton Babcock, ed., *Henry Wadsworth Longfellow: Selected Poems* (Peter Pauper Press, 1982), 38.

Since few or no regimes today (with the partial exception of Liechtenstein) claim to be Christian—as opposed to the multiplicity of states that claim to be Islamic or Buddhist—answering the question "what *is* Christendom?" needs to be preceded by understanding what it *was*.

In one sense, Christendom began at the Cenacle on that first Pentecost when the Church, as we know it, was born. From the beginning those first Catholics were armed with our Lord's dictum to "render unto Caesar what is Caesar's, and unto God what is God's" (Mt 22:21). Nevertheless, and despite prayer for their pagan sovereigns within and without the Roman Empire and yeoman service in the militaries of said sovereigns, persecution was their lot on every hand. But over the following two centuries, the work of conversion went on and bore fruit. The Kingdom of Edessa, led by its ruler Abgar V, was the first to convert. It was rapidly followed by Armenia, Georgia, Ethiopia, and Nubia. But it was the conversion of a Roman emperor that led directly to the creation of Christendom (Roman patronage of the faith in turn induced the Empire's then-chief foe, Persia—which had simply persecuted its Christians prior to that time—to encourage the local Church to adopt Nestorianism, distancing "their" Christians from those of Rome). Indeed, Emperor Theodosius the Great granted automatic imperial citizenship to those who received baptism. The Eastern half of the Empire survived, centred on Constantinople; the baptism of Clovis ensured the survival of the vision of Christendom in the barbarian kingdoms of the West. This last eventually resulted in the rise of Charlemagne and the birth of the Holy Roman Empire. All of these events taken together—and supplemented by the adventure of the Crusades—resulted in what we might call "the first Christendom," the *res publica christiana*.

Lasting from whenever a given area was Christianised until the Reformation, this period saw any number of horrors and mishaps during its sway—as every time does. But the institutions of society were expected to reflect, to the highest possible degree, the divine order as revealed by the Church.

So it was that emperors and kings began their reigns with the sublime rite of coronation; each had his own chaplains and publicly observed the holy days of the Church; each sponsored certain parishes and monasteries. Moreover, they provided for pilgrims to and supported institutions in Rome and the Holy Land, and gave oaths at their crownings that they would protect their people from heresy. The sessions of nascent parliaments were opened and closed with Masses, as were those of the courts; bishops and abbots often served in legislative and judicial roles. Priests accompanied the military into battle; the latter's fields of combat were limited by the Truce and Peace of God. In towns, merchants and trades organised into guilds, which looked after the spiritual as well as physical needs of their members. They and the confraternities often sponsored the processions and miracle and mystery plays that were such a big part of the celebration of holy days in towns. Agricultural life was organised around the feasts and fasts of the Church, as were fairs and markets. Universities placed their faculties of theology above those of law and the arts, and the chapels of their colleges were the centres of academic life. The monastic, mendicant, and military orders fanned out over Christendom, providing as tight a web of unity as did the dioceses and the network of pilgrims' shrines. When the age of discovery commenced, the kings of Spain and Portugal attempted to expand this Christendom to the ends of the earth.

To be sure, it is easy to romanticise this state of affairs; it could be bloody, anarchic, and corrupt from time to time, and of course it varied wildly from place to place. Nevertheless, its eulogies by such as Chateaubriand, Novalis, Digby, and Gautier were not entirely wrong.[2] And it might be argued that we moderns, seated happily as we are above millions of infant skulls, beneficiaries of innumerable atrocity-filled wars in the name of freedom, and proponents of an unprecedented moral code as regards marriage and sexuality, may not be the best judges of blood, anarchy, or corruption on the part of our Christian ancestors.

Regardless of what view one maintains of the first Christendom, it came to an end in the East with the Ottoman conquests of the fourteenth and fifteenth centuries, and in the

---

[2] See Viscount de Chateaubriand, *The Genius of Christianity: Or, the Spirit and Beauty of the Christian Religion* (Baltimore, 1856); Margaret Mahony Stoljar, trans., *Novalis: Philosophical Writings* (State University of New York Press, 1997), 137–52; Léon Gautier, *Chivalry* (London, 1891).

West with the Protestant Revolt in the sixteenth, and the revolutions of the eighteenth and nineteenth centuries — a process culminating in World War II. Oddly enough, Protestant Europe retains innumerable mummified remains of institutions dating from the first Christendom. Such phenomena as the royal rituals of the British, Danish, Swedish, and other Protestant monarchies; Protestantised remnants of the Order of St. John and the Teutonic Knights; guilds in London and the rest of England, Switzerland, Scotland, and elsewhere in northern Europe; Lutheran monasteries and chapters of canons (notably Brandenburg, Meissen, and Naumburg) in Germany; faculties of theology in state universities; bishops in the House of Lords; and many more continue to give a certain amount of charm to life in those regions. Ironically, this kind of thing was swept away more thoroughly in Catholic Europe by the militant children of the Enlightenment.

These successive assaults on Christendom brought forth heroic figures and martyrs ready to do or die against whatever the threat to faith and order *du jour* happened to be. Quite a few were sovereigns: Constantine XI, last Byzantine Emperor (considered a blessed by Catholics[3]); the House of Habsburg, especially its last reigning monarchs, Charles I and Zita; Louis XVI and Marie Antoinette of France, and their great-nephew, the rightful Henri V; the Anglican Charles I (who has both British and American admirers) and the Russian Orthodox Nicholas II are acclaimed as martyrs by their co-religionists. Much may be said also for the groups who rose in defence of such rulers — the Jacobites, the men of the Vendée, the Carlists, the Miguelists, the Papal Zouaves, and so forth. Nor were all such heads of state monarchs, as the nineteenth and twentieth centuries wore on: García Moreno, Dollfuss, Salazar, Franco — some would add Pétain — all fought in their time for some fragment of the ethos of Christendom in their countries. Innumerable counterrevolutionary thinkers sprang up, as well as political parties and groups. This resistance — in all its variety and failure — we may call the

---

[3] See "A Special Note Concerning the Status of Blessed Constantine XI," The Society of St. John Chrysostom of Ayatriada Rum Katoliki Kilise, http://rumkatkilise.org/statusconstantineXI.htm, archived June 22, 2017, at https://archive.ph/gl9u5.

second Christendom. In a real sense, it died at last in World War II, crushed between Hitler on one hand, and Stalin and Roosevelt on the other. Whether they joined the resistance or the collaboration, their efforts for Christendom were in vain, at least as the outward world may see it. Consciously or otherwise, the realisation of this defeat seeped into the consciousness of the senior clergy of the Church. Benedict XVI summed it up thusly: "In the period between the two World Wars and especially after the Second World War, Catholic statesmen demonstrated that a modern secular State could exist that was not neutral regarding values but alive, drawing from the great ethical sources opened by Christianity."[4] Therefore, "it was necessary to give a new definition to the relationship between the Church and the modern State that would make room impartially for citizens of various religions and ideologies, merely assuming responsibility for an orderly and tolerant coexistence among them and for the freedom to practise their own religion."[5] The more cynical might say that the Church had thrown in the towel in its struggle with the modern state.

Despite such figures as Adenauer, Schuman, De Gasperi, and Otto von Habsburg, who attempted after the ruin of World War II to salvage some place for the values of Christendom in the modern world of liberal or religiously neutral states, the optimism of the Fathers of Vatican II as expressed by Pope Benedict has been sadly disappointed. The second Christendom has ended, and the Church hierarchy has nothing to show for letting go of it so easily — except, perhaps, survival.

But what of today, in our era of secular states engaged in a never-ending quest to befoul themselves and their denizens as much as possible, whilst desultorily attempting to contain an Islam of renewed militancy? Well, there is a third Christendom, in my estimation, which differs from the first two by being far harder to identify. Rather than being divided by nationality, this new Christendom — which may be either a last gasp or a

---

[4] Benedict XVI, "Address of His Holiness Benedict XVI to the Roman Curia Offering Them His Christmas Greetings," December 22, 2005, www.vatican. va/content/benedict-xvi/en/speeches/2005/december/documents/hf_ben_ xvi_spe_20051222_roman-curia.html.
[5] Benedict XVI, "Address of His Holiness."

seedbed of the future—is broken into two major divisions: conscious and unconscious.

In the former camp may be found the network of traditionalist orders and movements, as well as the varied remnants of the second Christendom, whose proponents, however marginalised, soldier on. Were one to restrict one's vision to them alone, however (and I say this as both a traditionalist and a monarchist), he would have to be rather pessimistic.

But the second division holds much promise, both by being much larger and in a position to affect the Church and the world in a more powerful way. There are still areas of what was once Christendom where the faith remains deeply embedded in the hearts and customs of the locals: Germany's Eichsfeld, Italy's Abruzzo, Brittany, our own southern Louisiana and northern New Mexico, and, thank God, many other regions and provinces from the Philippines to Poland. There are innumerable shrines throughout the Catholic world where—however secular the surrounding area—within the confines of the place and among those who come to pray, Christendom lives on. It does so too on pilgrimage: not only on the roads to Chartres or Auriesville, but also in Compostela and many other places. In many monasteries and some of the new religious orders and Catholic movements also does Christendom live.

The devotional brotherhoods most common in Italy, France, Spain, and Latin America (but also to be found elsewhere) bring Christendom to life on certain feasts, as do the shooting fraternities in the Catholic German-speaking world. These last explicitly number among their goals "a united Christian Europe."[6] Indeed, in any town where the festivals of the Church are openly celebrated with religious solemnity and secular observance, there too is Christendom. It may be found for that matter in many of the initiatives of the "New Evangelisation," such as the Anglican Ordinariates and renewed attempts at healing the Eastern schism. It is up to those of us who consider ourselves conscious citizens of Christendom to help those engaged in all these efforts to see their work as part of a greater whole. Whatever scrap of Christendom may be left in our neighbourhood—be it a community observance

---

[6] "Data and Facts," EGS, accessed February 6, 2025, https://www.e-g-s.eu/.

with Catholic roots, an historic church or building, or a shrine, no matter how obscure—let us join the effort to preserve it, while kindly showing its other defenders its larger significance. Perhaps such efforts will be the foundation of a new Christendom, but certainly they will help save souls.

There is a fourth Christendom. It is at once older than the other three and newer than even ourselves. Ernest Oldmeadow describes it eloquently:

> Christ the King has other rebels besides Russia and Mexico and France. The map of His dominions shows not only the Empires and Kingdoms and Republics, but also the counties, the towns, the villages, the hamlets, and—like the ordnance maps of largest scale—the homesteads each and all. Indeed, it goes farther than the work of any human cartographer; because it shows the inmost places of every human heart. Even the humblest man or woman or child alive is, so to speak, a tiny province in the dominions of Christ the King: a province either submissive or disobedient, either loyal or rebellious.[7]

That fourth Christendom is in each of us, who by our baptism were made members of the Mystical Body of Christ, sons of the Church, and—by imperial decree, no less—subjects of the Holy Empire, the boundaries of which are wherever any of us happens to be, and regardless of whether or not a human emperor sits upon his throne. With St. Paul, we can say, "I am a Roman citizen" (Acts 22:28).

Our attempts at rebuilding Christendom must be intimately linked with performing the spiritual and corporal works of mercy. It may be that what we do in the temporal sphere lays the foundations for some future outward revival of Christendom—though what form that shall take is doubtless as impossible for us to imagine as the work of Justinian and Charlemagne was for Ss. Ambrose and Augustine, for all that duo's efforts were essential to both imperial revivals. But whether or not that happens, may our spiritual endeavours result in our becoming permanent subjects of that celestial realm of which any earthly expression of Christendom, however grand, is only a poor shadow and reflexion. Whatever discouragement

---

[7] Ernest Oldmeadow, *A Layman's Christian Year* (Burns, Oates & Washbourne, 1938), 277.

and temptations to despair we may feel in this glorious quest, we should remember the further words of Longfellow in the Christmas carol cited earlier:

> And in despair I bowed my head;
> "There is no peace on earth," I said;
> "For hate is strong
> And mocks the song
> Of peace on earth, good will to men!"
> Then pealed the bells more loud and deep:
> "God is not dead, nor doth He sleep!
> The wrong shall fail,
> The Right prevail,
> With peace on earth, good will to men!"[8]

---

[8] Babcock, *Henry Wadsworth Longfellow*, 39–40.

❧CHAPTER 6❧
Sacrum Imperium

𝕮 HRISTMAS BRINGS ALL SORTS OF JOY, FOR
all sorts of reasons. Readers of Dom Prosper Guéranger's *Liturgical Year* will be reminded in his first volume
for the season of three great historical events that took place
on Christmas Day—the conversion of Clovis, the conversion
of England, and the crowning of Charlemagne:

> Three hundred years after [St. Augustine of Canterbury's
> mass baptisms at York], God gives us another glorious
> event in honour of the Birthday of his Son. It was on
> this divine Anniversary, in the year 800, and at Rome,
> in the Basilica of St Peter, that the Holy Roman Empire
> was created, to which God assigned the grand mission of
> propagating the Kingdom of Christ among the barbarian
> nations of the North, and of upholding, under the direc-
> tion of the Sovereign Pontiffs, the confederation and unity
> of Europe. St Leo III crowned Charlemagne Emperor. Here,
> then, was a new Caesar, a new Augustus, on the earth;
> not, indeed, a successor of those ancient Lords of Pagan
> Rome, but one who was invested with the title and power
> by the Vicar of him who is called, in the Sacred Scriptures,
> *King of Kings and Lord of Lords.*[1]

Later on, in the same volume, wherein the good Benedictine
is describing the ceremonies of the seventh lesson of Christmas Matins (dealing with the order of Caesar Augustus for
the census which brought Mary and Joseph to Bethlehem) at
St. Peter's Basilica, he writes of how the emperor sings the
seventh Lesson, because it was none other than an Emperor's
"decrees [that] were the occasion of Mary and Joseph going
to Bethlehem, and so fulfilling the designs of God."[2] Indeed,
there is a great deal to be found throughout the *Liturgical
Year* about the imperial office; we saw too that the entry on
St. Leo III includes a marvelous description of the coronation

---

[1] Prosper Guéranger, OSB, *The Liturgical Year*, trans. Laurence Shepherd (Newman Press, 1950), vol. 2, "Christmas: Book 1," 112–13.
[2] Guéranger, *The Liturgical Year*, vol. 2, "Christmas: Book 1," 160. See full
quotation on pp. 75–76 below.

in Rome of a Holy Roman Emperor.[3] Yet again, during Holy
Week, when Dom Guéranger is describing the rites of Good
Friday, he mentions the prayer for the emperor which could
be found in the Roman Missal until Pius XII's revision of
1955.[4] Of this collect, he wrote: "The Church of Rome . . . had
in view the emperor of Germany, who was formerly the head
of the germanic confederation, and, in the middle ages, was
entrusted by the Church with the charge of propagating the
faith among the northern nations. This prayer is now omitted,
excepting in those countries which are subject to Austria."[5]
On Holy Saturday, the *Exsultet* contained, in parentheses, the
passage "Regard also our most devout Emperor *N.*, and since
Thou knowest, O God, the desires of his heart, grant by the
ineffable grace of Thy goodness and mercy that he may enjoy
with all his people the tranquillity of perpetual peace and
heavenly victory." Dom Guéranger comments that "The words
here put in parentheses are said only in those countries, which
are subject to the emperor of Austria."[6] On September 10,
1857, Bl. Pius IX issued the Bull *Imperii Galliarum*, by which
the Church in France was allowed to address these prayers to
God on behalf of Napoleon III. These, however, were far from
the only references to "the emperor" in the pre-1955 missal.
Among the "Occasional Prayers" (sets of Collects, Secrets, and
Postcommunions for various intentions, to be said by the
priest after finishing the day's orations), we find a set entitled "For the Emperor."[7]

Despite Dom Guéranger's references to the emperor of
Austria and Bl. Pius's to the emperor of the French, there is
a certain universality implied in all of these prayers. Indeed,
if one turns from the Roman to the Byzantine rite (Catholic or Orthodox), one stumbles upon similar prayers in the
older service books. The opening litany or Great Ektenia of
their liturgy of the catechumens prays, "For our most faithful
and God-protected Emperor *N.*, for all his palaces and armies,
that the Lord would aid him in all things, hasten to grant

---

[3] For the text, see pp. 74–75 below.
[4] See p. 76.
[5] Prosper Guéranger, OSB, *The Liturgical Year*, trans. Laurence Shepherd (Newman Press, 1952), vol. 6, "Passiontide & Holy Week," 482.
[6] Guéranger, *The Liturgical Year*, vol. 6, "Passiontide & Holy Week," 566.
[7] See p. 76.

him all his desires, and place under his feet every enemy and adversary." The Troparion for the Holy Cross implores: "Save Your people, O God, and bless Your inheritance. Grant victory to Your most faithful emperor over his enemies and protect Your people by Your Cross." In the Anaphora of the more commonly used Liturgy of St. John Chrysostom, God is asked to "Remember our most faithful emperor and all his palaces and armies. Grant him, O Lord, a peaceful reign, so that by his tranquility, 'we may lead quiet and peaceful lives in all godliness and purity.'" The rather more elaborate Liturgy of St. Basil, reserved for special feasts and seasons, prays in a manner somewhat reminiscent of the Roman Good Friday collect:

> Remember, O Lord, our most devout and faithful Emperor N., whom you have set to rule on the earth. Crown him with a weapon of truth, a weapon of good will; let your shadow fall upon his head in the day of war; strengthen his arm, exalt his right-hand, establish his empire; subdue beneath him all barbarous nations that desire to make war; grant him deep and enduring peace; speak good things to his heart for your Church and for all your people; so that by his tranquility we may lead quiet and peaceful lives, in all piety and purity.

In the last century, Ukrainian and Ruthenian Catholics placed the name of the Austrian kaiser in the appropriate spots, while their Russian Orthodox co-ritualists used that of the Russian tsar. But the prayers themselves predate both the Austrian and Russian Empires, first being composed for the emperor we call Byzantine but who referred to himself as "Roman"—even as did that sovereign whom we call "Holy Roman" but who did not use the first adjective for himself, reserving it for the Empire over which he ruled. Liturgically, symbolically, and philosophically, both the Holy Roman emperor and the Byzantine emperor (as well as the later Austrian and Russian rulers who claimed to succeed them—all of whom used the double-headed eagle as their device) claimed the same role: successor of the Caesars, temporal leader of all the Christian people throughout the world, and chief lay protector of the Church of Christ—in a word, the role seen for himself by Constantine the Great and consecrated by Pope St. Sylvester I.

This idea of the "Holy Empire," citizenship in which (after Emperor Theodosius I) was conferred alongside membership in the Church by baptism, is one which has haunted the Christian mind ever since. This is so despite innumerable blows dealt to it by such unpleasantries as imperial sponsorship of the Arian, monophysite, monothelite, and iconoclastic heresies; struggles by various popes for independence from both Eastern and Western emperors; the Great Schism; the investiture controversy; mutual betrayals during the Crusades; the Massacre of the Latins; the Fourth Crusade; the struggles between Guelphs and Ghibellines; the fall of Constantinople to the Turks; the Protestant Revolt; the Thirty Years' War; Josephinism (from which both Catholic and Orthodox monasticism and devotion suffered); the creation and suppression of the Uniates; the French Revolution; the ephemeral Bonaparte Empires; and the fall of the dynasties due to World War I.

All of these horrors and scandals cannot efface the more positive side of the coin — those sadly rare times when popes and emperors, East and West, collaborated for the common good. It is not merely that the events were not as frequent as one would hope; it is also that lovers of division, for whatever reason, have always preferred not to dwell upon them. But there were more than a few: the relationship between Pope St. Agapetus I and Emperor Justinian; the collaborations between Charlemagne and Empress Irene; the alliance between Emperors Louis II and Basil I; the marriage of Otto II and Theophanu, and the pan-Romanism of their son, Otto III; the reign of the latter's cousin, St. Henry; the cooperation of Alexios I and the First Crusaders; the attempts of Byzantine Emperors Michael VIII and John VIII to reunite East and West; Emperor Sigismund's contribution to ending the Western schism; the Westerners who came to the aid of Bl. Constantine XI in 1453; the marriage between Ivan III of Russia and Princess Sophia Palaiologina, arranged by Pope Paul II; the Holy League of 1684; Tsar Paul's protection of the Order of Malta; and Alexander I and the Holy Alliance — to touch upon a small number of episodes. It is significant that both Bl. Charles of Austria (and his Empress Zita) and Nicholas II and his family, the last reigning representatives of their respective imperial traditions, are considered saints by their coreligionists—and that the visit of Grand Duchess Maria Vladimirovna and her son George to Pope Benedict XVI, and the similar visit of the Archduke Otto von Habsburg and his subsequent funeral, should be considered newsworthy.

Practical history aside, the idea of the Holy Empire, of Christendom, of the Christian commonwealth, has continued to wield an extraordinary influence in such notions as the *renovatio imperii, translatio imperii,* and the Third Rome—just as mankind's seemingly overwhelming propensity to sin has not drowned the yearning for virtue. From Dante through Novalis to Soloviev, and even today, Christians have not ceased to yearn for political as well as religious unity, for an emperor who will set all things to right—a successor to Constantine and Justinian, Bl. Charlemagne and Frederick Barbarossa, Frederick II, Bl. Constantine XI, and Charles V—indeed, of Bl. Charles I and Nicholas II. From this yearning came the prophecy of the great monarch who will come before the Antichrist and, according to some, be defeated by him before the end. But from it also came the spurs for Spanish, Portuguese, and French colonisation and royal patronage of missionary activity—as well as, in a real sense, the British Empire, which, in its latter days, self-consciously modelled itself upon the Holy Empire of old—as the 1911 *Encyclopedia Britannica* concludes its article on empire: "The British Empire is, in a sense, an aspiration rather than a reality, a thought rather than a fact; but, just for that reason, it is like the old Empire of which we have spoken; and though it be neither Roman nor Holy, yet it has, like its prototype, one law, if not the law of Rome—one faith, if not in matters of religion, at any rate in the field of political and social ideals."[8]

Much the same could be said of that Empire's daughter, these United States, as its Constitution's authors had in mind the later Holy Roman Empire's institutions, alongside the influence of the Iroquois Confederacy, Montesquieu, St. Robert Bellarmine, and John Locke. The college of electors had some influence upon our own electoral college; the relationship of the imperial states with the emperor is reminiscent of the original view of states' rights.

---

[8] "Empire," in *Encyclopaedia Britannica: A Dictionary of Arts, Sciences, Literature and General Information* (Cambridge University Press, 1910), 9:356.

The idea of empire, however, influenced many other peoples. Long isolated from the rest of Christendom by Muslim invasion, the emperors of Ethiopia conducted themselves in ways recalling the Roman emperors. The Ottoman sultans claimed to be successors in some sense of the Byzantine emperors, which they combined with their own ideal of the caliphate; this was a vision picked up by their Persian and Mughal co-religionists. European missionaries and explorers saw much that reminded them of the Christian imperium in the rulers of China, Japan, and Vietnam, and so called them "emperors"—a title the late-nineteenth-century king of Korea seized when trying to assert independence from both of his neighbours. The two Napoleons' attempts to renew the Empire of Charlemagne we mentioned in passing earlier; their examples led newly independent nations in the New World—Mexico, Brazil, and Haiti—to claim the title. Here in California, we even had our own Emperor Norton I.

But although only the ruler of Japan is now called emperor, the imperial dream lives on today in unexpected ways—and not only in the innumerable institutions, customs, and buildings founded by imperial fiat. The European Union, in its earlier, Christian days, looked explicitly for inspiration to Charlemagne, as the works and comments of Coudenhove-Kalergi, Adenauer, Schuman, De Gasperi, Monnet, *Neues Abendland*, and the founders of the Karlspreis reveal. Despite the EU's present-day extremely anti-Christian bias, such groups as the Paneuropa Union and Identità Europea attempt to push it back along the routes suggested by those earlier men.

In similar wise, the notion of the United Nations is simply the most recent incarnation of the idea of a world state. Certainly, the global civilisation it encompasses is built upon the foundations of the nineteenth-century colonialism that was inspired—in various ways—by the Empire. Without a doubt, consciously or otherwise the attitude of the Holy See toward both the European Union (EU) and the United Nations (UN) is heavily influenced by the long history of papal-imperial relations—and the undying hope that perhaps this time a power can be found that will keep a universal peace that allows the Church to do her job of sanctification.

How real those hopes are is another issue. But what is certain is that the ruins and traces of the Holy Empire are all about us. An understanding of its history and continuing influence is key to understanding the practical implications of the social kingship of Christ—which idea, in so many ways, is the ideal successive emperors and their loyal subjects sought to follow on earth, and without which, as Pius XI taught in *Quas Primas*, real peace is impossible. Whether or not the great monarch returns in our day (and I for one would be happy to see him), it is good to know upon what basis such a sovereign would rule; if nothing else, this knowledge will show us what we ought to be able to expect of our rulers—and how far short they usually fall. That is the reason we must continually look, for lessons, to the founders of the Christian Empire: Constantine the Great, St. Helena the Empress, and Theodosius I—as well as such of their subjects as Ss. Ambrose, Augustine, Basil the Great, John Chrysostom, and Hilary of Poitiers who helped formulate the whole idea of the *sacrum imperium*.

CHAPTER 7

Europe and the Empire

𝔍 AM A EUROPEAN. THIS MAY SOUND RATHER strange, given that I was born in New York, have lived most of my life in Los Angeles, and will be buried in my family plot in Massachusetts. The first Coulombes to come to the New World arrived in the seventeenth century, and my immediate ancestors have served in the armed forces of the United States in every conflict this country has been involved in since 1900. I myself have so served, and once upon a time swore to defend the US Constitution from "all enemies, foreign and domestic." Nevertheless, I am indeed a European.

The fact is that, save for some native blood (visible in my Coulombe cousins, though not in myself), my ancestry hails from the mother continent. Mixed — French, Austrian, English, Russian, Scots, Irish, and various others — to be sure, but nevertheless all European. None of the languages I speak, however poorly — Canadian French, Yankee English, a fractured Viennese, and Los Angeles Mexican street Spanish — can be considered indigenous to the Americas, and as a result, all of the arts to be enjoyed in the languages I understand have European origins — from Shakespeare to Piaf. In the state of California, where I lived for many years, although the laws covering land, water, and minerals point up our origins as a colony of His Most Catholic Majesty of Spain, the rest of our governance, with its panoply of governor, legislature, judiciary, counties, sheriffs, mayors, coroners and on and on, show the English origins of the better part of our law and institutions. Above all, I belong to a religion centered in Rome, whose last pontiff said, shortly after his accession, "all Catholics are in some way Romans."[1] It is unlikely that he was referring either to Rome, New York, or Rome, Texas.

Of course, I am not alone in this position. It is true of the larger proportion of my fellow Americans ethnically, and

---

[1] Benedict XVI, Homily for the Mass of Possession of the Chair of the Bishop of Rome, May 7, 2005. This is the principal theme of Alan Fimister's *The Iron Sceptre of the Son of Man: Romanitas as a Note of the Church* (Os Justi Press, 2023).

virtually all of us culturally. It is especially true of the Blacks in this country, who have no real, identifiable ties to Africa (despite all the hype), except mere genetics. If anything, they are, save the Native Americans, the most completely American cultural element in the population. But that too makes them Europeans. The truth is, *pace* the Anti-Colonial League, we are the most successful of colonies, having succeeded so tremendously that we have dominated all our former metropoles and their neighbours. Moreover, most of us have forgotten our origins and unconsciously think of ourselves as autogenetic. But on a deeper level still, we know that it is not true. Old Europe still keeps a hold on our imaginations, no matter how much we may try to deny it. Moreover, the fact remains that none of us without tribal ancestry can stand on a bit of land in this country and say, "my people were here a thousand years ago." The equally unconscious ability of Europeans to do precisely that (and of those few Americans who visit to do likewise) quietly influences the relationship between the two sides of the Atlantic. Canadians are somewhat more aware of their origins, which gives them a separate mental universe entirely.

For my own part, a large segment of my work as a writer has been to asseverate the truth that we Americans are Europeans separated by time and space from our origins. But as with any colonial, it is not the Europe of Tony Blair, Bertie Ahern, Jacques Chirac, and rest of the "generation of '68" gone to seed that I have in mind. There is a reason why the seventeenth and eighteenth centuries can still be heard in the French, English, and Spanish spoken in various remote spots in the Americas. It is because we were settled by a different Europe.

The continent that produced our ancestors was the Europe of Dryden, Cervantes, and Molière — the realm of chivalry and guilds, shrines and legends. It was from Christendom that our fathers came, from *Abendland*. Echoes of this can be found in the more profound religiosity that characterizes most of the western hemisphere — even if much of that religiosity is Calvinism or sects still more bizarre. It has been only since the '60s that our elites have become more or less atheistic, and determined to impose their creeds upon the rest of us (a phenomenon to which neither Quebec nor Latin America have been immune, although in the latter case it is still somewhat moderated).

In any case, the malaise that has infected Europe since 1789, and has become more or less triumphant since 1945 and especially 1968, has not gone nearly as far here. In Europe herself, by way of contrast, American religious attitudes are well-nigh incomprehensible; public displays of religious ceremonial are quite common in Europe (although her current leaders do try to suppress or limit them when possible), to a degree unheard of in the United States; yet the personal faith that is a *sine qua non* in a politician here is considered rather strange on the other side of the ocean. Marriage and birth statistics reveal that such personal faith is also increasingly rare among the European citizenry at large (a lack noticeably absent in her growing Muslim population).

The Altar was one of the two foundations upon which Europe rested: the other was the Throne. Since 1776, we have done our best on this side of the water to minimise its contributions to our nationhood; Latin Americans have been doing so since the 1820s, and Canadian politicians and media folk got into the act in the 1960s. Yet, as earlier mentioned, all of our institutions come to us from Europe — from a *royal* Europe. The same anti-monarchical slant infected Europe in 1789 and received heavy boosts in 1918 and 1945. But European republics still house the dreary old politicians they call presidents in the royal palaces, surround them with more or less cut-rate royal pageantry (guards, households, and orders of knighthood), and pretend that somehow the whole charade has something to do with "rule by the people" — as though the general mass of the people were able to live as well as the politicians that batten on them! Much the same is true in Latin America, where current chiefs of state continue to use many of the appurtenances of the long-vanished viceroys.

For all of the differences between old Europe and her children, however, there can be no doubt that, despite the end of colonialism and the attempts at self-assertion by local politicians in such nations as Australia, Europe really extends from San Francisco to Vladivostok, and from North Cape to Cape Town and Buenos Aires. Like it or not, we are stuck with each other. Culturally and religiously, the health of the periphery still depends upon that of the mother continent.

Over here, Europe's health is frequently spoken of in terms of the European Union. But just what is that Union, and how true is it to the European soul, of which Hilaire Belloc once famously remarked that "the Faith is Europe, and Europe is the Faith"?[2]

One must say, given the disastrous course of European history in the twentieth century, that the origins of the EU were promising enough. Solid Christians like Jean Monnet, Paul-Henri Spaak, Robert Schuman, Konrad Adenauer, and Alcide De Gasperi hoped to pull out of the ruins of their countries a new Europe—rooted deeply in the religion and best traditions of her past, but freed of the national hatreds and social conflicts that had spilled so much of the best of her blood from 1914 to 1945. It was a noble dream, reflected in such efforts as the Karlspreis, the annual award by the city fathers of Aachen (also known as Charlemagne's Aix-la-Chapelle) to the individual who, in their opinion, had best demonstrated the "European idea" that year. In time, the Atlantic-Caribbean-Pacific (ACP) scheme was intended to allow the former imperial masters to aid their one-time colonies in a way consonant with those nations' self-respect. Moreover, European unity would allow Europe to play an effective role in world affairs, independent of both the United States and the Soviet Union. Yet at the same time, the principle of "subsidiarity" would allow towns, counties, and provinces (or their local equivalent) far more freedom to run their own affairs. Successive popes seconded this goal—and came to prefer it to the older vision enunciated by such as Salazar, Franco, and any number of Latin American rulers.

Alas, the reality was to be far different from what either pontiffs or founding politicians had hoped. For what we are faced with in the European Union is quite another thing entirely. Far from the sort of Europe envisaged by the Founders, the EU is, to begin with, ever more anti-Christian, as the abortive constitution's preamble and the Buttiglione case point up. Non-marital unions, contraception, abortion, euthanasia—anything calculated to worsen Europe's already plummeting demographics—are encouraged at every turn by the EU. Instead of subsidiarity, the local farmers, artisans, and regular folk throughout the Union find themselves ever more strangled

---

[2] Hilaire Belloc, *Europe and the Faith* (Paulist Press, 1921), viii.

by the Brussels bureaucracy. What seems to be emerging is a personally oppressive superstate upon a foundation of equally annoying national bureaucracies. Perhaps making up for this has been the EU's ineffectiveness in foreign affairs: the ACP idea is being abandoned, having done little to ameliorate Third World poverty and less to address bad governance there. Bosnia and Kosovo pointed up the New Europe's inability to address even nearby conflicts effectively. Needless to say, the US took little notice of Europe when dealing with Iraq — alas, perhaps, to no one's ultimate advantage. The only thing more pitiful than the awarding of the Karlspreis to Tony Blair in 1999 was Bill Clinton's reception of it the following year.

As a result, despite the best efforts of a well-oiled public relations machine, and the views of most European political parties, the EU has yet to win the affection of the common man in Europe. Instead, most folk respond with derision. Yet despite polls and plebiscites, the thing appears to be on its way to commanding ever-greater power over a supine continent. Since the 1980s, a common explanation was to blame the next country over for the EU. British blamed the French, Frenchmen blamed the Germans, Germans blamed the Italians, and so forth. In recent years, this sort of round robin of finger-pointing has subsided. That is probably just as well, because the plain truth is that the EU's failings are not to be laid at the door of any single nationality. Rather, responsibility for them rests communally with the greater part of the dominant elites in each country of Europe. Back in 2006, when I first wrote this chapter, we were looking at Blair and Ahern, Belgium's Guy Verhofstadt, Spain's José Luis Rodríguez Zapatero (he masculinised it from "Zapatera"; in light of his support of homosexual marriage, he need not have bothered), and the cashiered French and German premiers Jospin and Schröder. What all of these worthies and their numerous hangers-on, concubines, and flunkies in government, the judiciary, and media have in common is a shared vision. Products of the 1960s, they simply hate their respective countries, at least as they inherited them. The same pattern has only intensified in the political appointments of recent years.

Naturally, this hatred does not extend to the organs of power — ultimately the gift in most European countries of Bonaparte and such unconscious successors as Bismarck and

Cavour—but rather is aimed at *the countries themselves*, and at whatever gave each its own identity. In all cases, this includes not merely Christianity but the religion's effect on society and culture, on traditional mores in the family and in the arts. To make all things anew after their own image was the desire of the rebels of the '60s, and their successors today are no different. Yet each of these nations is a building block in what had been the very real but difficult-to-define entity called "Europe," *née* Christendom. Just as, in their hands, their respective countries have begun to morph into something very different from what they had been, so too with the European Union.

Nothing is sacred to these folk! Hunting and the House of Lords must go in Great Britain, indissoluble marriage in Ireland, school crucifixes in Belgium and Spain, strange and unusual means of producing goods in every rural hamlet on the continent, and smoking everywhere (were public health really a concern, these mandarins might turn their attention to limiting such things as the behaviours that spread AIDS). Behind these lie greater alterations—the selfsame all-important demography-busting marriage, life, and family issues earlier referred to.

Disastrous as these measures will doubtless be in the long-run, their practical harm is multiplied by the fact that they are all that the rulers of Europe have to throw back at militant Islam—which manages at once to convince the Muslims of their own moral supremacy and to limit the ability of Europe to resist. The problem is that the EU has been recast in the leadership's own image.

All of which having been said, we need to look and see if there is a viable alternative to what is on offer. I once told a German friend of mine (as it happened, in Aachen, outside of Charlemagne's resting place in the cathedral there), that I was not opposed to the union of Europe, but to *this* union of Europe! He responded, "No, Charles, you are really opposed to the union of *this* Europe." He was right, but is there another Europe to choose?

Indeed there is. The noted French royalist, Charles Maurras, coined the notion of France being divided into two: the *pays réel*, the real France, Catholic and royalist; and the *pays légal*, the legal France, anticlerical and republican. Georges Bernanos wrote of life in the former France in his brilliant work *Nous*

Autres Français (Gallimard, 1939) — *We Other French.* Perhaps inspired by Bernanos, Philippe de Villiers called his quondam organisation *Nous autres Européens.* It is the "other Europe," the Europe that drew its origin from Rome and Jerusalem, that we must look at, rather than the one that is rooted in Brussels (much as I personally love that pleasant city!).

Two centuries ago, faced with the similar problem posed by the new Europe then aborning, romantic writer Friedrich von Hardenberg (better known as Novalis) penned his best known essay, "Christendom or Europe." Its opening paragraph was a battle cry, a challenge thrown down to everything that had happened to Europe since the Reformation:

> There once were beautiful, splendid times when Europe was a Christian land, when *one* Christendom dwelt in this continent, shaped by human hand; *one* great common interest bound together the most distant provinces of this broad religious empire. Although he did not have extensive secular possessions, *one* supreme ruler guided and united the great political powers. A numerous guild which everyone could join ranked immediately below the ruler and carried out his wishes, eagerly striving to secure his beneficent might. Each member of this society was honored on all sides, and whenever the common people sought from him consolation or help, protection or advice, being glad in exchange to provide richly for his diverse needs, each also found protection, esteem, and a hearing from the more mighty ones, while all cared for these chosen men, who were armed with wondrous powers like children of heaven, and whose presence and favor spread many blessings. Childlike trust bound people to their pronouncements. How cheerfully each could accomplish his earthly tasks, since by virtue of these holy people a safe future was prepared for him, and every false step was forgiven by them, and every discolored mark in his life wiped away and made clear. They were the experienced helmsmen on the great unknown sea, under whose protection all storms could be made light of, and one could be confident of a safe arrival and landing on the shore of a world that was truly a fatherland.[3]

This was high-flown romanticism, to be sure, but not without some basis in historical fact, unlike the visions of the ruling revolutionaries of his day — or ours, for that matter. Certainly,

---

[3] Stoljar, *Novalis: Philosophical Writings,* 137.

Novalis had uncovered the ideal of medieval society in this passage, if not always its reality. One shudders to think of what the idealism of our current masters, with its glorification of perversion, conformity, and death, would look like, if reduced to writing.

At any rate, the medieval Christendom of which Novalis wrote so glowingly was not, like modern Europe, a patchwork of more or less stable nation-states, but rather a crazy quilt of minor fiefdoms, principalities, duchies, free cities, ecclesiastical lordships, and strange local groupings not easily described (like the first three forest cantons of Switzerland or Holstein's Dithmarschen). These in turn were grouped together, for the most part, into various kingdoms — although some of the lesser entities split their allegiance between two or more kings. The monarchs of these countries were sometimes elected but usually hereditary.

But they were not heads of state in the modern understanding of the term, because the countries they presided over were not states as we now know them. Lacking secret police or internal revenue services, they had none of the appurtenances of governance we would recognise. Indeed, to our eyes, these countries would have been mere bundles of anarchy.

This is because our ancestors lived in a very different mental universe from ours. Allegiance meant much more than merely being draughted or taxed. Although the king may not have had the ability through his guards to impose his will much beyond his palaces, his subjects loyally upheld the local equivalent of "the king's peace." Did a desperado "play the robber on the King's Highway?" The neighbours would send up the hue and cry, hunt him down, and kill him in the name of the king — and then consider "the king's peace" restored. The nation, in our way of thinking, was a mutually imagined illusion.

But it was certainly real to them, in the sense of Platonic realism. Key to understanding how the medieval kingdom worked is to realise the difference between power and authority: the former is the ability to make things happen, the latter the right to say how that power should be used. In medieval times, power was diffuse, with lords, churchmen, commoners, guilds, and so on all claiming their share. Authority, however, was in the hands of the king. A good king was like the conductor of an orchestra. But under a bad king, apart from annoyances meted out to his immediate companions, the result was not dictatorship in the modern fashion but anarchy. When such times occurred, locals would often group together to "keep the peace," forming a confraternity for that purpose. These bodies often served as local police and militia — such as the famous Santa Hermandades of Spain.

As a side note, it is fair to say that His Majesty King Charles III probably has little more power than did his pre-Tudor ancestors (who were as much the founders of the modern state as anyone else, like Louis XIV). But because, in our day, power is concentrated in the hands of the elite, while authority is scattered amongst a more or less oblivious electorate, his position looks much less impressive. Such is the modern state.

Binding all of these kingdoms and so on together were several institutions, first of which was the Church, with her several networks of dioceses and religious orders; she in turn gave her blessing to the complementary circuits of guilds and universities. Some of the same benediction touched chivalry, the "corporation," as it were, of knighthood; this would come in time to include the great military orders, which partook of both the Church and chivalry.

But in, with, and under all of these was the idea of the "Holy Empire," Roman in the West, Byzantine in the East. We need to take a close and somewhat detailed look at this imperial idea, because it provides the great alternative to the notion of the European Union. Despite many conflicts between the imperial and papal powers, there was an underlying unity between the two that was unbreakable. This is admirably summed up by James, Viscount Bryce:

> The realistic philosophy, and the needs of a time when the only notion of civil or religious order was submission to authority, required the World-State to be a monarchy: tradition, as well as the continued existence of a part of the ancient institutions, gave the monarch the name of Roman Emperor. A king could not be universal sovereign, for there were many kings: the Emperor must be universal, for there had never been but one Emperor; he had in older and brighter days been the actual lord of the civilized world; the seat of his power was placed beside that of the spiritual autocrat of Christendom. His functions will be

seen most clearly if we deduce them from the leading principle of mediaeval mythology, the exact correspondence
of earth and heaven. As God, in the midst of the celestial
hierarchy, rules blessed spirits in Paradise, so the Pope, His
vicar, raised above priests, bishops, metropolitans, reigns
over the souls of mortal men below. But as God is Lord
of earth as well as of heaven, so must he (the *Imperator
coelestis*) be represented by a second earthly viceroy, the
Emperor (*Imperator terrenus*), whose authority shall be of
and for this present life. And as in this present world the
soul cannot act save through the body, while yet the body
is no more than an instrument and means for the soul's
manifestation, so there must be a rule and care of men's
bodies as well as of their souls, yet subordinated always
to the well-being of that element which is the purer and
the more enduring. It is under the emblem of soul and
body that the relation of the papal and imperial power is
presented to us throughout the Middle Ages. The Pope, as
God's vicar in matters spiritual, is to lead men to eternal
life; the Emperor, as vicar in matters temporal, must so
control them in their dealings with one another that they
may be able to pursue undisturbed the spiritual life, and
thereby attain the same supreme and common end of ever-
lasting happiness. In view of this object his chief duty is
to maintain peace in the world, while towards the Church
his position is that of Advocate or Patron, a title borrowed
from the practice adopted by churches and monasteries of
choosing some powerful baron to protect their lands and
lead their tenants in war. The functions of Advocacy are
twofold: at home to make the Christian people obedient
to the priesthood, and to execute priestly decrees upon
heretics and sinners; abroad to propagate the faith among
the heathen, not sparing to use carnal weapons. Thus does
the Emperor answer in every point to his antitype the
Pope, his power being yet of a lower rank, created on the
analogy of the papal.... Thus the Holy Roman Church and
the Holy Roman Empire are one and the same thing, seen
from different sides; and Catholicism, the principle of the
universal Christian society, is also Romanism.[4]

To Voltaire, that great pioneer of the modern mindset, is often
attributed the gibe that the HRE was "neither Holy, nor Roman,
nor an Empire"—nor had been for many years. Indeed, that
was what any modern would see. But for most of its history,
as an overarching framework of Christendom, it was at least

---

[4] Bryce, *The Holy Roman Empire*, 103–6.

as real to its denizens as "France," "Germany," or "Poland." As with chivalry, any given guild, the "republic of letters" of the universities, or the Church herself, the Empire was as real as its subjects conceived it to be — no matter how much they might fight over (or even against) it.

Proof of this contention may be found in the work of Dom Prosper Guéranger, OSB, who, as both a nineteenth-century Frenchman (and restorer of the Benedictines in that country as well as of Gregorian Chant throughout the Church) and as an ultramontane (he was instrumental in bringing about the 1870 definition of papal infallibility), may not be accused of partiality in this matter. At the time of his writing, most commentators in English favoured the medieval emperors against the popes because of their partiality toward Prussia and the nascent German empire of Bismarck. This makes Dom Guéranger's description of the imperial coronation in his entry for St. Leo III in his magisterial *The Liturgical Year* all the more telling:

> Space fails us, or gladly would we here describe in detail the gorgeous liturgical function used during the Middle-ages, in the Ordination of an Emperor. The *Ordo Romanus* wherein these rites are handed down to us is full of the richest teachings clearly revealing the whole thought of the Church. The future Lieutenant of Christ, kissing the feet of the Vicar of the Man-God, first made his profession in due form: he "guaranteed, promised, and swore fidelity to God and blessed Peter, pledging himself on the holy Gospels, for the rest of his life, to protect and defend, according to his skill and ability, without fraud or ill intent, — the Roman Church and her Ruler, in all necessities or interests affecting the same." Then followed the solemn examination of the faith and morals of the elect, — almost identically word for word, the same as that marked in the Pontifical, at the Consecration of a Bishop. Not until the Church had thus taken sureties regarding him who was to become in her eyes, as it were, an extern Bishop, was she content to proceed to the Imperial ordination. Whilst the Apostolic Suzerain, the Pope, was being vested in pontifical attire for the celebration of the sacred Mysteries, — two Cardinals clad the Emperor elect, in amice and alb; then they presented him to the Pontiff, who made him a Clerk, and conceded to him, for the ceremony of his coronation, the use of the tunic, dalmatic, and cope, together with the pontifical shoes and the mitre. The anointing of the prince

was reserved to the Cardinal Bishop of Ostia, the official consecrator of Popes and Emperors. But the Vicar of Jesus Christ himself gave to the new Emperor, the infrangible seal of his faith, namely the ring; the sword, representing that of the Lord of armies, the Most Potent One chanted in the Psalm; the globe and sceptre images of the universal Empire and of the inflexible Justice of the King of kings; lastly, the crown, a sign of the glory reserved in endless ages as a reward for his fidelity, by this same Lord Jesus Christ, whose figure he had just been made. The giving of these august symbols took place during the Holy Sacrifice. At the Offertory, the Emperor laid aside the cope and the ensigns of his new dignity; then, clad simply in the dalmatic, he approached the altar and there fulfilled, at the Pontiff's side, the office of Subdeacon, the *Servitor*, as it were, of Holy Church and the official representative of the Christian people. Later on, even the stole was given him: as recently as 1530, Charles V. on the day of his coronation, assisted Clement VII. in quality of deacon, presenting to the Pope, the paten and the host, and offering the chalice together with him.[5]

The imperial office was considered as sacred with Charlemagne and his successors as it ever had been under Constantine, Theodosius, or Justinian. The emperor was enrolled as a canon of St. John Lateran and at the church at Aix-la-Chapelle. He was considered to have some power over the weather by the people — in Germany today, fine sunny weather is still called *Kaiserwetter*. Hence, as Dom Guéranger further tells us, this ceremony for the seventh lesson of Christmas Matins (dealing with the order of Caesar Augustus for the census which brought Mary and Joseph to Bethlehem) at St. Peter's:

This seventh Lesson, according to the Ceremonial of the Roman Church, is to be sung by the Emperor, if he happen to be in Rome at the time; and this is done in order to honour the Imperial power, whose decrees were the occasion of Mary and Joseph going to Bethlehem, and so fulfilling the designs of God, which he had revealed to the ancient Prophets. The Emperor is led to the Pope, in the same manner as the Knight who had to sing the fifth lesson; he puts on the Cope; two Cardinal-Deacons gird him with the sword, and go with him to the Ambo. The Lesson being

---

[5] Prosper Guéranger, OSB, *The Liturgical Year*, trans. Laurence Shepherd (Dublin, 1890), vol. 12, "Time After Pentecost: Book 3," 171–72.

concluded, the Emperor again goes before the Pope, and kisses his foot, as being the Vicar of the Christ whom he has just announced. This ceremony was observed in 1468, by the Emperor Frederic III, before the then Pope, Paul II.[6]

This was echoed by the prayers of the Roman Missal, until 1955. Among the "Occasional Prayers" — sets of Collects, Secrets, and Postcommunions for various intentions, to be said by the priest after finishing the Propers — we find the following "For the Emperor":

COLLECT. O God, the Protector of all kingdoms and in particular of the Christian Empire, grant to Thy servant our Emperor N. always to work wisely for the triumph of Thy power, that being s prince in virtue of Thy institution he may always continue mighty by virtue of Thy grace. Through our Lord.

SECRET. Accept, O Lord, the prayers and offerings of Thy Church for the safety of Thy suppliant servant, and work prodigies habitual to Thine arm for the protection of nations faithful to Thee: that, the enemies of peace having been overcome, Christian peace may allow of Thy being served in security. Through our Lord.

POSTCOMMUNION. O God, Who hast prepared the Roman Empire to serve for the preaching of the gospel of the eternal King: present Thy servant our Emperor N. with heavenly weapons, that the peace of the Churches may not be disturbed by the storms of war. Through our Lord.

Nor was this the only liturgical treatment the emperor received. Twice a year, all Catholics came into contact with the imperial idea. Among the Good Friday Collects was inserted the following:

Let us pray also for our most Christian Emperor N., that our God and Lord may, for our perpetual peace, subject all barbarous nations to him.

Let us pray. Let us kneel down. R. Arise.

O Almighty and Eternal God, in Whose hands are the powers of all men and the rights of all kingdoms; graciously look down upon the Roman Empire, that the nations that confide in their fierceness may be repressed by the power of Thy right hand. Through our Lord. R. Amen.

---

[6] Guéranger, *The Liturgical Year*, vol. 2, "Christmas: Book 1," 160.

Then again, on Holy Saturday, during the *Exsultet*, the prayer blessing the Paschal Candle, the priest would chant:

> Regard also our most devout Emperor *N.*, and since Thou knowest, O God, the desires of his heart, grant by the ineffable grace of Thy goodness and mercy that he may enjoy with all his people the tranquillity of perpetual peace and heavenly victory.

The Empire in the East fell to the Turks in 1453, after which the Russian tsars claimed that post for themselves. The last Holy Roman Emperor abdicated in 1806, and this is generally accepted as the end of the institution, although legal experts always point out that the abdication of a sovereign does not dissolve his throne. This last emperor had, two years earlier, declared himself emperor of Austria. That line continued until 1918, when Bl. Charles I (of Austria — he would have been Charles VIII of the Holy Roman Empire) was forced off the throne at the behest of Woodrow Wilson.

It is rather ironic that the line begun with one Charles I, who is a blessed, should have ended with another Charles I. The year before, Nicholas II abdicated the Russian throne. No longer does any government claim connexion with Constantine.

What is the importance of all of this history for the modern age? As Valentin Tomberg put it:

> The *post* of the Emperor...what an abundance of ideas concerning the post — its historical mission, its functions in the light of natural right, and its role in the light of divine right — of the Emperor of Christendom are to be found amongst mediaeval authors!
>
> As it is suitable that the institution of a city or a kingdom be made according to the model of the institution of the world, similarly it is necessary to draw from divine government the order (*ratio*) of the government of a city — this is the fundamental thesis advanced on this subject by St. Thomas Aquinas (*De regno* xiv, 1). This is why authors of the Middle Ages could not imagine Christianity without an Emperor, just as they could not imagine the Universal Church without a Pope. Because if the world is governed hierarchically, Christianity or the *Sanctum Imperium* cannot be otherwise. Hierarchy is a pyramid which exists only when it is complete. And it is the Emperor who is at its summit. Then come the kings, dukes, noblemen, citizens and peasants. But it is

the crown of the Emperor which confers royalty to the royal crowns from which the ducal crowns and all the other crowns in turn derive their authority.

The post of the Emperor is nevertheless not only that of the last (or, rather, the first) instance of sole legitimacy. It was also *magical*, if we understand by magic the action of correspondences between that which is below and that which is above. It was the principle itself of authority from which all lesser authorities derived not only their legitimacy but also their hold over the consciousness of the people. This is why royal crowns one after another lost their luster and were eclipsed after the imperial crown was eclipsed. Monarchies are unable to exist for long without the Monarchy; kings cannot apportion the crown and sceptre of the Emperor among themselves and pose as emperors in their particular countries, because the shadow of the Emperor is always present. And if in the past it was the Emperor who gave luster to the royal crowns, it was later the shadow of the absent Emperor which obscured the royal crowns and, consequently, all the other crowns — those of dukes, princes, counts, etc. A pyramid is not complete without its summit; hierarchy *does not exist* when it is incomplete. Without an Emperor, there will be, sooner or later, no more kings. When there are no kings, there will be, sooner or later, no more nobility. When there is no more nobility, there will be, sooner or later, no more bourgeoisie or peasants. This is how one arrives at the dictatorship of the *proletariat*, the class hostile to the hierarchical principle, which latter, however, is the reflection of divine order. This is why the proletariat professes atheism.

Europe is haunted by the shadow of the Emperor. One senses his absence just as vividly as in former times one sensed his presence. Because the emptiness of the wound *speaks*, that which we miss knows how to make us sense it.

Napoleon, eye-witness to the French Revolution, understood the direction which Europe had taken — the direction towards the complete destruction of hierarchy. And he sensed the shadow of the Emperor. He knew what had to be restored in Europe, which was not the royal throne of France — because kings cannot exist for long without the Emperor — but rather the imperial throne of Europe. So he decided to fill the gap himself. He made himself Emperor and he made his brothers kings. But it was to the sword that he took recourse. Instead of ruling by the *sceptre* — the globe bearing the cross — he made the decision to rule by the sword. But, "all who take up the sword will perish by the sword" (Matthew xxvi, 52). Hitler also had the delirium of desire to occupy the empty place of the Emperor. He believed he could establish the "thousand-year empire" of tyranny by means of the sword. But again — "all those who take up the sword will perish by the sword."

No, the post of the Emperor does not belong any longer either to those who desire it or to the choice of the people. It is reserved to the choice of heaven alone. It has become occult. And the crown, the sceptre, the throne, the coat-of-arms of the Emperor are to be found in the *catacombs*... in the catacombs — this means to say: under absolute protection.[7]

We are dealing with deep and strange matters here. But the fact remains that the Empire, both East and West, is gone. The vision of the Holy Empire haunted the soldiers and administrators who pioneered the Spanish, Portuguese, French, and British colonial empires. The First World War would weaken that Empire fatally, even as it would destroy the German Empire, the other great Protestant exponent of the imperial idea.

In any case, across Europe, and in Latin America, Canada, the Philippines, and elsewhere, in institutions, customs, and buildings, the mark of the Empire can be seen. Even in our own United States, in places settled before independence or by the French and Spanish, there yet linger traces; visible only to those who know what to look for, perhaps (like the double-eagle over the Spanish Governor's Palace in San Antonio, Texas), but still present. In many ways, starting with the United States and its electoral college, such federal unions as Canada, Australia, South Africa, Mexico, Brazil, Argentina, and India all owe elements of their constitutions to the Empire, and its idea of unity within diversity.

The founders of the European Union hoped that their creation would, in some way, take its place, as did all the popes from Pius XII to Benedict XVI. Instead, we have what we have.

But does this matter? Indeed it does, especially as the aging hippies of Brussels seem hell-bent on taking the place of Bonaparte and Hitler, albeit in a dull, "compassionate" kind of way. Back in 1900, the great Russian philosopher, Vladimir Soloviev, declared:

---

[7] Anonymous [Valentin Tomberg], *Meditations on the Tarot: A Journey into Christian Hermeticism*, trans. Robert Powell (Jeremy P. Tarcher/Penguin, 2002), 85–87, ellipses in original.

For lack of an imperial power genuinely Christian and Catholic, the Church has not succeeded in establishing social and political justice in Europe. The nations and states of modern times, freed since the Reformation from ecclesiastical surveillance, have attempted to improve upon the work of the Church. The results of the experiment are plain to see. The idea of Christendom as a real though admittedly inadequate unity embracing all the nations of Europe has vanished; the philosophy of the revolutionaries has made praiseworthy attempts to substitute for this unity the unity of the human race—with what success is well known. A universal militarism transforming whole nations into hostile armies and itself inspired by a national hatred such as the Middle Ages never knew; a deep and irreconcilable social conflict; a class struggle which threatens to whelm everything in fire and blood; and a continuous lessening of moral power in individuals, witnessed to by the constant increase in mental collapse, suicide and crime—such is the sum total of the progress which secularised Europe has made in the last three or four centuries.

The two great historic experiments, that of the Middle Ages and that of modern times, seem to demonstrate conclusively that neither the Church lacking the assistance of a secular power which is distinct from but responsible to her, nor the secular State relying upon its own resources, can succeed in establishing Christian justice and peace on the earth. The close alliance and organic union of the two powers *without confusion and without division* is the indispensable condition of true social progress. It remains to enquire whether there is in the Christian world a power capable of taking up the work of Constantine and Charlemagne with better hope of success.[8]

More recent authors have written in much the same vein. Journalist Gary Potter writes:

Words express ideas, and some of them now being quoted signify notions likely to be totally foreign to anyone unfamiliar with history prior to a few decades ago: "world emperor," "imperial office," AEIOU [*Austriae est imperare orbi universo*—"all the world is subject to Austria"] itself. This is not the place to lay out all the history needed to be known for thoroughly grasping the notions. However, the principal one was adumbrated by Our Lord Himself in the last command His followers received from Him: to make

---

[8] Vladimir Solovyev, *Russia and the Universal Church*, trans. Herbert Rees (Geoffrey Bles, 1948), 30–31.

disciples of *all* the nations. In a word, the idea of a universal Christian commonwealth is what we are talking about.

To date, it has never existed. Today there is not even a Christian government anywhere. However, from the conversion of Constantine until August, 1806 — with an interruption (in the West) from Romulus Augustulus in 475 to Charlemagne in 800 — there was *the* Empire. It was the heart of what was once known as Christendom. Under its aegis serious European settlement of the Western Hemisphere began and the Americas' native inhabitants were first baptized, which is why the feather cloak of Montezuma is to be seen today in a museum in Vienna. After 1806 a kind of shadow of the Empire, the Austro-Hungarian one, endured until the end of World War I, when its abolition was imposed as a condition of peace by U. S. President Woodrow Wilson. Since 1438, when Albert V, cousin of Frederick III, was crowned Roman Emperor, all the Emperors were Habsburgs. The last was Archduke Otto's father, Karl.[9]

The malaise of Europe and her daughters is, in great part, traceable to her renunciation of the faith that created her. But that renunciation itself owed much to the death of the imperial idea and the philosophical basis upon which it rested. The horrors Soloviev described have only worsened — not only on the national and continental levels, but on the personal one as well.

Given this difficulty, and the others concerning demographics and Islam earlier mentioned, just what is to be done? It is evident that the Zapateros of the world will rarely, if ever, wake up to reality (and Blair's conversion to Catholicism after leaving office may only mean he spends his dotage condemning the evils resulting from his own policies, without ever noticing their ultimate origins). It is just as evident that the rulership of Europe is committed to the EU becoming an ever more encompassing superstate.

It is a truism to say that "the rulers rule and the subjects serve," but they do in all societies, and never more so than in the twenty-first century. In all likelihood, things will continue along the route they are proceeding, until at last the EU is a true prison of the nations, or Islam cleans Europe's cuckoo clocks in a bath of blood. Neither is a particularly appetizing outcome, in all honesty.

---

[9] Gary Potter, *In Reaction* (Neumann Press, 1991), 55.

However, "while there is life, there is hope," to quote a cliché, and much can yet be done. The first thing is an acceptance of reality. Despite the best (and truly noble) efforts of the Eurosceptics — and occasional partial and temporary victories here or there — I think that it must be admitted that the European institutions at Brussels, Strasbourg, and Luxembourg, with their attendant bureaucracies, are not going away, nor are their hideous buildings. In a political sense, then, the struggle for control of these bodies must be begun in earnest. What is required is a sort of political counterrevolution.

But counterrevolutions most often fail because their leadership (and sometimes their rank and file) has no real political ideas or ideology of its own, save opposition to the usurpers. Indeed, it often shares many of its opponents' basic beliefs, so successful has the revolution become. Moreover, conservatives, men of the right — call them what you will — are not usually driven by hatred and envy, as they are usually not driven much at all. Why bother about a seemingly abstract cause and some distant future, when the present can be so enjoyable?

Yet if Europe is not to sink beneath a sea of either blood, boredom, or both, those with the love of her as she was and to some degree yet remains, at heart must be animated by a desire for political success the equal of her present rulers. Thankfully, the bits and pieces are still around to be picked up and perhaps resewn into a new garment.

The EU has divided European conservatives in twain. On the one hand, there are the Eurosceptics, who quite rightly fear the loss of national, regional, and provincial liberties. On the other, conservative proponents of an integrally united Europe, such as the Paneuropa Union, invoke the Crown of Charlemagne for their work. These two sets must realise that in reality, they complement one another and ought not to be opposed. France and Estonia, Asturias and Bavaria — all need to be preserved as fully functioning entities with legitimate lives and ethoi all their own; but this understanding needs to be blended with a true realisation of Europe's legitimate cultural and spiritual unity, the need in today's world for this unity to be expressed in a concrete way (especially in terms of trade and defence), and the importance of the civilisation that unity has engendered for the rest of the world — especially, but far from solely, the daughter nations. Nor should these realisations be restricted by race. Many a Goan, Tahitian, or Cape Coloured is a better European than those who crawl the corridors of power in the mother continent. Much the same could be said for the Christians dying for their faith in China, the Sudan, India, Pakistan, or Indonesia.

This brings up another point, doubtless an uncomfortable one for many. That is the religious dimension. As earlier quoted, dear old Belloc declared, "the Faith is Europe, and Europe is the Faith." Now, as many of the aforementioned Christians in Africa and Asia might tell you, there is some oversimplification there — but only some. Since Europe has, after 1945, done her best not to be united to the faith, she has done an extremely effective job of being nothing at all. But Islam's challenge cannot be countered with mere affirmations of an empty and weary pluralism. A positive thing can be checked only by another positive thing, not by a negation.

Nor can this be a mere question of, as some churchmen have put it, Europe regaining a sense of her Christian "roots" and "values," any more than Islamic "roots" and "values" are posing a serious threat to the West. It is the conviction of individual Muslim militants that their personal salvation is bound up with their political and military actions that make them formidable, even as it was a similar conviction on the part of Christians that allowed first the establishment of Europe herself, and then her expansion across the globe. Cynical historians may point to the part that lust for power and thirst for wealth played in these developments, and they are certainly correct to a degree. But those elements alone would never have brought armies of settlers across the seas, nor battalions of missionaries to exceedingly unpleasant climes. However given up to the worship of mammon in all his forms my home may be, it was neither the quest for power nor wealth that led to the founding of this City of Angels.

Even though such figures of the right as Maurras, Bolingbroke, and Santayana might have been comfortable as unbelievers, citing religion's mere utility in preserving the culture and institutions they loved, personal belief is required for the Europe of the future to be one worth living in. It was for this reason that, in his homily on the occasion of the beatification of Emperor Charles I of Austria, John Paul II declared:

> From the beginning, the Emperor Charles conceived of his
> office as a holy service to his people. His chief concern was
> to *follow the Christian vocation to holiness also in his political
> actions*. For this reason, his thoughts turned to social assis-
> tance. May he be an example for all of us, especially for
> those who have political responsibilities in Europe today![10]

I will outrage modern sensibilities even further and say that
a vague "Christianity" will not serve for this purpose. Rather,
that Church that gave birth to Christendom in the first place
is the only one that can truly serve as a religious basis for a
revivified Europe. But for that to happen, she must regain
the sense of self she has dissipated since the 1960s — a need
her current rulers seem utterly ignorant of as they waste their
energies and ours on the liberal causes *du jour*. Catholics, if they
are to be politically effective, must learn to think once more
of personal salvation, and of political, social, and charitable
action as a means to that end. Many of the newer orders and
movements in the Church, as well as revivals of older ones
(like the Templars in Italy and the Hieronymites in Spain) are
hopeful signs in that direction, and so are the younger clergy.

In this light, ecumenism will have to be rethought. On the
one hand, dialogue with moribund ecclesial bodies that are no
longer sure of doctrinal realities is pointless. But dialogue in
search of union with such groups as the Traditional Anglican
Church, the *Hochkirchliche Vereinigung,* and the Nordic Catholic
Church (which body received apostolic succession from the
Polish National Catholics, with papal approval and encouragement) assumes a real urgency. All of that is even truer
as regards the Orthodox and "lesser" Eastern Churches. The
rediscovery of pilgrimages and refurbishing of pre-Reformation
shrines in Northern Europe that has gone on since 2000 is a
promising development along these lines. Official bodies (such
as the European Institute of Cultural Routes) and private ones
(like the Confraternities of St. James in various countries)
have done much to revive the pilgrims' routes (especially to
Compostela) that did so much to bring the peoples of Catholic
Europe together in both movement and devotion.

---

[10] John Paul II, "Beatification of Five Servants of God," October 3, 2024,
https://www.vatican.va/content/john-paul-ii/en/homilies/2004/documents/
hf_jp-ii_hom_20041003_beatifications.html.

We also need to regain a love for Europe as Christendom, for our own country's heroes and traditions, as well as those of others. From Aetius and Arthur to von Stauffenberg, the great ones who defended Europe against her enemies and spread her religion and civilisation throughout the world, should be vindicated. No longer ought we to apologise for the Crusades (save for when folly or treachery on the part of those paladins frustrated their high purpose). We should honour, as part of our common heritage, folk like the Chouans and Vendéens in France, the Cristeros in Mexico, the Cavaliers and Jacobites in the British Isles, the Carlists in Spain, the Pontifical Zouaves, and on and on. It needs also to be remembered that, at their best, they fought under the standard of Jesus and Mary; at their worst, they were still better, as men, than the "heroes" the modern world offers us, such as Norman Bethune, Margaret Sanger, and Che Guevara.

This being the case, it would be well for theologians and others concerned with European institutions and holding at least some of the views heretofore outlined to take another look at the vision of the Empire. This too is already happening. As we saw earlier, Fr. Aidan Nichols, OP, clearly recognises the providential role of the Holy Roman Empire and calls for its restoration.[11] It is far from impossible that some future pope may see the need for the sort of restoration here envisaged. If such a pontiff mounts the throne of St. Peter at a time when the then-leadership of the European Union feels a need to animate its machinery with a soul, we may see something of a new empire emerge. This development would profoundly affect the European daughter nations of the Americas, Australasia, and elsewhere; moreover, it might be the only real answer Western civilization can make to a resurgent Islam.

Eurosceptics, pan-Europeans, Catholic activists, neo-imperialists—none of these need agree on all points at this stage. What they must do is talk with each other and write up their ideas. A body of discourse should be built, "knitting up the fragments," as it were, of past traditions and present needs. Above all, folk minded in this direction who do not care to go into European or national politics (or find no opportunity

---

[11] See the passage on p. 16.

therein) should consider two equally or even more important areas of endeavour: academia and the production of reference materials, such as encyclopaedias and dictionaries. Samuel Johnson saw the importance of this latter area of the conflict, and it has been well said that the history of the world, at least its English-speaking component, would have been far different had the *Encyclopaedia Britannica* been produced at Oxford rather than at Cambridge.

All of this labour in the macrocosm may well take generations, even as the opposition's work did—and it could certainly be that we do not have the time. Worse still, most of us will never play any role at all on the continental or national stage, whether in a political, academic, or literary role. What, then about the rest of us? Ought we simply to sit back and hope for the best?

By no means! Each of us needs to cultivate a personal faith, simply because, presuming we have souls, each of us will be around far longer than the current political scene, and our own damnation or salvation depends upon it. Beyond that, though, the creeping of "that hideous strength" into every corner of Europe and the West requires resistance—resistance in our own particular sphere in which we find ourselves. Whether it be larger issues, such as abortion or euthanasia, or smaller local ones, such as protection of the built heritage or unspoiled areas, looking after the poor or disabled, defending monarchy, hunting, or other traditional institutions and practises, or just fighting for the right of local cheese or sausage makers to continue their craft as their fathers did, we each have a battle to fight. But if we are in Europe, we should remember that in what appear to be parochial conflicts, we are fighting the local battles of a great war, and we should get in touch with similarly engaged folk throughout the continent, exchanging ideas and tactics. The threat is Europe-wide—so should be the defence.

What of the future? Who knows? Should ever something along the lines of Fr. Nichols's proposal become likely, the case can be made that the abdication of Francis II in 1806, which is generally considered to be the act that ended the Empire, simply began a new interregnum, comparable to that opened by Romulus Augustulus's renunciation of the throne in AD 476, and concluded by Charlemagne's coronation in 800 (although, to be sure, the Eastern Empire continued uninterruptedly all that time). As Viscount Bryce himself points out:

> Great Britain had refused in 1806 to recognize the dissolution of the Empire. And it may indeed be maintained that in point of law the Empire was never extinguished at all, but lived on as a sort of disembodied spirit. For it is clear that, technically speaking, the abdication of a sovereign destroys only his own rights, and does not dissolve the state over which he presides. Perhaps the Elector of Saxony might, legally, as imperial Vicar during an interregnum, have summoned the electoral college to meet and choose a new Emperor.[12]

What made Great Britain's refusal to recognise the emperor's act so important is that her king, at that time elector of Hanover, had a voice in the governance of the Empire and a vote in the election of any future emperor. Much the same case is made by Klaus Epstein:

> While there is no question that Francis was personally entitled to abdicate a crown he was no longer willing to wear, he certainly had no constitutional power to dissolve the fabric of imperial obligation per se. The empire, like all sovereign states, was intended to be perpetual and the emperor had sworn to maintain it to the best of his ability. He broke his coronation oath when he declared it dissolved, and he failed to consult the *Stände* assembled at Regensburg about his highly irregular procedure. One can argue, therefore, that the imperial death warrant was technically *ultra vires* and therefore null and void, and that the empire "legally" continued to exist after 1806.[13]

Should such a pontiff emerge as we just spoke of, given that by the Empire's law the pope was in fact "imperial vicar" during an interregnum (*pace* Viscount Bryce), he would have a firm legal base from which to conjure the Empire back into existence.

But that is all speculation. Should Europe be overwhelmed by external enemies or collapse into some horrible Orwellian nightmare, or both, the faith and the notion of the Empire will survive her. No doubt a new civilisation will arise on her ruins,

---

[12] Bryce, *The Holy Roman Empire*, 416.
[13] Klaus Epstein, *The Genesis of German Conservatism* (Princeton University Press, 1966), 668.

even as she did on those of old Rome. Yet there will be continuity of some kind; it may be that Brazilians or Congolese will free the mother continent from her occupiers and retransform her cathedrals from mosques into churches once more, as happened so many times in Spain and Hungary. In truth, while we may be confident of future victory, at this time we can no more predict what form that victory will take than Ss. Ambrose and Augustine could have foretold Clovis and Justinian.

But what of us as individuals? What have we to look forward to? The work that has been laid before us, done with all our might, as part of our quest for heaven. In one way, Bl. Charles of Austria was a complete failure. Nothing he tried in the political sphere succeeded: World War I did not end early, his peoples were not able to settle down as equal partners in one house, and even his attempts to regain Hungary came to miserable ends. He died a tubercular exile on a far-off island. Bl. Thomas Percy tried, in the Rising in the North, to restore England's Church and state; he failed, and was executed in the Tower of London. St. Louis IX attempted to reignite the Crusades and died a prisoner of the Turks. The Church did not raise these men to her altars for their political efforts but for their personal holiness; nevertheless, those efforts played a role in their ascension to heaven. So may it be for us, God willing, regardless of whatever may come from our poor actions this side of the grave.

The crown of Charlemagne rests in Vienna's Hofburg, while his throne is in the upper gallery at Aachen's cathedral. Though the last imperial claimant went into exile in 1918, the ghost of the Empire remains; it will continue to, so long as there are folk of faith and valour left upon the earth. Those who come after may look more like Indians, Chinese, or Africans than ourselves, but they will be worthy successors of Arthur, Charlemagne, and Godfrey of Bouillon all the same.

CHAPTER 8

Disembodied Church and Zombie State

T HE FIRST SUNDAY IN LENT IS, IN THE BYZ-
antine calendar used by both Catholics and Orthodox
of that rite, the Sunday of Orthodoxy. It is an observance that honours the triumph by the orthodox Catholics of
East and West over the Iconoclasts at the Second Ecumenical
Council of Nicaea in 787, at a time when Rome and Constantinople stood firmly united. Although a Latin Christian of the
Anglican Ordinariate myself (though a cradle Catholic), this
year I found myself carrying an icon of Bl. Emperor-King Karl
of Austria-Hungary in the traditional procession with icons
that is a feature of the day's observances. It was with that in
mind that—after the equally traditional denunciation of various heresies that follows—I listened to the commemorations
of various degrees of believers, including:

> To the most holy Emperor Constantine, equal to the Apos-
> tles, to his mother Helena; to the orthodox Emperors Theo-
> dosius the Great, Theodosius the Younger, Justinian; to the
> most pious Grand Duke Vladimir, equal to the Apostles, to
> the Grand Duchess Olga, and all other orthodox emperors
> and empresses, princes and princesses, eternal memory!

This prompted many musings indeed. For one thing, many
of those present were Ukrainians or Ruthenians; they have
friends and relations at this moment fighting the Russians—
who in turn commemorate Ss. Vladimir and Olga in exactly
the same manner this day, equally claiming them as their
forbears with Ukrainians and Belarusians. For another, the
Byzantine rite prayers for the emperor in the liturgies of Ss.
Basil and John Chrysostom were used equally for Bl. Karl and
for his wartime opponent, Tsar Nicholas II (although Karl was
also named in the Latin rite prayers for Good Friday and Holy
Saturday). There is a certain fittingness in this last, because
Habsburgs and Romanoffs were in some sense successors to

the Holy Roman and Byzantine emperors; Aachen/Vienna and Moscow/St. Petersburg thus carried on the traditions of imperial Rome and Constantinople.

Such thoughts led further to considerations of how Theodosius the Great had made baptism entrance into Roman citizenship as well as membership of the Church—thus incarnating, as it were, Christ's union of His Davidic kingship with the *communio* of the Church at the Last Supper. From that time on, both in the various imperial manifestations of East and West, as well as in the kingdoms from Ireland to Russia that formed on "their" soil and were ruled by kings that claimed to be subject to them, Church and state were seen as two distinct facets of the same *res publica Christiana*. This notion survived not only the various schisms between East and West but also the Protestant Revolt (although Catholics suddenly found themselves shoved out of the body politic in countries where the new religion prevailed—and its adherents received the same treatment where it did not). However, the horrors and the bloodshed of that time led directly to the rise of deism, the Enlightenment, and the far worse bloodshed of the French and subsequent revolutions, all of which targeted Christianity in its various forms. By turns violent and peaceful, the rise of secularism eventually pushed Catholicism, Orthodoxy, and Protestantism out of any real say over policy in their respective countries. Indeed, the experience of Covid has shown that in the vast majority of nations, the Church is not considered in any sense an equal partner with the state but a mere private association, like the Rotary Club—and with no more rights than the Rotary Club has. Sadly, this is a situation in which the vast majority of ecclesiastical hierarchs have happily acquiesced.

Nevertheless, wherever it is considered advantageous by the secular and progressivist governments, bits and pieces of the old arrangements with Christianity are retained—either out of a desire to clothe the ugly realities of current public life in somewhat more presentable garb, or else to wring some real advantage out of the remaining band of believers. In the United States, where Thomas Jefferson coined the phrase "separation of Church and state,"[1] this is expressed in a number of ways.

---

[1] This phrase does not appear in our Constitution, since several of our first states retained established Churches when that document was ratified, and as

Apart from the Episcopalian National Cathedral acting as the backdrop for much of our civic ceremonial (and similar scenes taking place in each of our state capitals), clerical chaplains are actively recruited to encourage soldiers, sailors, airmen, policemen, and firemen to continue to risk their lives. Government tolerates any "faith-based initiatives" that spend money (and so save the government some expense) without proselytising. The National Conference of Catholic Bishops and each state's Catholic conference are listened to when what they have to say echoes existing government policy, and ignored when it does not. Christmas is a national holiday — and in a few areas, Good Friday, Epiphany, and All Saints' Day as well.

Indeed, in almost all post-Catholic and in some other countries, Catholic military dioceses are welcome, for the same reason they are in the USA. The same goes for such post-Christian countries as Britain and the Crown Commonwealth, Scandinavia, and Benelux. But there are other bits and pieces retained as curiosities or for some minor political advantage. Most formerly believing nations retain presences in Rome (embassies to the Holy See and sometimes the Order of Malta, national churches, academies, national seminaries, and pilgrim hospices), and the Holy Land (sponsored churches, monasteries, and yet more pilgrim hospices). In the latter place, France, Spain, Italy, and Belgium are "consular" nations receiving special privileges from the Franciscan "Custody of the Holy Land"; even the double eagle remains there in shadow: the Austrian Hospice and the Russian Mission to the Holy Land — both begun and endowed by kaisers and tsars. For that matter, around the globe, the Carthusians still pray for the restoration of the Latin Kingdom of Jerusalem — of which the last major remnant, the Order of the Holy Sepulchre, struggles manfully to keep the Catholic Church in the Holy Land funded.

Although the vestigial nature of official Christianity in Britain is often invoked in that country's monarchical ceremonial — which reached a crescendo in the coronation of King Charles III — such also survives elsewhere. The president of France, heir of Robespierre, has nevertheless inherited a canonry of

late as 1892 the Supreme Court maintained that the United States comprises a "Christian nation" (*Church of the Holy Trinity v. United States*, 143 U. S. 457, 471) — whatever that might mean.

St. John Lateran from the Most Christian Kings, while the king of Spain has a similar honour over at St. Mary Major. Macron must approve the bishops appointed to France — and, indeed, many countries retain such privileges as codified in the nation's concordat, if it has one. Needless to say, regardless of how anti-Christian a government's policies may be, they do tend to continue to observe something of the Church's liturgical year in the calendar of holidays and in tolerance or encouragement of the various customs thereof. But as much as this writer enjoys the ritual invocation of Almighty God in American courts, the Regimental Collects of the British Army, the annual march of civic officials in European Corpus Christi processions, and the handful of New England villages whose meetinghouses continue to shelter both the town government and a Congregationalist (or Unitarian) parish as they have done since colonial days, he cannot help but see it all as a bit of theatre or make-believe — though no less gripping for all that.

The raw truth is very different. Lovely as all of these trappings are, they would vanish in a heartbeat if the local ecclesiastical leadership seriously challenged the powers-that-be in regard to things like euthanasia, abortion, or gender confusion. The archbishop of Canterbury would be immediately out of a job, while Cardinal McElroy would find, at the very least, that a Democrat president would not show up for the Red Mass at St. Matthew's Cathedral. One wonders how long the German bishops would enjoy the Church Tax if they were committed to the Catholic faith. Even in Russia, where at least lip service is paid to Christian morality (although abortion remains legal, as it has been since 1918), the extravagant support given to the Russian Orthodox Church would vanish if it seriously dissented from government policy. Indeed, these days the only opponents bishops seem disposed to attack are those who hold to the Church's traditions — knowing, of course, that those hapless traditionalists have no recourse. It is ever the mark of the bully that he abuses the weak while kowtowing to the powerful.

One might see the Church as having been the *form* of society in the ages of faith, as the state was its matter. For the medievals, the separation of the body's form — the soul — from its matter was the very definition of death. Today, the Churches, whether Catholic, Orthodox, or Protestant, are quite as effectively separated from the states they formerly animated as any soul from any corpse. Many of their leaders flit about, intent on proving themselves relevant to the mouldering pile of flesh which once they ensouled. But it is a pointless task, really, as the corpse cares nothing about them. Indeed, in the tragic case of so many Catholic parishes in America, during the Covid lockdown their websites counselled their parishioners to "make a perfect act of contrition and a spiritual communion, and donate *here*." A clearer insistence on one's own spiritual irrelevance would be harder to envision — nor a better inducement to ending donations.

But let us not think that the corpse of the state lies empty and quiet — by no means! Every society requires a state Church of some kind to operate, an animating philosophy of some sort to give authority and legitimacy to its rulership and some kind of "morality" to its subjects. Islam, Judaism, Buddhism, Hinduism, and Shinto all animate various nations around the planet. Nature abhors a vacuum, and in those countries formed by the now-effectively-banished-from-public-life Christianity, the faith of their fathers has been replaced by a quasi-religious faith that sees barren sexuality and infanticide as sacred, death as the greatest evil (which paradoxically may be freely dealt out to the defenceless), and the masters of the state as the wisest of all who must be obeyed unquestioningly by their servants. They must be obeyed, whether that means shutting down half a nation's farms against their owners' wills, seizing the bank accounts of supposed enemies who speak out against the rulership, or just shutting down a nation's economy. It would perhaps not be so bad if these measures — draconian and dictatorial as they are — ever worked to the advantage of the populace whom the masters claim to represent; but they do not. Blind to and uncaring about their subjects' needs, they do as they please. These are the creatures who appear to be lurching like the walking dead toward nuclear war.

Even if that supreme catastrophe should be avoided and sanity at least momentarily prevails in Washington and Moscow, there is no guarantee that they and their similar blind fellow leaders shall not steer us into other and perhaps worse mischief. If the European nations have lost their souls, as many commentators have said, the same is no less true for the countries of Europe beyond the seas, from San Francisco to Vladivostok, and from Buenos Aires to Cape Town and Sydney.

While the soul — like the Church — is indeed immortal, neither the body nor the state is. The zombie governments of this world shall continue to bounce off each other — unless these be the last days — until they rot completely, and are replaced by entirely different entities and societies, which the Church shall have to evangelise in their turn ... or perhaps the existing lands of what was once Christendom can be restored to life.

But first, the Catholic Church must reconcile herself with her tradition and inherent structure; she must have a leadership committed to the faith, practised as her Lord and founder once delivered it to her. The rupture with and within the Eastern Churches must be healed, and as presaged by the Ordinariates, those elements of the state churches and *Landeskirchen* of Northern Europe that still retain a desire for Christian orthodoxy must be brought back into the fold of the Church Universal. Yet essential as these things are for the restoration of political health to the West, they must be done not for political ends but for purely spiritual and salvific ones: "Seek ye therefore first the kingdom of God, and his justice, and all these things shall be added unto you" (Matt 6:33).

CHAPTER 9

The Quest for a Catholic State

AFTER THE FRENCH REVOLUTION, COUNT Joseph de Maistre, probably the greatest of counterrevolutionary thinkers, uttered this warning: "Know how to be a royalist: in the past it was instinct, today it is a science."[1] He was fully aware that traditional loyalties and institutions had been questioned by the revolutionary turmoil; in particular, rationalism and illuminism attacked the Throne and the Altar and pursued a strategy of laicisation of state and unchristianisation of society. They fought sacred monarchies because they denied that authority is derived from God and rejected the idea that society is a natural development of families, is founded on traditions, and is an organic entity. Against this they proposed the notion of a hypothetical social contract. De Maistre knew very well that political battles must first be won in the field of ideas—a teaching which was to be stressed by another great French monarchist, Charles Maurras—and that the revolution, even if defeated on the battlefield, still lay in wait.[2]

Up until 1848, Catholic social theorists and politicians alike had, to a great degree, simply ignored the industrial proletariat. While they continued to fight for Catholic monarchy, local liberties and traditions, and the countryside over the town, they had ignored the growth of the proletariat and what was called the "social question"—the reduction of the industrial workers to semi-permanent misery. The result was the loss of the faith among such masses and the corresponding rise of socialism and communism. The revolutions of 1848 and the following few years made Catholic leaders aware of two important facts: the Church had to face the industrial age, and just as they had been forced by the revolutions to turn what

---

[1] Joseph de Maistre, *Lettres d'un royaliste savoisien à ses compatriotes* (H. Pelagaud fils et Roblot, 1793), 28.
[2] See Massimo de Leonardis, "Monarchism in Italy," *Royal Stuart Review* 8, no. 1 (1990): 5.

had previously been an instinctual acceptance of the natural order of things into a conscious philosophy, so too must they now find a way to apply that philosophy — developed initially in defense of traditional and rural institutions — to modern life.

In the first part of the nineteenth century, men like de Maistre, de Bonald, von Baader, and Müller arose to elaborate and popularize the Church's social teachings; in the second half it was no different. As early as 1869, German bishop Wilhelm von Ketteler declared that the working classes required six things:

1) increase of wages corresponding to the true value of labor;
2) shorter hours of labor;
3) days of rest;
4) abolition of child labor in factories;
5) prohibition of the employment of women, particularly mothers, in factories; and
6) prohibition of the employment of young girls in factories.[3]

The fact that these proposals seemed radical then says much about conditions at the time. Soon, men like von Ketteler all over Europe would be attempting to unite the older strand of Catholic social thought with the new conditions. Always, however, they would be hampered by the fact that, by this time, the reins of power in most of Europe were in liberal hands.

Already, though, the world had seen at least one government in integrally Catholic hands, showing what the Church's teachings could give the nation and the ruler who dared to apply them. The country so blessed was Ecuador, and the ruler, Gabriel García Moreno.

The coming of independence to Latin America saw the formation in every country there of two parties: Liberal and Conservative. The latter looked to Spain in particular and Europe in general for social and political inspiration. They wished to retain the Catholic Church in the position which she had had from the first settlement; further, they wanted the great estates to remain like those of Europe — self-contained communities

---

[3] See Rupert J. Ederer, ed., *The Social Teachings of Wilhelm Emmanuel von Ketteler: Bishop of Mainz (1811–1877)* (University Press of America, 1981), 444–59. Lest the latter two seem horribly sexist, it should be remembered that then, as now, family life was disrupted when mothers had to work, and young girls could be employed at a fraction of the pittance paid men.

which, while they may not have made their owners a great deal of money, did build social stability. The Liberals looked to the United States as a guide, wanted separation of Church and state, and wished to turn the great estates into money-making concerns, like factories. These two groups had clashed since independence. The Conservatives had indeed produced some great leaders, like Mexico's Agustín I and Guatemala's Rafael Carrera. But these were inevitably opposed by powerful US-backed forces. In any case, as the nineteenth century progressed, both parties were faced with the impact such inventions as the railroad must make on their countries.

Born in 1821 to an aristocratic family of Ecuador's capital, Quito, García Moreno studied theology in the university there. Thinking he had a vocation to the priesthood, he received minor orders and the tonsure, but his closest friends and his own interests convinced him to pursue a more worldly career. Graduating in 1844, he was admitted to the bar. Starting his career as both a lawyer and a journalist (opposed to the Liberal government in power) he made little headway. In 1849, he embarked on a two-year visit to Europe for a firsthand look at the effects of the 1848 revolutions. He made a second trip in 1854–1856. Louis Veulliot (himself a great champion of the faith in the press) described what these trips did for García Moreno:

> On a foreign soil, alone, unknown, but sustained by the faith and love of his great heart, García Moreno prepared himself to reign if such were the will of God. With this view alone he prayed and studied. Paris, where Providence had called him, was the real workshop for such an apprentice. Paris, Christian on the one hand and savage on the other, gives the world the spectacle of a fight between two opposing elements. It has schools for priests and martyrs, and others for antichrists, idols, and executioners. The future President and Missioner of Ecuador had before his eyes good and evil. When he returned to his distant home, his choice was made.[4]

He returned home in 1856 to find his country in the grip of strident anticlericals; he was elected a senator and joined the opposition. Although himself a monarchist (he would have liked to have seen a Spanish prince on the throne), he bowed

---

[4] Augustine Berthe, CSSR, *Garcia Moreno*, trans. Lady Herbert (Dolorosa Press, 2006), 113.

to circumstances and allowed himself to be made president after a civil war the year after his return — so great had his stint in the country's Senate made his reputation. In 1861, this was confirmed in a popular election for a four-year term. Unhappily, his successor was deposed by the Liberals in 1867. Two years later, however, Moreno was reelected, and then again in 1875. During his period in office, he propelled his nation forward, all the while uniting her more closely to the faith.

Personally pious (he attended Mass daily, as well as visiting the Blessed Sacrament; he received Communion every Sunday — a rare practice before St. Pius X — and belonged to the workingmen's section of the sodality, in which he was quite active), he believed that the first duty of the state was to promote and support Catholicism. Church and state were united, but by the terms of the new concordat, the state's power over appointments of bishops, which it had inherited from Spain, was done away with — at García Moreno's insistence. The 1869 constitution made Catholicism the religion of the state and required that both candidates and voters for office be Catholic. He was the only ruler in the world to protest the pope's loss of the Papal States, and two years later had the legislature consecrate Ecuador to the Sacred Heart.

In more worldly considerations, he came to office with an empty treasury and an enormous debt. To overcome this, he reorganized government spending on a more stringent basis, abolished useless positions, and eliminated the corruption that siphoned off tax dollars. As a result, he was able to provide Ecuadoreans with more for less. Slavery was abolished, but slaveowners were fully compensated (saving both them and their former slaves from economic ruin). The army was reformed, with officers being sent to Prussia to study and illiterate recruits taught basic skills. Houses of prostitution were closed, and hospitals opened in all the major towns. Railroads and national highways were built, the telegraph network extended, and the postal and water systems improved. City streets were paved and local bandits suppressed. García Moreno further reformed the universities, established two polytechnic and agricultural colleges and a military school, and increased the number of primary schools from 200 to 500. The number of students in them grew from 8,000 to 32,000. To staff the enormously expanded health-care and educational facilities, foreign religious were brought in. All of this was done while expanding the franchise and guaranteeing equal rights under the law to every Ecuadorean.

But the Liberals (not without contacts and support in the American embassy) hated García Moreno; when he was elected a third time in 1875, it was considered to be his death warrant. He wrote immediately to Pius IX asking for his blessing before inauguration day on August 30:

> But I wished to let you know [of my election] today, so as to obtain from Heaven the light and strength which I need now, more than at any other time, to remain the devoted son of our Holy Redeemer and the loyal and obedient servant of His Vicar.
>
> Today, when all the Masonic lodges, excited by those in Germany and Belgium, utter against me the vilest and most horrible calumnies, and are moving heaven and earth to find means to assassinate me, I need more than ever the Divine protection, so as to live and die for the defense of our holy religion and of this dear Republic which God has called upon me to govern.[5]

García Moreno's prediction was correct; he was assassinated coming out of the cathedral in Quito, struck down with knives and revolvers. So passed from the scene one of the greatest Catholic statesmen the world has ever seen. He showed that making Catholicism the basis of public policy will not doom a country to poverty, but quite the opposite; all Catholic Latin American politicians who have followed since owe him a great debt.

In Europe, there were few truly Catholic governments. Even in Austria-Hungary, Liberals often had the upper hand. If they were not quite able to destroy what Catholicism remained in public life, they were able to prevent it from applying real solutions in response to the social question.

Yet following the leads of Bishop von Ketteler and García Moreno, Catholic social theorists continued to work. In France, one such was Charles, Marquis de La Tour du Pin (1834–1924). A nobleman, he owned and ran a large estate that his old and distinguished family had successfully preserved through the Revolution. His first taste of practical social Catholicism was

---

[5] Berthe, *Garcia Moreno*, 318.

his father's admonition: "Never forget that you will be only the administrator of these lands for their inhabitants."[6] After a decorated military career that ended in 1882, he threw himself into the fight to build a just nation out of France's Third Republic. Horrified by both the poverty of Parisian workingmen and their profound alienation from Church and nation, he collaborated with Albert, Count de Mun in forming workingmen's circles. These would provide centers where industrial laborers could find entertainment, fellowship, education and mutual assistance — under Catholic auspices — and so be both uplifted and made immune to communist propaganda. This was a valuable experience for La Tour du Pin; together with his convictions that Catholicism must regain its rightful place in the life of France and that France must once again have a king, it was the origin of his unique social and political vision. Because of the influence of La Tour du Pin's teachings on future events, we will quote a detailed description of them:

> Men must have certain personal rights, and also certain common rights, due to the social organization, which it is the duty of government to recognize. These rights are a part of the national constitution. Whether codified or not, the real constitution of a country is what is traditional, permanent, and essential to the principles of its political institutions. It is an historic product; the sum total of solutions given to the eternal problem of reconciling authority with the desire for liberty.
>
> In the past this problem was less acute, for men had a different conception of liberty. To us today liberty is individualistic and means the absence of restraints; to them, because they were more truly Christian, it was social, and meant the free play of the institutions which ensure social justice, that is to say, an equitable distribution of the burdens and advantages of society.
>
> The true basis of such institutions is the association of men according to their functions. Thus only is the sense of social solidarity developed. To be genuine, a representative system must make room for all social collectivities. Both the feudal and the corporative regimes were just such organizations of men, not according to classes, but according to functions.

[6] André Caudron, "La Tour du Pin Chambly, René, marquis de la Charce," *Le Maitron*, March 30, 2010, https://maitron.fr/spip.php?article82173; translation mine.

A political body should represent, not individuals, but social bodies, organic elements, such as bishoprics, fiefs, cities, communes, corporations. When laws are to be elaborated, it is only from such organized bodies that one can expect competence, independence, and prudence. When classes and interests are represented there is a constant current, and no violent movements occur, but when the parliament is based on an unorganized universal suffrage, only opinion is represented, and all is ephemeral—it is a mere demagogy.

La Tour du Pin was favorable to the creation of an aristocracy. There have never been closed castes in Christian countries, he pointed out, but only classes. These will always exist, for a society necessarily develops an aristocracy, which is the mainspring of its civilization. If society is not to be a chaos, a natural selection of families by means of heredity must be allowed to take place. The hereditary possession of the land is the truest source of distinction and authority; it alone can create a genuine nobility.

When a parliament represents permanent forces, as it does in countries like England[7] (where the absolutism of the *ancien régime* did not penetrate), when a peerage is a real House of Lords, that is to say, of those possessing great fiefs, and representing the families which have always shared in the sovereignty, the result is good. But in France the nobility had ceased during the *ancien régime* to be a political order, and had become a mere social class. This was one of the reasons why at the Restoration it was so difficult to reconstruct a representative system.

In addition to the peerage, which already represents the class of landowners and the profession of soldiers, there are three types of interests which should be represented. They are (1) the taxpayers, (2) constituted bodies in the State, and (3) professional associations. As to the first category, the family is the primordial unit of representation, as it is of society. Each head of a family has a right to select mandataries who will consent to taxation. Widows and unmarried women should here have in this respect equal rights with fathers, for they represent a family. Electoral colleges may be formed of these heads of families. They should be divided into three classes, according to the amount of taxes which they pay, and the burden should be distributed equally among these three groups.

As to the second category, churches, universities, and legal bodies, as well as the professional corporations, must have representation. It cannot be regulated, however, as in

---

[7] Or did, until the change of constitution in 1911.—*Author.*

the case of the taxpayers; it must be based on the hierarchical principle which is the very structure of these bodies.

Most important of all is professional representation. The
corporative régime must be introduced into all occupations,
and become the basis of economic, social, and political life.
All occupations create common rights and interests, and
the associations which arise from these should be organized, and erected into political as well as economic units.

The representatives of the taxpayers would constitute
the administrative organs, which would be autonomous in
the communes, and in the State would exercise a control
over the use of public monies, through a chamber of dep-
uties, which would vote the budget. The budget, however,
should normally be voted for a number of years ahead,
unless there is some unusual expense to be provided for.

Another chamber should exist, formed by the representatives of the social bodies, which would have the right
to be consulted on all technical and economic matters.
This would secure a balance between the opinion of the
moment, represented by the taxpayers' delegates, and the
permanent interests of the country, represented by the delegates of the organized bodies. The consent of both chambers would be necessary for measures which concerned all.

The chambers are not, however, to have a supreme
authority, either in legislation or in administration. It
is the king in his council who governs, and the States
[namely, legislatures], Provincial or General, have merely
rights of consent and control. They are not to sit in permanence, or be convoked regularly, for this would lead
to a divided sovereignty, and perpetual struggle.

This political structure as conceived by La Tour du Pin
was founded on the corporative organization of industry,
professions, and the land. His ideas with regard to this
corporative regime are precise. What should the contract
of labor provide for the worker, for the owner, and for
society? he asked. This contract is an exchange of services.
Both capitalist and laborer must procure a living from
it, each according to his condition, and living implies a
home and the means of rearing a family.

The corporative régime is not socialistic; it admits that
inequalities of social condition must be respected. Its basis
is the fact that labor and capital are mutually dependent.
Its principle is the admission of a right and a duty for
each member of the association, and of reciprocal rights
and duties between the association and the State. The
corporation is, like the commune, a state within the State,
a social institution, with a fixed place in the community,
and obligations to it.

In the Middle Ages the land was for the peasant, and the tool for the worker. Today the laborer has no real rights, no guaranty of fixed work, no safe tomorrow. Socialism, on the contrary, gives no rights at all to capital. The corporative régime gives rights to both.

A corporation should include all who are engaged in a given industry, in whatever capacity, for they are all interdependent, and the salary or profit of each, according to his place, will depend alike on the state of the industry.

The fundamental functions of a corporation are: first, the formation of a corporate patrimony, i.e., an insurance fund, to be levied partly on the profits of capital, and partly on the wages of labor, and to serve both as a protection for the workers, in old age and illness, and as a reserve for the industry itself, to enable it to survive times of stress; and second, the verification of professional capacity, both of workers and directors, and the supervision of the quality of production. This will limit, but will not do away with competition, and access to trades and professions. It will protect the public and safeguard the skill which is the laborers' capital. A third function would be the representation of each element in a corporative government. This will allow disputes as to wages and the conditions of labor to be settled by those who are actually interested in the industry in question, either as workers or as owners.

The land, like the tools of industry, must yield the means of subsistence to those who cultivate it. It belongs to the poor as well as to the rich. Society has rights in it, and the individual only a tenancy.

In every case the duties, not the rights of property owners should be stressed. Property is the basis of society only if it is reasonably accessible to all. The masses to become conservative must be given a stake in the community. Liberalism destroyed the old corporations, in which everyone had some interest, and free competition lowered the standard of living, and did not respect the needs of family life. The State exists only to protect society, and if misery becomes so great that a large number of members do not want society to be preserved, the State will not be able to act.

La Tour du Pin saw the need of decentralization. He thought that it could best be realized by means of indirect professional representation. All professional associations should send delegates to a local syndical chamber, in which owners and workers would be equally represented. These local chambers would send delegates to a body which would have its place of meeting in the chief town of the arrondissement. These in turn would send delegates to provincial chambers. Thus agriculture and industry, producers and retailers, as well as the liberal professions, would each possess a provincial chamber, and these chambers could unite, when necessary, to discuss their common interests. They would then form a body much like the old Provincial Estates. These chambers should be presided over by a permanent official, emissary of the central power, and there should also be a central office in each province to permit the government to keep in touch with the local corporations.

La Tour du Pin was hostile to the liberal conception of a free Church in a free State. In practice, he said, this had proved unfavorable to religion. The Church once had the right of ministry, that of teaching, and that of administering justice where its interests or its members were concerned. Today only the first of these is left, for the Church's judicial power has disappeared, and her right to teach is strongly contested.

Both the idea that religion is a private matter, and the belief that the Church should be submitted to the control of the State are errors. "Man," he said, "is a religious being, and the social order always corresponds more or less closely to a religious idea." Religious society is the best society, and its precepts must be practiced. No attack upon it must be allowed. All that is not Christian in the spirit and habits of society must be banished. Dissidents may be tolerated, but they should be treated, not as members of the community, but as strangers.[8]

This very long quotation is useful because it shows not only what La Tour du Pin arrived at by the late nineteenth century, but what most other Catholic social theorists had arrived at as well—the idea of the corporate state. Men like Ramón Nocedal in Spain, Karl, Baron von Vogelsang in Austria, and Giuseppe Toniolo in Italy elaborated the same ideas in their own countries. The latter was influential in persuading Leo XIII to accept these notions; the result was the groundbreaking 1891 encyclical *Rerum Novarum*. In this, Leo XIII held up corporatism as the Catholic ideal.

As a result, the Catholic or Christian Social Parties in Austria-Hungary, Germany, Belgium, and the Netherlands all adopted the corporate state as their long-term goal. In France, the chance to form such a group was ironically scuttled by Pope

---

[8] Charlotte Touzalin Muret, *French Royalist Doctrines Since the Revolution* (Columbia University Press, 1933), 207–13.

Leo's order that French Catholics should abandon royalism and "rally to the republic" (see his encyclical *Au Milieu des Sollicitudes*);[9] this in hopes of convincing the government not to seize the churches. While Leo's strategy failed to preserve the property, it did manage to split the most activist French Catholics into two factions. In Italy, no Catholic party was formed, because to take part in electoral politics would have entailed recognition of the Italian government's legitimacy (impossible due to its usurpation of Rome).

In Spain and Portugal too, the Catholics were split by dynastic disputes. In any case, since the whole nature of electoral politics as we know it and in which the Catholic parties had to function is and was liberal, these groups often had to defer any work on the corporate state to some unknown future and spend the present working for easier goals—often including piecemeal parts of the total program. So it was as the new twentieth century dawned.

The First World War destroyed much of value, including the Habsburg Empire of Austria-Hungary. But it also destroyed faith in the liberal vision of progress; its horrible devastation led many to think more of the next world. Further, the unleashing of communism in Russia (and its bloody attempts at rule in Finland, Hungary, Bavaria, Slovakia, and elsewhere) brought many to think more seriously of non-liberal capitalist alternatives. But it was the worldwide Depression in 1929, threatening the very foundations of the international capitalist economy, that led many folk in many lands to ponder the corporate state anew. Although monarchism and Catholicism were bound up together with corporatism in the view of many, the three were not necessarily identical, as attempts to put them into practice showed. At any rate, Pius XI reinforced and updated his predecessor's endorsement of corporatism in his encyclical *Quadragesimo Anno*, issued in 1931.

Portugal had suffered a revolution in 1910, which expelled King Manuel II and put in an anticlerical regime. On May 27, 1926, a popular rising against the regime began in Braga, in the north. On June 17, the rebels entered Lisbon. The presidency

---

[9] For more on this failed strategy, see Roberto de Mattei, "The *Ralliement* of Leo XIII: A Pastoral Experience that Moved Away from Doctrine," *Rorate Caeli*, March 19, 2015, https://rorate-caeli.blogspot.com/2015/03/the-ralliement-of-leo-xiii-pastoral.html.

was given to General Óscar Carmona. He summoned to the capital one Professor António de Oliveira Salazar, an instructor of economics at the University of Coimbra. Like García Moreno, Salazar had been ordained in the minor orders and was a fervent Catholic. Moreover, at Coimbra he was a student of the writings of La Tour du Pin. Eventually, he became prime minister, and in 1932 he gave his country a new, corporative constitution. In this document, the ideas articulated by La Tour du Pin were erected into law. The result was called the Estado Novo, the New State. Corporations representing labor and capital in every branch of industry were erected.

The economy of Portugal had been in foreign hands for a long time; Salazar restored the position of the Portuguese fishermen, farmers, and artisans. The Church reassumed her rightful place in the national life. He declared that when the country was ready, he would bring back her king. Above all, Salazar tried, as had La Tour du Pin, von Vogelsang, and the other corporate theorists, to put an end to the rule of party and faction. In his own words:

> We seek to construct a social and corporative State corresponding exactly with the natural structure of society. The families, the parishes, the townships, the corporations, where all the citizens are to be found with their fundamental juridical liberties, are the organisms which make up the nation, and as such they ought to take a direct part in the constitution of the supreme bodies of the State. Here is an expression of the representative system that is more faithful than any other.[10]

What was the result? Throughout the 1930s, World War II, and the '50s, Portugal did rather well. The corporations continued to grow and the standard of living rose. But in the early '60s, revolts against Portuguese rule broke out in the African possessions of Angola, Mozambique, and Portuguese Guinea. Although the guerrillas were armed by both the Soviet Union and the United States, Salazar resolved to fight. Incapacitated by a stroke in 1968, he died two years later. His successors were not as able as he, and in time the strain of fighting the world's two superpowers by proxy ruined the national economy. A coup in 1974 ended Salazar's experiment. But what would

---

[10] Michael Derrick, *The Portugal of Salazar* (Campion Books, 1939), 133.

have been the outcome had the New State been allowed to develop in peace is a question, which, while unanswerable, deserves a good deal of thought.

Another attempt to inaugurate a Catholic, corporate state took place in Austria. The rump remaining from the German-speaking areas of the former Empire was always in a rather precarious economic position. The Depression hit the country badly. The rise of the Nazis to power in Germany caught the country in a vice; to stave off Hitler, successive Austrian governments had to turn to Mussolini. Moreover, the socialists and communists were very active. Surrounded by dangers internal and external, Austrians looked for strong Catholic leadership. They found it in Engelbert Dollfuss.

Born in 1892, Dollfuss had studied law and economics at Vienna. He became secretary to the Lower Austrian Peasants' Union, and in 1927 he helped found and became a director of the regional Chamber of Agriculture of Lower Austria. In 1931 he became chancellor of Austria. At the Christian Social Party conference in April 1933, the need to reconstruct Austrian society if it was to stave off its enemies was of paramount concern. At that conference, Dollfuss's assistant, Kurt von Schuschnigg declared that the "reconstruction of the state" was "indivisibly connected with the reform of society,"[11] and that *Quadragesimo Anno* was the guide. A new corporative constitution was adopted on June 19, 1934.

It is a remarkable document. Its preamble reads: "In the name of almighty God from Whom all justice emanates, the Austrian people receives for its Christian, German Federal State on a corporative foundation this constitution."[12] In keeping with this, the Concordat of 1933 with the Holy See was elevated to constitutional law. Corporative legislative bodies like the Federal Cultural Council and the Federal Economic Council were erected. Dollfuss, lover of Austrian institutions that he was, favoured a Habsburg restoration. Although he gave his country a good constitution, he did not see it in operation for long.

---

[11] Cecil Schmid, "Kurt Schuschnigg und die 'österreichische Identität': Verortung einer Österreich-Ideologie zwischen zweitem deutschen Staat, Reichsgedanken und österreichischer Sendung" (master's thesis, University of Vienna, 2021), 71, https://doi.org/10.25365/thesis.66145; translation mine.
[12] From the translation of the Constitution in *British and Foreign State Papers*, vol. 141 (1950).

The Austrian Nazis were fearful that Dollfuss's activities would prevent the country's annexation by Germany. On July 25, 1934, a group of 150–200 Nazis seized the chancellery and murdered Dollfuss. Although the attempted coup was put down, it was nevertheless a great blow to Austrian independence.

Dollfuss's constitution did survive him — for four years. At last, abandoned by the West, Austria submitted to her northern neighbour. For the short period that Dollfuss's reforms were in effect, they produced some excellent results. Unhappily, we shall never know the full extent of the results that could have followed, had they been allowed to flourish.

Lithuania also attempted a similar solution to the problems of the Great Depression, communism, and Nazism. After a pro-communist government was deposed in 1926, Antanas Smetona, who had led the nation to independence in 1918, returned to power. Under his sponsorship, a new constitution in 1931 made Catholicism the religion of the state and established the Chamber of Commerce and the Chamber of Agriculture to function in typical corporative style. A 1935 law created the Chamber of Labor to safeguard the workers' cultural, economic, and social interests. Here again, only five years would pass before Soviet troops ended the experiment — but what was accomplished in the meantime showed great promise.

The next year, Lithuania's neighbour to the north, Latvia, adopted a corporative government; this even though only 29 percent of Latvians were Catholic. Still, it conformed to the general pattern:

> A corporative form of government came into effect with the formation, in January 1936, of a National Economic Council, made up of the elected boards of the newly created chambers of commerce, industry, agriculture, artisans, and labor. A State Cultural Council was also created, consisting of the boards of the Chamber of Professions, and the Chamber of Literature and Art. These councils were allowed to collaborate with the respective government departments, individually and jointly. The two National Councils constituted the Joint Economic and Cultural State Council, which was convoked by the President of the Republic, and worked in close collaboration with the Cabinet of Ministers. The Joint State Council represented all sections of the nation, including the national minorities. It passed resolutions by a simple majority vote of its members.

> The reorganization of the producing population on a guild basis was paralleled by a readjustment in municipal and rural self-government, where elections were now held along guild rather than political lines. A new communal law provided for an organic coordination between the various corporative chambers and the self-governing territorial administrations. It was generally conceded at the time that the direct participation of every producing socio-economic group in the governmental machinery insured that national unity which both public opinion and the men in office sought as a remedy for the current ills and a new foundation for the future security of the state.[13]

Needless to say, the Soviets put an end to all of that, too, in 1940.

The year 1936 also saw the beginning of the Spanish Civil War. The Falange, the coalition of Carlists, Alfonsinos, and corporatists who won that conflict in 1939, maintained the following point along with the 27 others in their program:

> 9. We consider Spain, in economic terms, to be one gigantic workers' union of producers. We will organize Spanish society corporatively through a system of vertical unions, based on branches of production, at the service of national economic wholeness.[14]

The Falange did form some of these syndicates; moreover, they spread the idea of corporatism throughout Latin America. Even in the American-held Philippines, a branch of the Falange existed, organized by Andrés Soriano and Enrique Zóbel.

But by 1937, some of these nations had their own native Catholic corporatist movements, friendly to but independent of the Spanish Falange. The Sinarquistas of Mexico maintained as one of their sixteen points:

> The members of the same craft or profession must unite, building corporate groups. Over these professional or corporate groups, a superior power must be established, in charge of their mutual relationships and directing them to the common good. Similar professional corporations must unite within themselves, submitting to a supreme authority embodied in the political structure of the Nation.[15]

---

[13] Alfred Bilmanis, *A History of Latvia* (Princeton University Press, 1951), 360–61.
[14] Justin Crumbaugh and Nil Santiáñez, eds., *Spanish Fascist Writing*, trans. María Soledad Barbón et al. (University of Toronto Press, 2021), 111–12.
[15] Allan Chase, *Falange: The Axis Secret Army in the Americas* (G. P. Putnam's Sons, 1943), 168. N. B.: this document as a whole advocates a very different viewpoint from the one I am advocating.

Laureano Gómez, head of the Colombian Conservative Party after 1930, and president from 1950 to 1953, was interested in corporatism; so too was José Uriburu, Argentine president from 1930–1931. But in order to be friendly with the US, Franco tacitly dropped corporatism after 1955, and most Latin Americans followed suit. *Quadragesimo Anno* made such an impression in the Netherlands that corporations were actually formed at the behest of the minority Catholic party and endowed with a certain amount of governmental power in the 1938 constitution; World War II and German occupation ended this experiment. In Belgium, Robert Poulet, a journalist, played an important part in the Reaction group. This consisted of men of letters, war veterans, corporatists, etc. Established in 1932, its organ for the next two years was the *Revue réactionnaire*. It tried to foster a "powerful current of opinion against parliament and democracy"; it felt that the old parties must disappear and "abdicate their sovereignty into the hands of the king."[16] The king, who would govern with the help of a corporatist system, would be given the most extensive powers, including legislation. In 1935 the *Revue réactionnaire* was succeeded by the *Revue de l'Ordre Corporatif* (1935–1940) which continued the struggle for a "corporate monarchy." The previous year, Poulet and various other *Reaction* members took over the *Nation Belge*. This latter held that the parliamementary regime was dying and should be replaced by a corporatist state organized around the king. Of similar views were Pierre Nothomb (1887–1966), writer and orator, founder of the weekly *L'Action Nationale* (1924–1930), and Paul Hoonaert, who was executed by the Nazis.

In Ireland, corporatism inspired the work of Fr. Denis Fahey and Fr. E. Cahill; it also had some influence on the 1937 constitution.

As might be expected, corporatist ideas were not unknown in France, home of La Tour du Pin. They were popularized by the famed Charles Maurras of Action Française. Due to his influence and that of those like him, the regime of Marshal Pétain at Vichy experimented with corporatism during the two years of its partial independence from the German occupiers in 1940–42. After that date, former socialists like Pierre Laval

---

[16] Hans Rogger, *The European Right: A Historical Profile* (University of California Press, 1965), 146.

were forced into positions of power by the Germans; these soon ended the corporatist effort.

Corporatism crossed over to Quebec from France; the movement Action Française Canadienne, led by Fr. Lionel Groulx, became so influential that Cardinal Villeneuve himself opined on April 17, 1937, "We have here and there some bits of social justice, but these appearances of remedies do not suffice. We need more than that: full corporatism."[17] As Sinarquismo came across the border to the Southwest, so did folk inspired by Groulx come with the French Canadians to New England. Thus was founded the '20s-era paper in Woonsocket, Rhode Island, *La Sentinelle*, edited by Elphège J. Daignault (1879–1937).

Unfortunately, Mussolini and Hitler attempted to claim corporatism for themselves, leading some to claim that it is merely fascism. But this attempt is belied by two important facts. The one is that in true corporatism, as elaborated by popes and lay theorists and politicians, the corporations are organic, that is, true developments from the grass roots. The great dictators tried to make them artificially; it did not work well, and in the case of Italy, the attempt was given up after 1937.

The other important point is that many of their opponents were true corporatists. Fr. Luigi Sturzo's Popular Party (Catholics could vote in Italy after World War I) was among the bitterest opponents of the fascists. It had as its motto *Libertas*, a liberty which was not "the liberal, individualist, antiorganic, atomic conception . . . based on the [false] conception of the sovereignty of the people."[18] In Germany, the heroic Claus, Count von Stauffenberg, who attempted to assassinate Hitler as part of a coup on July 20, 1944, was surrounded by corporatists. Apart from emphasizing the need for Christianity in general and Catholicism in particular in German public life, von Stauffenberg had some very corporatist things to say:

> How can people fit to govern be recruited from all sections of the population? Is it possible, and if so how, to establish popular representation in Germany, perhaps on an entirely different basis than that of conventional political parties — perhaps building on the political reality

---

[17] Mason Wade, *The French Canadians 1760–1945* (The Macmillan Company, 1955), 909.
[18] Edward R. Tannenbaum, *The Fascist Experience* (Basic Books, 1972), 183.

of a system of local communities, vocational groups, or
associations of common interests which might be given
a public voice of their own in Parliament instead of devi-
ously pursuing their objectives through self-interested
parties or by parleying with such parties.

Relations between entrepreneurs and workers must be
based on their common tasks, and their joint responsibility toward the community as a whole and towards the
individual human being.[19]

Von Stauffenberg was, by all accounts, a great man; one wonders how, had he been successful, he would have served his
country and his continent. Is it not odd that Nazi, fascist,
communist, and capitalist alike all opposed these corporatists?
One might be tempted to say that destruction of the unique
Catholic social and economic vision was the one thing that
united both Allies and Axis in World War II.

But why bother with all this old news now? What can this
pack of lost opportunities tell us today?

Three things. First, corporatism was an attempt to apply the
never-changing teachings of the Church in the social sphere
to the changed conditions brought on by industrialism. The
shift in developed countries over the last few decades from an
industrial to an information and service economy is as great a
shift, and quite as traumatic. Surely it needs to be addressed
from a Catholic viewpoint.

Second, having been in the grip of a recession deeper than
any we have had since the Great Depression, we are driven by
economic scarcity to question whether or not there are better
alternatives to our present economic and political system.

Thirdly, it will be apparent from all that has been written
here that in many ways, we in these United States are the acme
of classical liberalism. Apart from the Mexican and French-
Canadian immigrants spoken of and the late Fr. Charles E.
Coughlin, no one has ever seriously suggested that the social
and financial life of this county ought to be organized upon
Catholic principles. For good reason; to do so would require
our nation's conversion.

We have such an admirable band of predecessors, as we
have just read. It would be good if we could emulate them.

---

[19] Peter Hoffmann, *The History of the German Resistance, 1933–1945* (MIT Press, 1977).

CHAPTER 10

Bl. Karl, Clericalism, and Lay Church Governance

WHAT IS CLERICALISM?

There has been on every side over the past few years denunciations of clericalism in the Church—not least by the Holy Father. The same word can be used, however, to cover a multitude of meanings. If, for instance, one uses it to mean reserving various liturgical and sacramental actions or governance of parishes to members of the clergy, that could, I suppose, be called clericalism. But by the same token, the various changes in the liturgy, to say nothing of recent attempts to alter Church teaching, might also be called clericalism, since the ability to do such things is entirely in the keeping of the clergy, high and low, and is generally done with no reference to the laity whatsoever. When Pius XII decided to change the rites of Holy Week, abolish the octaves of a number of major feasts, and the like, no laity were consulted. So too when Pope John XXIII deleted from the calendar all feasts that he thought "repetitive." These, of course, paved the way for the oceans of changes liturgical and otherwise that Paul VI inflicted upon the Church—including eliminating most lay positions from the Papal Court. None of these things were asked for by the laity; they arose simply from the idea of the reigning pontiffs that they or their clerical cohorts understood the faith better than their predecessors who had gone before or the laity. One sees in these actions clericalism of the deepest dye.

But where did it begin? Paradoxically, one might trace present-day clericalism to the fall of the Papal States. Prior to 1870, the Popes ruled over a small but nevertheless real country. It had strengths and problems like any other nation, but it allowed the papacy to be independent of any temporal ruler on the one hand—in an age when most Catholics lived

under Catholic rulers — and on the other made them cognizant
of the actual difficulties rulers have. Reigning over both nobility and commoners, successive popes perforce had to provide
for the needs of their laity. While this dual role of pope and
temporal ruler was fraught with many difficulties, it anchored
each pope in the world his subjects had to live in. After the
fall of Rome to the Sardinians, so the popular mythology has
run, the popes were "freed" to devote themselves entirely to
spiritual issues; moreover, it is asserted that this temporal
rule was responsible for various of the worst popes the Church
has had to endure through history. But it may well be argued
that since 1870, popes have become ever further divorced from
the experience of both laity and law, which has made them
increasingly oblivious to either. Moreover, if the temporal rule
of the popes was responsible for the bad ones, to what do we
attribute the far greater number of saints in their number,
who were just as intimately involved with temporal concerns?

THE LAY GOVERNANCE OF THE CHURCH

At any rate, if the popes were once concerned with temporal issues in their domains, in the traditional Catholic state
emperors and kings were very much concerned with religious
ones. Each had an ecclesiastical household with chaplains; they
founded cathedrals and abbeys and petitioned the Holy See for
approval of new feasts and devotions. The Holy Roman Emperors and the kings of France, Spain, and England were honorary
canons of major Roman basilicas and had specific liturgical roles
at papal Masses when visiting Rome. They publicly observed in
various ways the great feasts of the Church — most notably the
footwashing of the poor on Maundy Thursday and processing
after the Blessed Sacrament on Corpus Christi. Bishops and
abbots served in provincial and national legislatures, and very
often, the primate of the given country crowned the monarch.
The Crown supported the Church financially — and, in the case
of the French, Spanish, and Portuguese colonial empires, footed
the entire bill for the evangelisation of those countries. As the
pope had the power of veto over any number of imperial and
royal ecclesiastical measures, so the Holy Roman Emperor and
the kings of France and Spain had the power to exclude any
particular cardinal from consideration in the papal conclave.

In the countries sheared off from Christendom by the Protestant Revolt, a similar connexion was kept with the newly created Protestant state churches of Northern Europe. The French Revolution began the destruction of this relationship in Catholic Europe, and by 1914, it survived intact in two countries alone: Spain (which, however, had compromised in several key areas with liberalism, as our Carlist friends will tell you) and the Austro-Hungarian monarchy.

EMPEROR FRANZ JOSEPH

In many ways, Austro-Hungarian Emperor-King Franz Joseph epitomised the traditional relationship between the lay and clerical powers of the Church. As with the other crowned heads of Europe, he had inherited a particular style of Catholic devotion peculiar to his own dynasty—the *Pietas Austriaca*. Bound up with a veneration of the True Cross and the Passion, the Blessed Sacrament and the Sacred Heart, the Blessed Virgin and St. Joseph (the family patron), this religiosity had led to the tremendous collection of relics at the Hofburg, the Imperial Palace in Vienna. The Maundy Thursday footwashing and the Corpus Christi procession were highlights of court life in Vienna, and in 1898 Franz Joseph led the imperial family in the Consecration of All Mankind to the Sacred Heart, in a spiritual union with Leo XIII in Rome. In the canon of the Mass, the Good Friday Collects, and the Holy Saturday *Exsultet*, the emperor was prayed for by name.

Franz Joseph was crowned and anointed king of Hungary in 1867. As emperor-king, he appointed the cardinals, archbishops, and bishops, subject to papal approval. Exempt from this were Salzburg and Olomouc, their metropolitans being elected by the cathedral chapters, and the former "Salzburg dioceses" of Seckau, Lavant, and Gurk. The archbishop of Salzburg had the right of appointment for Seckau and Lavant, while the occupation of Gurk was regulated in a mixed manner, that is, the emperor proposed two candidates and the subsequent nomination was made by the archbishop of Salzburg. The nuncio had to be consulted to make sure that the choice was not obnoxious to the pope—disapproval would derail the process. The separate Austrian and Hungarian ministries of worship and education would do the research, but it was Franz Joseph who had to approve the choices, for both Latin and Eastern rite Catholic bishops. Moreover, he had to bear in mind that some of his appointees would sit in one or more legislatures within the monarchy.

There were three national parliaments. In the upper house — the House of Lords (*Herrenhaus*) of the Austrian Parliament — could be found the prince-archbishops of Vienna, Prague, Salzburg, Görz, and Olmütz, the archbishops of Lemberg and Zara, the Byzantine Catholic archbishop of Lemberg, the Armenian Catholic archbishop of Lemberg, and the Greek Orthodox archbishop of Czernowitz, as well as the prince-bishops of Brixen, Breslau (although located in what was then Germany, for the diocesan territory in Austrian Silesia), Krakau, Seckau, Trient, Laibach, Lavant, and Gurk. The Hungarian upper house, the *Főrendiház* or "House of Magnates," had an even higher proportion of ecclesiastical members — although it was also more interfaith than Austria's: forty-two dignitaries of the Catholic and Orthodox Churches, including the primate, archbishops, bishops, abbots, and various other high officials, and thirteen representatives of the Protestant confessions. The annexation of Bosnia in 1908 presented a challenge in creating representative institutions for a region that had never known them. But while the Bosnian diet (*sabor*) would have only one house, it would also have religious representatives appointed by the monarch. These were, in deference to the Muslim majority, the reis, who was the principal of the Muslims' granted lands, and the Muslims' regional leader from Mostar; four metropolitans and the president of the Orthodox community; the Catholic archbishop and two province members of the Franciscan order of Bosnia and Herzegovina; and the Sephardic rabbi of the higher order. The various provincial diets in the Austrian half of the monarchy also included the local Catholic bishops in their number.

Another religious duty that Franz Joseph took very seriously was that of funding missions — even though Austria-Hungary had no colonies. The Catholic Church in Scandinavia, Albania, and Bulgaria (Latin and Byzantine in that case) was heavily funded by the emperor, as was the Church in the Holy Land and Egypt (the Coptic Catholic Church was funded from its beginning thereby, and Franz Joseph paid for the building of the Latin Catholic cathedral of St. Catherine in Alexandria, where, ironically, the remains of his wartime enemy King Victor Emmanuel III would rest until their recent repatriation to Italy). But since 1826, very largely out of funds given by both Franz Joseph and his two immediate predecessors, a large amount of this largesse went to the Church in the United States. Through an organisation called the *Leopoldinenstiftung*—the "Leopoldine Foundation"—the Habsburgs and many of their subjects poured millions of dollars into the American Church, founding 400 parishes, subsidising wholly or partly 300 missionaries (such as St. John Neumann and Ven. Bishop Baraga), and sending an endless flow of vestments, statues, stained glass, liturgical implements, and the like. A great deal of dynastic money went to Eastern rite churches in the United States as well. Unfortunately, the outbreak of war in 1914 ended the flow of generosity—which, of course, would be repaid by Woodrow Wilson's insistence on the deposition, exile, and partition of the domains of Franz Joseph's successor.

BL. EMPEROR KARL

That successor was Bl. Emperor Karl, who succeed Franz Joseph in 1916. As all the Catholic world knows, he was beatified for his personal piety and virtue. As a boy, he had made the Consecration to the Sacred Heart in the family chapel, when illness prevented him from going to Vienna with his parents for the aforementioned Sacred Heart observance in 1898. Whenever possible, from childhood until his untimely death in exile in 1922, he went to daily Mass. Despite personal betrayal by Vienna's Cardinal Piffl (who urged Austrians to rally to the republic, declaring it to be a "religious duty," and persuaded most of the other Austrian bishops to join him in his stand), Karl never lost his love of the Church nor his reverence for the clergy.

Responding to Piffl's move in a January 15, 1919 letter delivered by his secretary, Baron Karl Werkmann, the emperor asked the cardinal to influence the Catholics of all the dioceses of Austria, through the priests, to achieve not only a Christian but a monarchist election result. The emperor argued that the Church in Austria would soon perish without the monarchy, as shown by the revolutionary government's many anti-church laws (immoral marriage legislation, allowance of Freemasonry, etc.). As for his own stance toward his office, Bl. Karl declared that, as rightful ruler of German-Austria, he had never abdicated and would never abdicate:

> The current government is a revolutionary government because it has eliminated the state power instituted by God. I am always surprised when Catholics are led to believe that Pope Leo XIII approved the republics; this is fundamentally wrong. A republic that has set aside the rights of others can never, according to the views of the great Pope, be a legitimate form of government for Catholics.[1]

While a few bishops (Ignaz Rieder of Salzburg, Sigismund Waitz of Brixen, Johannes Maria Gföllner of Linz, János Mikes of Szombathely, and a few others) remained loyal to the exiled emperor-king and his son, Otto, most did not. But there were others also on the road to canonisation who did. Cardinal Mindszenty is the best known of these, but one might also mention the Hungarian Bl. Zoltán Meszlényi, who in 1921 wrote a study entitled "The King and the National Assembly," in which he declared that the king's will is above that of his national assembly. Of course, his greatest loyalist in both earthly and heavenly rank is John Paul II, whose father named him Karol after the emperor, and who, when meeting Karl's widow, Servant of God Zita, declared that it was an honour to finally meet "my empress."

In an age when many laymen feel left out, ignored, and even victimized by a large part of the hierarchy, the example and intercession of Bl. Karl and his consort have never been more important. And while the relationship between the lay and clerical powers of the Church in almost every country today may be very different from what it was—and that of Christendom has even been condemned by many theologians in recent decades—the latter system produced and was endorsed by many saints, not least of which was Bl. Karl.

---

[1] Quoted in Elisabeth Kovács, "Kaiser und König Karl I. (IV.) und die Bischöfe der Österreichisch-ungarischen Monarchie (1916–1922)," *Mitteilungen des Instituts für Österreichische Geschichtsforschung* 109 (2001), 163–64; translation mine.

CHAPTER 11

Guelphs and Ghibellines Revisited

"There is no Christian prince left. These other countries are even as Britain, or else sunk deeper still in the disease."

"Then we must go higher. We must go to him whose office it is to put down tyrants and give life to dying kingdoms. We must call on the Emperor."

"There is no Emperor."

—C. S. Lewis[1]

HEN I WAS YOUNG, "GUELPHS AND GHI-bellines" was such a phrase as "Hatfields and McCoys," "Cops and Robbers," "Montagues and Capulets," and "Cowboys and Indians"—a stock line indicating two irreconcilable groups. Today I do not know if most college-aged people would recognise any of these folk. Nevertheless, the first-named are key to understanding a great deal of medieval European history; moreover, the recent rift between the Orthodox patriarchates of Constantinople and Moscow and the scandals in the Catholic Church bring the issues over which their long-ago battles were fought back into focus.

From the time that Constantine the Great legalised Catholicism and Theodosius the Great made citizenship in the Roman Empire coeval with membership in the Church via baptism, the relationship between the religious and temporal heads of the *res publica Christiana* has been tense. After 800 there were two rival Empires, and after 1054 two rival Churches; but the issues in their relationships and, as it were, their sociologies, are interchangeable with each other *and* the pattern prior to 800. Before the crowning of Charlemagne, there was no disagreement that the pope of Rome was the supreme spiritual head of the Christian people and that the emperor at Constantinople (certainly since 476) was their supreme temporal leader. Justinian in his famous *Code* quotes a letter he received from Pope John II:

---

[1] C. S. Lewis, *That Hideous Strength* (Scribner, 1996), 290.

> That this See is truly the head of all churches, both the
> regulations of the fathers and the statutes of emperors
> declare, as the most reverent utterances of Your Piety also
> attest. It is clear, therefore, that in You will be fulfilled
> what the scriptures say: "By me kings reign and the pow-
> erful decree justice." For there is nothing that burns with
> a brighter light than correct faith in an emperor; there is
> nothing less subject to decline than true religion. For as
> both behold the author of life or light, they rightly both
> reject darkness and know not how to succumb to eclipse.
>
> Wherefore, Most Glorious of Emperors, divine might
> will be entreated in all our prayers, so that it may, without
> fail, long preserve Your Piety in this ardor of faith, in this
> devotion of mind, in this zeal for untainted religion. We
> believe this is also for the good of the holy churches. For
> it is written, "the king rules by his lips," and again: "the
> king's heart is in the hand of God: He turneth it whither-
> soever He will." For it is this that strengthens Your rule;
> this that preserves Your reign. For the peace of the Church
> and the unity of religion protect its author with grateful
> tranquility, when he has been borne up on high (after
> death). For no small thanks will be bestowed by divine
> might on him through whom the Church has been divided
> and sundered by no cracks; through whom it has been
> tainted by no blemishes. For it is written: "when a just
> king sits upon his throne, no evil will oppose him."[2]

Also included in the Code is Justinian's response:

> We have therefore hastened to make all priests of the
> whole Orient subject to the See of Your Holiness and to
> unite them with it. And We therefore deemed it neces-
> sary to bring to the notice of Your Holiness what action
> presently has been taken here, although it is clear and
> unquestioned and has ever been resolutely observed and
> preached by all priests in accord with the teaching of
> Your Apostolic See. For We permit no action to be taken
> concerning the status of the churches, however clear and
> unquestioned it may be, but that it should come to the
> notice of Your Holiness, because You are the head of all
> holy churches. For in all ways, as stated, We strive to
> increase the honor and authority of Your See.[3]

This seems relatively clear. In the manual *de Ceremoniis* of Constantine VII, 400 years later, the same amity and understanding

---

[2] Bruce W. Frier, ed., *The Codex of Justinian*, trans. Fred H. Blume (Cambridge
University Press, 2016), vol. 1, 31–33.
[3] Frier, *The Codex of Justinian*, 33–35.

of their complementary roles seems to dominate the ritualized dialogue between papal envoy and emperor:

> The foremost of the Holy Apostles protect you: Peter the keyholder of heaven, and Paul teacher of the nations (*ethne*). Our spiritual father (*pneumatikos pater*) [N.][4] the most holy and ecumenical patriarch, together with the holiest bishops, priests and deacons, and the whole clerical order of the holy Church of the Romans (*Romaioi*) send you, Emperor, faithful prayers through our humble persons. The most honored princeps (*prinkips*) of the elder Rome with the leading men (*archontes*) and the whole people subject to them convey to your imperial person the most faithful obeisance (*doulosis*).[5]

The logothete inquires on the emperor's behalf:

> How is the most holy bishop of Rome, the spiritual father of our holy Emperor? How are all the bishops and priests and deacons and the other clergy of the holy church of the Romans? How is the most honoured [N.] princeps of the elder Rome?[6]

Despite this apparent unanimity, there were in reality strains and stresses of all sorts. Justinian may well have been committed to papal supremacy — and certainly papal support was needed for his reconquest of Italy from the Ostrogoths. But he believed that as his predecessors had the right to convoke ecumenical councils, he had the right to interfere in disputed papal elections — for example, choosing Vigilius as pope over Silverius. Nevertheless, as had his uncle, Justin I, when Pope St. John I came to Constantinople, so too did Justinian take advantage of Pope St. Agapetus's visit to get a second coronation. It was perhaps with this memory in mind that Pope St. Leo III chose to crown Bl. Charlemagne on Christmas Day 800 and so revive the Empire in the West. The power to crown the emperor — as a matter of course in the West, by deputation in the East (save for rare Eastern visits) — underlined the spiritual power's authority over the temporal.

Nevertheless, it is important to bear in mind that — theoretically anyway — Constantine and Theodosius, Justinian and

---

[4] The formula is *ho deina*, or "a certain," for which should be substituted the name of the individual in question.

[5] Edward N. Luttwak, *The Grand Strategy of the Byzantine Empire* (Belknap Press, 2009), 133.

[6] Luttwak, *The Grand Strategy*, 133–34.

Bl. Charlemagne, Basil II and Otto III, and their various successors were all inheritors of the imperial mantle; that mantle would see Emperor Sigismund, for example, play the biggest role in convoking the Council of Constance to end the Great Schism, when no other power on earth could do so—even as Otto III definitively ended the Pornocracy. The spiritual power, all agreed, was generally superior to the temporal; but if the Church went off the tracks and its usual leadership was incapable of righting things, it was also generally accepted that the emperor must set things right.

But as we know, the devil is in the details. The distinction between papal and imperial power might be clear enough in the abstract. In the concrete, however, issues frequently arose in an age when bishops were at once feudal and spiritual lords. To which of the two masters they served did the prelates owe their first loyalty? Moreover, experience had shown the popes the necessity of two things if they would avoid becoming a sort of domestic chaplain to the emperor, as the patriarch of Constantinople appeared to be in relation to the Eastern emperor: first, temporal independence—as in the Papal States; second, temporal allies other than the emperor. The Investiture Controversy (1075–1122), although featuring such exciting episodes as the Walk at Canossa, exhausted both sides without solving the question of dominance.

When Emperor Frederick Barbarossa attempted in the 1140s to subject Italy, many of the Italian city-states bonded together to oppose him in the Lombard League, with the tacit alliance of the pope. Thus were formed the two great parties whose strife would ensure anarchy in Italy—the pro-papal Guelphs and the pro-imperial Ghibellines. Some Italian cities came to favour one side "traditionally," others the other, and existing factions within a town would file in on one side or the other, often because of preexistent feuds. Ultimately, the conflict between papacy and empire would greatly facilitate the ruin of the Hohenstaufens and the ushering in of the interregnum, which ended only in 1273 with election of Rudolf von Habsburg. In the meantime, the modern national state began to emerge amid civil wars and chaos: the 1214 battle of Bouvines, after which France considered itself independent, conflicts between Spanish factions, and, of course, Latins and Byzantines playing each false, from the latter's Slaughter of the Latins to the former's Fourth Crusade. The result of all of this was the failure of the Crusades and eventually the fall of Constantinople. But in the east, the dying flame bequeathed by the murdered Bl. Constantine XI was claimed by Moscow, thanks to the wedding of a Muscovite prince to a Byzantine princess.

In any case, the two factions continued to exist as names in Italy until Emperor Charles V asserted his control of Italy in 1529. Charles V was probably the last legitimate "Roman emperor" thus far to achieve the traditional goal of a united Christendom—and the first upon whose Empire "the sun never set." But this dream was broken by four tacitly connected "Guelph" partners: the nascent Protestant heresy, the Turks, the French, and the papacy. His successors, Emperors Ferdinand II and III, would relive the same agony with the same cast of opponents. The result was the Peace of Westphalia; Louis XIV of France would attempt to take up the work of him whom he considered his forebear, Charlemagne—only to find a similar coalition raised successfully against him. In 1755, the reconciliation between the two major Catholic powers—and claimants to Charlemagne's throne—finally took place, with the wedding of Louis the Dauphin (later Louis XVI) and Marie Antoinette. Perhaps had such a wedding been brokered by the popes a century or two earlier, things would have been better.

The chaos of the French Revolution led to the rise of Napoleon, who—despite the disadvantage of having no blood claim to any such throne—attempted to construct a new Empire of Charlemagne from whole cloth, while snuffing out what was left of the real thing. It came and went; at the Congress of Vienna there was an attempt to rebuild something of Christendom, and Tsar Alexander I attempted to play the role of emperor with his Holy Alliance. A whole host of writers, from de Maistre to von Haller and von Baader talked about the need to revive the organic Catholic state—with the monarchy at its apex and some sort of imperium over that—and such advocacy would continue into the twentieth century. The two imperial claimants, Russia and Austria, clung to their double eagles, whilst liberal regimes came and went in Britain, France, Spain, and Portugal. Furthermore, new liberal monarchies were erected in Germany and Italy. The course of the latter's creation was particularly rich in historical irony. After the Peace of Westphalia, the dukes of Savoy remained loyal to the idea of the Empire, and so were given the title of "Perpetual Vicar of the Empire in Italy." Two hundred years later, the king of Sardinia—still bearing the title—put himself at the head of the unification movement. His adherents were called "neo-Ghibellines" because of their desire to seize the Papal States. Those who wanted a federation of the Italian princes under the presidency of the pope were called "neo-Guelphs." In the end, both sides came together and Bl. Pius IX was dispossessed.

By the dawn of the twentieth century, the double eagle and the kind of rule it represented was confined to Austria and Russia. In 1903's papal conclave, Franz Joseph exercised the *jus exclusivae* against Cardinal Rampolla; this last gasp of "Ghibillinery" gave us Pope St. Pius X. Then the horrors of World War I descended upon Europe, and when the smoke was cleared, there were no more double eagles. It might be thought that the Guelph dream had come true at last. There was no emperor.

But at what cost? It might well be thought that the subservient position of the Orthodox Churches in their lands of origin were in their way an illustration of what would happen were the Ghibelline idea to prevail. And indeed, long after 1453 and 1917, disputes between the patriarchates of Moscow and Constantinople often revolve around their respective relationships with the "former imperial power."[7]

World War I did not help matters in this area, and World War II much less so. When the conflict, with its imitation Reich, was over, a great many European thinkers began to look in the same direction Soloviev had. In Germany, in addition to men like Valentin Tomberg and Richard Coudenhove-Kalergi, the whole *Neues Abendland* school and *Abendländische Bewegung* emerged in Germany and Austria. Italy saw such folk as Attilio Mordini, Giulio Attilio Schettini, Giovanni Cantoni, and *Il Ghibellino*. Thierry Maulnier, Robert Aron, Henri Daniel-Rops,

---

[7] See the remarks of Vladimir Soloviev on p. 80.

Jean de Fabrègues, Alexandre Marc, Denis de Rougemont, and *La Federation* might be named in France. And there were many more—all looking to reconstruct a Christian Europe that would be free, social, and true to the example of such as Charlemagne. Most prominent of them all was the Archduke Otto von Habsburg, heir to Austria-Hungary. This to a large degree was the vision that inspired the original founders of the EU—Schuman, Adenauer, De Gasperi, and the rest. And it was just such a (more or less unconscious) yearning for the old imperial idea that has led the postwar popes to endorse the EU and the UN fervently.

The problem is that the Generation of '68 hijacked the EU and have turned it into an instrument of secularisation and cultural ruin. What then, is to be done? I think Fr. Aidan Nichols reveals part of the answer in calling us to "dare to exercise a Christian political imagination on an as yet unspecifiable future."[8] The truth is that we live in a world where Guelph and Ghibelline effectively cancelled each other out. But we see that groups with fervent imaginations have shaped the reality in which we live—a reality in which, effectively, there is neither God nor gender nor even humanity. So let it be our turn to exercise that imagination. Let us re-examine the many writers of this tradition; let us look carefully at the world around us, scooping up and revivifying such remnants of Christendom, of *Abendland*, of *l'Occident*, of *sanctum imperium* as still remain and evangelising as we can. Perhaps one day we shall have a world both sides would approve of.

---

[8] Nichols, *Christendom Awake*, 84. See p. 16 for full quotation.

PART III

Recent Intellectual Engagement with Monarchy

CHAPTER 12

Romantic Conservatives: The Inklings in Their Political Context

BEFORE WE BEGIN THIS CHAPTER, I MUST invite my readers to forget everything they believe they know about such words as "liberal" and "conservative." All of us have been programmed to have immediate reactions to them—good or bad—but such will be very unhelpful in dealing with the Inklings and their political views.

It is not too much to say that J. R. R. Tolkien, C. S. Lewis, and Charles Williams were, in descending order, arguably the most influential twentieth-century writers in English, certainly in the fantasy genre. As the success of the three *Lord of the Rings* films and the release of three movies based upon *The Chronicles of Narnia* show, a new, less literate generation is discovering the Inklings' magic. Lest purists sniff too loudly at this, watching the movies has led many a younger person to the books themselves. Of course, Williams has yet to be translated to celluloid. At a guess, this writer would bet on *All Hallows' Eve* (Faber & Faber, 1945) being the first such effort onscreen, if any of his works make it.

In any case, the Inklings have actually had influence in three areas. Their literary impact is too obvious to comment much upon here. Their religious views have also generated a great deal of both examination and agreement, although their influence here is far from being as great. But perhaps least looked at are their strictly political views. Of course, they would be the last to speak of their own political views as separate from their religious or literary, simply because in all three men these impulses were united. None of the three held to the American myth of separation of Church and state, and they would certainly have denounced any attempt to separate literature from either.

Nevertheless, although there will necessarily be some over-
lap, it is precisely their politics and the tradition from which
it sprang that we will examine. The first thing to remember is
that while we tend to see the Inklings as a bloc, a sort of "Chesterbelloc," they certainly did not see themselves as such. On
the literary plane, although Tolkien enjoyed Lewis's *The Space
Trilogy* (particularly the first two installments), he had little
use for Narnia, which he considered rather a thrown-together
hodgepodge of incongruous myths — and worse still, allegory.
For Williams's novels, Tolkien had even less use. Religiously, the
Catholic-Anglican split was an ever-present source of tension
among the company. This carried over into political questions:
Tolkien was, as were most Catholics aware of communist atroc-
ities during the Spanish Civil War, a sturdy supporter of Franco
and the Nationalists. Lewis, on the other hand, was not. In a letter to his son Christopher on October 6, 1944, Tolkien described
the meeting of himself and Lewis with Roy Campbell. The latter
was a South African poet, a convert to Catholicism of Ulster
Scot descent who had fought for Franco. Therein, Tolkien wrote:

> C. S. L.'s reactions were odd. Nothing is a greater tribute to
> Red propaganda than the fact that he (who knows they are
> in all other subjects liars and traducers) believes all that is
> said against Franco, and nothing that is said for him. Even
> Churchill's open speech in Parliament left him unshaken.
> But hatred of our church is after all the real only final
> foundation of the C of E [Church of England] — so deep
> laid that it remains even when the superstructure seems
> removed (C. S. L. for instance reveres the Blessed Sacra-
> ment, and admires nuns!). Yet if a Lutheran is put in jail he
> is up in arms; but if Catholic priests are slaughtered — he
> disbelieves it (and I daresay really thinks they asked for it).[1]

Even so, despite their internal divisions, they appear mono-
lithic in comparison to the most widely held views of our
time. As John Wain, a staunch Labour supporter and occasional participant in the Inklings' evenings has written, "The
group had a corporate mind, as all effective groups must; the
death of Williams had sadly stunned and impoverished this
mind, but it was still powerful and clearly defined. Politically
conservative, not to say reactionary; in religion, Anglo- or

[1] Humphrey Carpenter, ed., *The Letters of J. R. R. Tolkien* (Houghton Mifflin,
1981), 96.

Roman Catholic; in art, frankly hostile to any manifestation of the 'modern' spirit."[2] The latter two observations are obvious, but what of the first? Just what did the phrase "conservative" mean, in the Inklings' context? Certainly, it did not mean a mere adherence to the Conservative Party. None of the trio was a notable advocate of Stanley Baldwin, or Harold MacMillan, either. It is anyone's guess what they would think of today's Conservatives, transformed by Lady Thatcher, as some wags would have it, into a mere copy of the American Republicans (the same sort would maintain that Mr. Blair has turned Labour into a corresponding imitation of the US Democrats, but that is another matter).

"Conservative" is one of those words that is meaningless without clarification as regards its use in a particular case. Europe and Latin America traditionally defined it quite differently from the United States, in a political sense. What Americans called "liberals" their cousins to the east and south named socialists; American "conservatives" would be "liberals" in Europe and Latin America; what the latter folk would call "conservatives" really have not existed in the United States as an organised political force on the national level since the Loyalists were forced into exile or silenced in 1783. In a nutshell, "conservative" at the very least meant opposition to the French and succeeding revolutions, and adherence to Altar and Throne, among other things. These other things will require closer examination shortly.

But first let us see precisely what the Inklings did believe politically. Of J. R. R. Tolkien's political views, Humphrey Carpenter wrote:

> His view of the world, in which each man belonged or ought to belong to a specific "estate," whether high or low, meant that in one sense he was an old-fashioned conservative. But in another sense it made him highly sympathetic to his fellow-men, for it is those who are unsure of their status in the world, who feel they have to prove themselves and if necessary put down other men to do so, who are the truly ruthless. Tolkien was, in modern jargon, "right-wing" in that he honoured his monarch and his country and did not believe in the rule of the people; but he opposed democracy simply because he

---

[2] Humphrey Carpenter, *The Inklings: C. S. Lewis, J. R. R. Tolkien, Charles Williams, and Their Friends* (Houghton Mifflin, 1979), 206.

believed that in the end his fellow-men would not benefit from it. He once wrote: "I am not a 'democrat,' if only because 'humility' and equality are spiritual principles corrupted by the attempt to mechanize and formalize them, with the result that we get not universal smallness and humility, but universal greatness and pride, till some Orc gets hold of a ring of power — and then we get and are getting slavery." As to the virtues of an old-fashioned feudal society, this is what he said once about respect for one's superiors: "Touching your cap to the Squire may be damn bad for the Squire but it's damn good for you."[3]

This was radical stuff in Tolkien's day, to be sure, but it is revolutionary in ours. Nevertheless, whatever Tolkien's attitudes toward Charles Williams's religious and artistic views and work, in the light of the foregoing it would seem obvious that he found Williams's politics congenial, as they were set forth by Alice Hadfield:

> [Williams] had grown up much aware of political structure. He saw the *res publica*, the matter of public life, the political community, presented in the experience of love and the family, in Victorian poetry, in eighteenth-century thought in France and England, in mediaeval feeling, as a balance between equality and hierarchy. Though youthfully a very temporary republican, he slowly created for himself over the years a synthesis in which all men and women were equal and yet different within their hierarchies of excellence and distinction, in which above political equality everyone's distinctness was embodied in the single person of the monarch, as everyone's personal equality and distinctness was held in Christ. He retained his sense of monarchy, hereditary in that it must have a blood link with the long history of England, visible to high and low, free from fashion, choice or vote, apex of an administration free, equal and yet hierarchical in public distinction.[4]

So, too, with C. S. Lewis. On the one hand, unlike Tolkien and Williams, he was quite happy to call himself a "democrat." But this must be understood in the sense in which he himself meant it:

[3] Humphrey Carpenter, *J. R. R. Tolkien: A Biography* (Houghton Mifflin, 2000), 132–33.
[4] Alice Mary Hadfield, *Charles Williams: An Exploration of His Life and Work* (Oxford University Press, 1983), 21.

> Being a democrat, I am opposed to all very drastic
> and sudden changes of society (in whatever direction)
> because they never in fact take place except by a par-
> ticular technique. That technique involves the seizure of
> power by a small, highly disciplined group of people; the
> terror and the secret police follow, it would seem, auto-
> matically. I do not think any such group good enough
> to have such power. They are men of like passions with
> ourselves. The secrecy and discipline of their organisation
> will have already inflamed in them that passion for the
> inner ring which I think as corrupting as avarice; and
> their high ideological pretensions will have lent all their
> passions the dangerous prestige of the Cause. Hence, in
> whatever direction change is made, it is for me damned
> by its *modus operandi*. The worst of all public dangers is
> the committee of public safety. The character in *That
> Hideous Strength* whom the Professor never mentions is
> Miss Hardcastle, the chief of the secret police. She is
> the common factor in all revolutions; and, as she says,
> you won't get anyone to do her job well unless they get
> some kick out of it.[5]

That he shared the basic outlook of his confreres is evidenced
by his view of the monarchy. In *That Hideous Strength*, arguably
Lewis's most overtly political work of fiction, Ransom responds
to Merlin's urging that the Pendragon and his followers overthrow the powerless King of Great Britain, "I have no wish to
overthrow him. He is the king. He was crowned and anointed
by the Archbishop. In the order of Logres I may be Pendragon,
but in the order of Britain I am the King's man."[6] His views
here went beyond fiction:

> Monarchy can easily be debunked, but watch the faces,
> mark well the accents of the debunkers. These are the men
> whose taproot in Eden has been cut: whom no rumour of
> the polyphony, the dance, can reach — men to whom peb-
> bles laid in a row are more beautiful than an arch. Yet even
> if they desire mere equality, they cannot reach it. Where
> men are forbidden to honour a king they honour million-
> aires, athletes, or film stars instead: even famous prosti-
> tutes or gangsters. For spiritual nature, like bodily nature,
> will be served: deny it food and it will gobble poison.[7]

---

[5] C. S. Lewis, *Of This and Other Worlds* (Fount, 2000), 89.
[6] Lewis, *That Hideous Strength*, 289.
[7] Elizabeth Freeman, ed., *The Traditionalist's Anthology* (Farnham Printing
Company, 1986), 161.

In sum, the political areas of agreement among the trio were greater than their disagreements. All three in actuality had little use for politics as commonly defined in their time (and in ours). This was because the Inklings did not separate reality into little boxes marked "politics," "religion," "art," "science," or "literature." Rather, for all three reality is a seamless thing in which all of these areas intertwine and affect the others, for good or ill.

For all their shared adherence to monarchy, to fully understand the political element in their work one must start with the individual. As believing Christians, they held that God created each man on earth "to know Him, to love Him, and to serve Him in this world, and to be happy with Him forever in the next."[8] From this simple sentence stemmed their view of his dignity as a child of God, from which reality stems all of his rights, first of which is the right, so long as he obeys the law, to be left alone. Throughout *The Lord of the Rings*, *The Chronicles of Narnia*, *The Space Trilogy*, and Williams's seven novels we are presented with an endless parade of dreadful would-be "organisers" and "rationalisers" of their fellow man, from Lotho Sackville-Baggins to Jadis of Charn to the N. I. C. E. to Sir Giles Tumulty. Much of their villainy derives from their contempt for the humble.

Their love of the common man and hatred of any who would enslave him is mirrored in their shared love of both nature and the built heritage. Whether one looks at Sharkey's work in the Shire or the plans of the N. I. C. E. for Edgestow and environs, one sees an identification of oppressors of the individual with despoilers of the landscape. What Patrick Curry says of Tolkien in his masterful *Defending Middle-Earth* can, I think, safely be said of all three of our authors:

> We cannot simply drop the Shire and the Sea, the social and spiritual dimensions; rather, they must be integrated into nature's centrality. Their final synthesis, I think, is that Tolkien's work urges *a new ethic* of human conviviality, respect for life, and ultimate humility. That ethic is to be based on the experience of life on Earth, and therefore the lineaments of life — good earth, clean water, fresh air and the like — as sacred. Finally, for that resacralization to succeed, it must be deeply rooted in culture, through being celebrated and communicated in local and traditional ways. The result is not simply a negative critique of

---

[8] *Baltimore Catechism II* (TAN Books, 2010), 8.

"positivist, mechanist, urbanized, and rationalist culture"
but a positive vision of what one reader well described
as "sanity and sanctity."[9]

Lewis's depiction of the N.I.C.E.'s opposition to the mere existence, for example, of the small village of Cure Hardy ("you can
bet it's insanitary," observes Cosser[10]) with its "undesirable" population of small *rentiers* and agricultural labourers is in much the
same vein. Studdock finds upon actually meeting these sorts of
folk that he likes them better than his colleagues. All three of our
authors were great believers in the wide distribution of property
amongst country livers — that is, in the proliferation of small-
holders, "brewing their own beer, and baking their own bread."

As implied in this and in the Carpenter and Hadfield quota-
tions regarding Tolkien's and Williams's politics, the Inklings,
while believing in the innate dignity of the individual and his
equality before God and the law, also believed in class distinc-
tions and hierarchy. But this hierarchy, to be authentic, must
be organic and natural, an earthly reflection of that hierarchy
that prevails in heaven. Moreover, like the Kingship of Christ
and the authority of the clergy, it must be based upon service to
those beneath the officeholders: with privilege comes responsibility. Further, it must be a reflection of that legitimacy of
order that ought to characterise society and the nation as a
whole. A perfect illustration is the speech of the mayor of Rich
in Williams's *Many Dimensions*, when that worthy is faced with
the healings in his town by the fragment of the Philosopher's
Stone that has come to it:

> "Good people," he said in a stentorian voice, "you all know
> me. I will ask you to return to your homes and leave me
> to discover the truth about this matter. I am the Mayor of
> Rich, and if the people of Rich have been injured it is my
> business to remedy it and help them. If, as appears, the
> Stone of which we have heard is able to heal illness, and
> if the Government are using it, as swiftly as may be, for
> that purpose, it is the duty of all good citizens to accept
> what delay the common good of all demands. But it is
> equally their right to be assured that the Government is
> doing its utmost in the matter, day and night, so that not

---

[9] Patrick Curry, *Defending Middle-Earth: Tolkien, Myth and Modernity* (St. Martin's Press, 1997), 154.
[10] Lewis, *That Hideous Strength*, 83.

a single moment may be lost in freeing as many as may
be from pain and suffering. I shall make it my concern to
discover this at once. I know the hindrances which must,
and I fear those which may, follow on what has happened.
I will myself go to London." He paused a moment, then he
went on. "Some of you may know that my son is dying of
cancer. If it is a matter of ensuring swiftness and order
he and I will be the last in all the country to claim assistance. But I tell you this that you may be very sure that
he shall not suffer an hour longer than need be because
of the doubts or fears or stupidities of the servants of
the people. Return to your homes and tomorrow at this
time you shall know all that I know." He paused again
and ended with a loud cry, "God save the King."

"God save the King!" yelled Oliver in a thrill of delight,
and assisted the Mayor to descend. Who turned on him
at once and went on talking before the Chief Constable
could interrupt. "I shall want you," he said. "I want all
the information you can give me, and I may need your
personal help. Are you free? But it doesn't matter whether
you are or not. I demand your presence in the name of
the King and by the authority of my office."[11]

Their ideal society would no doubt endorse the traditional
rhyme:

Oh let us love our occupations,
Bless the squire and his relations,
Live upon our daily rations,
And always know our proper stations.[12]

Yet by the same token, they held out for the ability of those
gifted with superior virtue and ability to rise by pluck and
luck, as witnessed by Sam Gamgee — all the while respecting
the integrity of those remaining in the humbler place birth
had put them: a birth seen, not as accident, but as the delib-
erate work of the God who presides over the great tapestry
of human society, so far as human free will permits Him to.

All three writers had a love of the traditional offices of Great
Britain and the country's ceremonial idiosyncrasies. These are
reflected in such characters as Tolkien's mayor of Michel Delv-
ing, master of Buckland, and thain of the Shire; as Williams's
aforementioned mayor of Rich and, in *War in Heaven*, the duke

---

[11] Charles Williams, *Many Dimensions* (Faber & Faber, 1931), 149–50.
[12] Charles Dickens, *The Chimes* (Baker & Taylor Company, 1908), 93.

of the North Ridings, "Marquis of Craigmullen and Plessing, Earl and Viscount, Count of the Holy Roman Empire, Knight of the Sword and Cape, and several other ridiculous fantasies";[13] and in Lewis's obvious hatred of the "progressive element's" dismantling of traditional collegiate ritual at Bracton College. It is not just that these things are pleasant and pleasing in themselves, lending mundane life a touch of colour; it is also that they are seen by the Inklings as remnants or signs of greater things, which may spring back into action as needed. The placing of the sovereign over this hierarchy is obvious.

Just as obvious is the love of the trio for England herself and for her towns and shires. But what about the rest of the world? Certainly, Tolkien was notorious for disliking the French (yet another area where this Francophone must dissent from the master—but of course Tolkien never forgave the Norman invasion). Lewis was, thanks to his Ulster background, provincial to the core. Williams seems to have been the most cosmopolitan, culturally. But it would be incorrect to think of any of them as "nationalist" in the modern sense. For in differing ways, all of them saw their beloved England as a part of a greater whole, even as their favourite places were all essential components of England.

That greater whole was Europe—not, however, a sort of sterile mechanism as the EU appears headed for, but as a religious and cultural entity: Christendom, or, as earlier thinkers would have it, the Holy Empire. That is to say, a higher unity that did not repress local or national liberties. As Tolkien wrote to his son, Christopher, in a letter dated July 28, 1944, "I should have hated the Roman Empire [that is, the pre-Christian one] in its day (as I do), and remained a patriotic Roman citizen, while preferring a free Gaul and seeing good in Carthaginians."[14] That he applied that view to current events may be seen by another letter to his son, of December 9, 1943: "I love England (not Great Britain and certainly not the British Commonwealth (grr!))."[15] Certainly, the Shire is his idealized vision of England—self-governing, and that government itself extremely limited in day-to-day affairs.

---

[13] Charles Williams, *War in Heaven* (Faber & Faber, 1962), 97.
[14] Carpenter, *Letters of J. R. R. Tolkien*, 89.
[15] Carpenter, 65.

But the Shire-folk are also bound (however tenuously prior to the War of the Ring) to a greater unit — the Kingdom of Arnor. Where Tolkien hates the grinding power of the Roman Empire prior to Constantine, his Númenórean realms in exile mirror the Christian Empire. Arnor itself is very like the Western Empire; counting progressively less militarily as the decades pass, it nevertheless survives in the minds of its subjects, even after the end of its actual existence. Its revival under Aragorn (or Elessar, as we must call him at that stage) bears a striking resemblance to the Carolingian revival. Gondor, on the other hand, reminds one of the Eastern Roman Empire, an analogy expressly made by Tolkien in a letter to Milton Waldman in late 1950, wherein he speaks of Gondor's initial glory, "almost reflecting Númenor," and then fading "slowly to decayed Middle Age, a kind of proud, venerable, but increasingly impotent Byzantium."[16] As opposed to the mere force of arms and weight of government machinery that Tolkien hated in the pagan Roman Empire, the restored kingdom under Elessar exemplified the "unity-in-diversity," the preservation of local freedoms under an overarching monarch, that medieval theorists ascribed to the Holy Roman Empire. In 1963, he wrote to a fan: "A Númenórean King was *monarch*, with the power of unquestioned decision in debate; but he governed the realm with the frame of ancient law, of which he was administrator (and interpreter) but not the maker."[17] Another Holy Roman Emperor manqué was Ingwë, chief of the Vanyar and high king of all the Elves.

That Tolkien, in reality as in fiction, saw his beloved England as properly a part of such an organic whole may be seen from his February 8, 1967 reply to the first draught of an article about him by Charlotte and Denis Plimmer:

> Auden has asserted that for me 'the North is a sacred direction'. That is not true. The North-west of Europe, where I (and most of my ancestors) have lived, has my affection, as a man's home should. I love its atmosphere, and know more of its histories and languages than I do of other parts; but it is not 'sacred', nor does it exhaust my affections. I have, for instance, a particular love of the

[16] Carpenter, 157.
[17] Carpenter, 324.

> Latin language, and among its descendants for Spanish.
> That it is untrue for my story, a mere reading of the syn-
> opses would show. The North was the seat of the fortresses
> of the Devil. The progress of the tale ends in what is far
> more like the re-establishment of an effective Holy Roman
> Empire with its seat in Rome than anything that would
> be devised by a "Nordic."[18]

One of the reasons (though by no means a major one) for
his love of the Catholic Church was its universality; this was
part of the reason he disliked the abandonment of Latin in
the liturgy and its replacement by the vernacular. With C.S.
Lewis, one finds, as might be expected, greater insularity. But
despite that, he too had an appreciation of sorts for at least
the historic unity of Christendom. One would be hard put to
define the role of the Christian Emperor as seen by contemporary writers better than Merlin's advice to the Pendragon
in *That Hideous Strength:* "Then we must go higher. We must
go to him whose office it is to put down tyrants and give life
to dying kingdoms. We must call on the Emperor."[19] For a
moment, we almost share the old wizard's shock when Ransom
replies, "there is no Emperor."[20]

But Lewis appreciated the fact that the ideal England he
believed in was, while certainly legitimate in its own sphere,
not the be-all and end-all. It is a part of a greater whole. Thus,
Dr. Dimble expostulates:

> "Don't you feel it? The very quality of England. If we've got
> an ass's head, it is by walking in a fairy wood. We've heard
> something better than we can do, but we can't quite for-
> get it . . . can't you see it in everything English — a kind of
> awkward grace, a humble, humorous incompleteness? How
> right Sam Weller was when he called Mr. Pickwick an angel
> in gaiters! Everything here is either better or worse than — "
> "Dimble!" said Ransom. Dimble, whose tone had become
> a little impassioned, stopped and looked towards him. He
> hesitated and (as Jane thought) almost blushed before he
> began again.
> "You're right, Sir," he said with a smile. "I was forget-
> ting what you have warned me always to remember. This
> haunting is no peculiarity of ours. Every people has its

---

[18] Carpenter, 376.
[19] Lewis, *That Hideous Strength*, 290.
[20] Lewis, 290.

own haunter. There's no special privilege for England — no nonsense about a chosen nation. We speak about Logres because it is *our* haunting, the one we know about."

"But this," said MacPhee, "seems a very round-about way of saying that there's good and bad men everywhere."

"It's not a way of saying that at all," answered Dimble. "You see, MacPhee, if one is thinking simply of goodness in the abstract, one soon reaches the fatal idea of something standardised — some common kind of life to which all nations ought to progress. Of course, there are universal rules to which all goodness must conform. But that's only the grammar of virtue. It's not there that the sap is. He doesn't make two blades of grass the same: how much less two saints, two nations, two angels. The whole work of healing Tellus depends on nursing that little spark, on incarnating that ghost, which is still alive in every real people, and different in each. When Logres really dominates Britain, when the goddess Reason, the divine clearness, is really enthroned in France, when the order of Heaven is really followed in China — why, then it will be spring. But meantime, our concern is with Logres."[21]

Despite his apologia for the Reformation and his love-hate relationship with Rome, Lewis was very conscious of (and nostalgic for) the old, pre-Reformation — I had almost written pre-political — unity of Christendom. He was enough of a Latinist to carry on a correspondence in that language with an Italian priest, Don Giovanni Calabria. While they are writing back and forth about the Continent's future, Lewis observes, "Let us beware lest, while we rack ourselves in vain about the fate of Europe, we neglect either Verona or Oxford."[22] Here again, in the universal language, we see the ongoing juxtaposition of the local and the supra-national.

Williams was the author of the Logres/Britain dichotomy Lewis deals with so well in *That Hideous Strength*. But while so much of his work is as deeply English as those of our other two authors, Williams also sees that what he loves in his own country is found — in different ways — elsewhere. In describing the visit of a fictional Zulu king in *Shadows of Ecstasy*, he writes:

> For a few moments royalty — a dark alien royalty — had appeared in the room, imposed upon all of them by the

---

[21] Lewis, 368–69.
[22] Martin Moynihan, trans., *Letters: C. S. Lewis/Don Giovanni Calabria* (Servant Books, 1988), 19.

mere intensity of the Zulu chieftain's own strength and conviction. By virtue of that wide reading which both she and her husband loved, she had felt a shadow of it at times; in the superb lines of Marlowe or Shakespeare, in the rolling titles heard on ceremonial occasions at Church or in local celebrations: "The King's Most Excellent Majesty," "His Majesty the King-Emperor," "The Government of His Britannic Majesty."[23]

But kingship is not the only motif to transcend boundaries in Williams's work. The Mass of the Grail in *War in Heaven* is perceived by each of its witnesses on precisely their own terms. Williams's description of the effect it has on the Catholic Duke of the North Ridings is all the more striking given his own Anglicanism:

> In each of them differently the spirit was moved and exalted—most perhaps in the Duke. He was aware of a sense of the adoration of kings—the great tradition of his house stirred within him. The memories of proscribed and martyred priests awoke; masses said swiftly and in the midst of the fearful breathing of a small group of the faithful; the ninth Duke who had served the Roman Pontiff at his private mass; the Roman Order he himself wore; the fidelity of his family to the Faith under the anger of Henry and the cold suspicion of Elizabeth; the duels fought in Richmond Park by the thirteenth Duke in defence of the honour of our Lady, when he met and killed three antagonists consecutively—all these things, not so formulated but certainly there, drew his mind into a vivid consciousness of all the royal and sacerdotal figures of the world adoring before this consecrated shrine. "Jhesu, Rex et Sacerdos," he prayed...[24]

Given the very sympathetic way he had written of the first Protestants in various of his histories and plays, Williams was certainly a man who could see past his own positions.

But it is in his poetry that the figure of the Christian Empire becomes an explicit motif. Agnes Sibley well describes the view of the Empire that Williams conjures up in *Taliessin Through Logres* (Oxford University Press, 1938) and *The Region of the Summer Stars* (Oxford University Press, 1944):

---

[23] Charles Williams, *Shadows of Ecstasy* (Faber & Faber, 1931), 61.
[24] Williams, *War in Heaven*, 135–35.

> The universe of the poems is sixth-century Europe, where
> the historical Arthur might have lived. Logres is a province
> ("theme") of the Byzantine Empire, the seat of the Roman
> Empire after the provincial tribes had captured Rome.
> Williams chose Byzantium as a symbol of wholeness, a
> perfect balance of body and soul—possibly because under
> Byzantine rule the church and secular society were more
> nearly unified than at any other period of history.
>
> The Empire, as Williams sees it, is not only a unified
> community but also a symbol of the "whole nature of
> man," including, of course, his body. For the first edition
> of *Taliessin through Logres*, a friend of Williams's drew a
> map of Europe in the form of a woman's body, the parts
> of which are frequently mentioned in the poems. Logres
> is the woman's head; her buttocks (Caucasia) represent
> the natural, physical side of the human being; and her
> hands are at Rome, where the Pope performs with his
> hands the Eucharist, in which body and soul are of equal
> importance and are seen as one in Christ.[25]

Logres, and the Empire of which it forms an integral part, is
held together, not by force, but by its shared faith and the
resulting "co-inherence," in which each part of the Empire is
connected to every other, as are the individuals that inhabit
the provinces. It is love, in essence, that gives the Empire
unity—and maintains Arthur's kingdom as a constituent part
of it. All of this is maintained by "exchange," accepting one
another's burdens, and by prayer—most famously, the "Prayers
of the Pope," in the poem of the same name.

In the simultaneous embrace of the local, the national,
and the supranational, the Inklings were not proposing the
construction of a specific political arrangement; rather, they
believed that society on all levels ought to reflect a higher
reality. As believing Christian medievalists, each of the three
had absorbed a great deal of Neoplatonism, to a great degree
through St. Augustine, but also through other Church Fathers
and directly from Plato himself.

This influence expresses itself in their political views insofar
as they held that the divine order is at once concealed and
symbolised by the earthly, and that legitimacy in government
derives from the governing folk attempting to realise in this
world the order that reigns in heaven. But the Augustinian

---

[25] Agnes Sibley, *Charles Williams* (Twayne Publishers, 1982), 91.

view opposing the City of God to the city of Man is also present in their thought: the latter city becomes evil to the degree that it deviates from the norm offered by the former, and all good men are required to struggle, one way or another, against that deviance; but at the same time, the two cities are distinct, and that of man can never replicate exactly that of God—it can only become somewhat closer. Yet this seemingly endless and unwinnable (in earthly terms) struggle can help the individual attain eternal salvation, and at times, as a bonus, actually improve the situation for a while. Paradoxically, however, attempts to replicate the City of God using illegitimate or evil ends must inevitably bring about worse evils than those being struggled against—as Galadriel reminds us when refusing the ring.

DISTRIBUTISM AND ITS WIDER POLITICAL CONTEXT

This, then, was the common political teaching of the Inklings. But whence did it come? What name can we give it? Was it autogenetic, or were they part of a larger stream? Did any of their contemporaries hold similar views?

The reply to the last question is—certainly! The distributists, led by G. K. Chesterton and Hilaire Belloc, are the most obvious seconders of the views of the Inklings; as a rather well known group in England between the Wars, our authors were extremely aware of their views regarding little England, the widespread distribution of property (from whence the title came), and the like. In *That Hideous Strength*, Curry says of Denniston, "A brilliant man at that time, of course, but he seems to have gone quite off the rails with all his Distributivism and what not."[26] In fact, the Chesterbelloc had a tremendous effect on the three authors, literarily, religiously, and politically.

Mention of them, however, automatically brings into play a host of writers of the period: Maurice Baring, Christopher Hollis, Douglas Woodruff, T. S. Eliot (whose work Lewis initially loathed but came to appreciate), and many, many more, whose complex interaction was so masterfully chronicled by Joseph Pearce.[27] Alongside the host of characters Pearce explored,

---

[26] Lewis, *That Hideous Strength*, 17.
[27] Joseph Pearce, *Literary Converts: Spiritual Inspiration in an Age of Unbelief* (Ignatius Press, 1999).

however, there were other figures such as fantasist and horror writer Arthur Machen, whose similar religious and political opinions were set forth in such works as *Dr. Stiggins: His Views and Principles* (Alfred A. Knopf, 1925) and *Dog and Duck* (Alfred A. Knopf, 1924); naturalist and organic farmer H. J. Massingham, co-founder of the Soil Association, who combined defence of the countryside and organic farming with Catholicism and distributism; and Halliday Sutherland, travel writer, medical doctor, and anti-contraception writer. There were all sorts of political movements like guild socialism and social credit that aimed at reorganising society and the economy on a non-Marxist and non-capitalist basis, deriving inspiration from various aspects of the medieval past and advocating, in addition to their particular mechanical solutions to the problems raised by the Depression, renewed devotion to Altar and Throne. As with the Inklings, these individuals and groups were extremely disparate among themselves but were similar enough to find common expression in the pages of such publications as Douglas Jerrold's *English Review* and Alfred Orage's *New Age*. In such a milieu of writers, artists, and thinkers (for very few were practical politicians), the politics of the Inklings was unremarkable, however eccentric it might have appeared to the media and political classes of their time—to say nothing of our own.

But whence came this family of views? Well, there actually is a line of descent to be traced. To begin with, all of these ideas might be described, as John Wain did, as "conservative." But just what did that word mean in this case? As mentioned earlier, it did not necessarily mean adherence to the party of Stanley Baldwin. Certainly the Conservative Party in some sense traditionally encompassed loyalty to both the Crown and the Established Church—or at least the once-Established Church. But as early as 1844 in his novel *Coningsby*, Benjamin Disraeli jibed about "A sound Conservative government . . . Tory men and Whig measures."[28] At that time, the fiery anti-slavery, anti-child labour, and anti-poverty Tory reformer Richard Oastler was rousing the factory workers with his battle cry of "Altar, Throne, and cottage!" We can see, looking at such men as Oastler, William Cobbett, and Sir Francis Burdett why the

---

[28] Benjamin Disraeli, *Coningsby* (London, 1844), 103.

first Labourites, men such as R. H. Tawney, were accused of being "the new Tories." It is in this direction we must look, if we are to place the Inklings in context.

It has often been remarked that Tolkien, Lewis, and Williams—as well as their circle—were late manifestations of English romanticism, and this is also true of their non-Inkling contemporaries who held similar ideals. This has been considered to be particularly true as regards their theology. But it applies to their politics as well. As we have seen, medievalism played a large part in the social worldview of the Inklings and like-minded contemporaries. But it was a medievalism filtered through the nineteenth century and owing its origins to Sir Walter Scott, the foremost practitioner of romanticism (of which more later) in Great Britain.[29]

Powerful as was Sir Walter's influence on the literature of his day, it was just as strong, ultimately, in religious, social, and political matters. For rather than portraying the age of *Ivanhoe* (Edinburgh, 1820) as the realm of superstition and oppression denounced by the writers of the Enlightenment throughout Europe, Sir Walter presented it as a time when society was an organic whole, when oppressors were—despite whatever office in either institution they might have held, even the highest—rebels against the order of Church and state, rather than as their prototypes. He also recast the Jacobites in the popular mind as heroic loyalists to a dying but worthier state of affairs, rather than as the obscurantist traitors to which they had been reduced. In so doing, he turned the minds of many of the intelligentsia of Britain in an entirely new direction.

One of his disciples, Kenelm Digby, produced *The Broad Stone of Honour: or, Rules for the Gentlemen of England* (London, 1822), a book whose influence in its own time is equalled only by its almost complete obscurity in our own. An attempt to show the young men of the time how they might lead the sorts of chivalrous lives that they had read of in Sir Walter's novels, it took young Oxbridge intellectuals by storm. It had, of course, its more ludicrous results: the celebrated Eglinton Tournament of 1839, for example, when rain drenched the

---

[29] See Joseph Shaw, "Medievalism, from Ruskin to Tolkien," in idem, ed., *The Latin Mass and the Intellectuals* (Arouca Press, 2023), 272–81.

attempts at jousting by a sort of nineteenth-century English Society for Creative Anachronism. But it created an atmosphere from whence came rather more lasting results. Digby, who converted to Catholicism, made the idea of returning to the old religion more respectable through his work, showing that the faith was more than just the tribal belief of old Catholic gentry and nobility or poverty-stricken Irish immigrants. The Oxford movement, which transformed the ritual life of Anglicanism and created an important (if never dominant) party in the Church of England wedded to medieval religion, owed much to Digby. The code of the gentleman, which so dominated much of Victorian social life, finds its origin in him as well.

There were also political results. The first and most obvious was Young England, whose leading proponents, George Smythe (later 7th Viscount Strangford), Lord John Manners (later 7th Duke of Rutland), Henry Hope, Alexander Baillie-Cochrane, and the young Benjamin Disraeli, launched their political effort in 1841. Influenced by Digby and by the Oxford movement, as well as by such as Cobbett, Oastler, and Burdett, Young England strove to restore the class unity of medieval England and to limit the power of industry over agriculture. In Lord John Manners's 1841 *England's Trust, and Other Poems* he "falls into a reverie before St Albans Abbey. Reflecting on episodes from the early days of Christianity in England, he regrets the passing of the ancient Church. . . . He sees rationalism as a spiritual sickness of modern times."[30] Lord John mourns "the loss of values and disruption of social order that he attributes to the absence of a strong monarch and Church, and he finds hope for England's future in its fictional medieval past," when

> Each knew his place — king, peasant, peer, or priest —
> The greatest owned connexion with the least;
> From rank to rank the generous feeling ran,
> And linked society as man to man.[31]

As its few members were all in the House of Commons, they backed up their writings with votes, using their influence in favour of various schemes for industrial reform and amelioration of the misery of the poor, toleration for Catholics and Jews,

[30] Louis Cazamian, *The Social Novel in England 1830–1850*, trans. Martin Fido (Routledge & Kegan Paul, 1973), 98.
[31] John Manners, *England's Trust, and Other Poems* (London, 1841), 16.

and opposition to the weakening of the Established Church and the monarchy. In the end, the group began to splinter when Disraeli, out of opposition to the prime minister, Robert Peel, voted against the Maynooth Grant Bill in 1845. This measure, providing a subsidy to the Irish Catholic seminary of that name, was typical of the things Young England had supported. But Disraeli could not resist a chance to embarrass Peel.

Nevertheless, the end of Young England was not the end of English romantic conservatism. For from the influence of the Oxford movement also emerged Pre-Raphaelitism on the artistic front, and such of its practitioners as Dante Rossetti and William Morris applied their romanticism first to literature and, in the latter case, to politics. The social implications of Morris's Arts and Crafts movement were an important part of the rise of guild and other non-Marxist socialisms. Here we see the ideological origins of men such as R. H. Tawney, whose analysis of capitalism as a product of the Reformation[32] was shared by the distributists. Furthermore, F. D. Maurice and others began a strain of Anglican (and even Anglo-Catholic) socialism firmly rooted in the romantic view of the Middle Ages.

But some of Young England's views continued to be seen in the ranks of the second rung of Tory Party leadership in the late nineteenth and early twentieth centuries. On the one hand, some of the circle called the Souls, especially George Wyndham (not surprisingly, a close friend of Belloc) continued to push for romantic conservative ideals — not just for the political goals of social union under the Altar and Throne, but also in literature.

Another result was nineteenth-century neo-Jacobitism, finding its ultimate roots in Scott's *Waverley* novels, but receiving an impetus from the Oxford movement's revival of Anglican devotion to Charles I as a saint and martyr and a desire to find a dynasty that would reinvigorate the monarchy. This led not only to the foundation of the Order of the White Rose (a group that attracted a number of nineteenth-century artists, such as Whistler, and eventually became a co-founder of today's Royal Stuart Society) but also, alongside the influence of a resurgent Irish nationalism, to the origins of Cornish, Welsh, and Scottish nationalism. Not surprisingly — although they would

---

[32] R. H. Tawney, *Religion and the Rise of Capitalism: A Historical Study* (Harcourt, Brace and Company, 1926).

take a leftward turn after World War II—the Plaid Cymru and the Scottish National Party numbered a great many Catholic distributists among their pre-war founders.

At any rate, it is to this historical development that we must look for the origins of the political ideas espoused by the Inklings and their like-minded contemporaries. Yet, if the social notions dominant at the manor of St. Anne's, the citadel of Minas Tirith, and the rectory at Fardles owe their origin, as it would seem at the moment, to Sir Walter Scott, is romantic conservatism a purely British phenomenon, with a purely British relevance? By no means.

As mentioned, Sir Walter Scott was indeed the foremost *British* literary practitioner of romanticism. But it must be remembered that romanticism was a Europe-wide phenomenon, and so one may well speak of it as a European family of ideas. We must now take a look at it in itself and then take an-all-too-speedy look at some of its parallel developments in the various nations of the West.

To begin with, just what is romanticism, anyway? There do seem to be as many definitions as there are writers; but it is as accurate a one as any might be to call it Europe's artistic and philosophical reaction to the arid rationalism of the Enlightenment, the horrors of the French revolutionary wars, and the centralising hand of Napoleon Bonaparte. As with any other current of thought, romanticism did not spring from a vacuum, and scholars trace it origins back before the Revolution to the German *Sturm und Drang*, the cult of sensibility, and various other interesting phenomena. What is certain is that it began in Germany with such folk as Novalis, Görres, and the like; France picked it up with Chateaubriand, and then the British Isles gave us Coleridge, Wordsworth, and of course, Sir Walter Scott. From there it spread throughout Europe and the Americas.

Opposing the Enlightenment's emphasis on rational thought and individual freedom (and noting how these contradicted themselves in the revolutionary bloodshed inspired by them), the romantics looked to intuition and traditional wisdom (especially religious and folkloric). To the Enlightenment's love of classical antiquity, the romantics replied with an exaltation of the "barbarous" Middle Ages, and where the enlightened, revolutionaries and Bonapartists alike, attempted to overthrow both hierarchies and local peculiarities, the romantics revelled in both. Not too strangely, after 1806 they rallied to the fight against Napoleon; from the critiques the romantics mounted against their foes emerged a sort of conservatism of which Klaus Epstein has said, speaking of the German variety in that year, "The Romantic movement—appealing to the eternal human craving for miracle, mystery, and authority—had begun to put the *Aufklärung* [Enlightenment] on the defensive in German cultural life."[33]

By 1815, it was the same throughout Europe, and in many ways the Congress of Vienna was the high-water mark of political romanticism. The Holy Alliance represented the effort of Tsar Alexander I (a romantic if ever there was one) to unite Europe's sovereigns on a basis of shared mysticism. It seemed as though a golden age had arrived.

It had not, however. Many romantics were eventually disappointed with the regimes that succeeded Napoleon—hence the transformation of such as Victor Hugo, who had written an ode for Charles X's coronation, into a republican. Thus was born romantic liberalism. For those who remained attached to romantic conservatism, the steady march after 1830 of a decidedly unromantic liberalism (of which the Manchester school was the leading British exponent), with its industrialisation, its governmental centralisation, its secularism, its republicanism (or at least, its limitation of the monarchy where retained), and its substitution of bankers and industrialists for nobility and gentry, of a proletariat for peasantry, called for their contempt and their resistance. This latter occurred in many different fields—literary, political, and even military. As in Britain, this contributed to both a Catholic revival and, where Protestant state churches existed, a "High Church" movement.

So in Germany and Austria, men like Friedrich Schlegel and Adam Müller rallied to the House of Austria, in hopes of recalling the glories of the Holy Roman Empire. After 1866, when the Habsburgs were definitively ejected from Germany, these folk looked to a spiritual and literary revival of the Empire—and to hatred of what they saw as the Bismarckian "pseudo-empire";

---

[33] Epstein, *The Genesis of German Conservatism*, 674.

hence such disparate groups as Richard Kralik's Gralbund and the Stefan George Circle.

Chateaubriand, de Maistre, de Bonald, and their many disciples acted as the ideologues of the Restoration in France. After the overthrow of Charles X in 1830, their successors, men like Barbey d'Aurevilly, Blanc de St. Bonnet, and Paul Bourget, wrote both defences of Altar and Throne and, in many cases, fantastic literature.

Spain and Portugal saw civil wars that pitted traditionalist proponents of the two royal families' senior lines, of the position of the Church within the state, and of traditional local liberties against liberals. Defeat coming in both cases, they transferred their efforts to the literary field. In Ibero-America, similar folk continued, after independence, to write on behalf of Hispanidad and Lusofonia, which represented closer ties between the former colonies and their motherlands. These folk worked and wrote particularly against the dominating efforts of the United States.

In Italy, the effort to unite the country split into a romantic or neo-Guelph wing, which advocated a federation under the pope, and a liberal wing that wished to bring all the Italian states under the sway of Savoy. Still other romantics pressed for continued independence or autonomy for these little entities.

Russian romanticism resulted in the Slavophile movement, which sought to reject Western European influence in favour of native tradition. But perhaps the greatest later exponent of Russian romanticism was Vladimir Soloviev, who evolved from Slavophilism to a desire to reconcile Russia with papacy, and to have the tsar take the lead in the spiritual regeneration of all of Europe.

In the rest of Eastern Europe, as in Scandinavia, romanticism led also to movements in favour of reviving native traditions — in the former case, to reviving national sentiment among such suppressed minorities as the Serbs and Slovaks. Even the Meiji Restoration in Japan and the abortive similar attempt in China owed a little to romanticism.

In the United States, as mentioned, political conservatism of the European type died in 1783. Even so, such romantics as Washington Irving, Nathaniel Hawthorne, Edgar Allan Poe, and Fitz-Greene Halleck (son of a Loyalist and notorious public defender of both Catholicism and monarchy) were, in the first three cases, as close to romantic conservatives as an American could be. The South, in love with Sir Walter Scott, provided fertile ground for it; defeat in the War Between the States sealed this, resulting in the 1930s in the Southern Agrarians. A coming together between these and the British distributists was perhaps to be expected. Even in New England, however, men such as Ralph Adams Cram—famous writer and architect, as well as American head of the Order of the White Rose—joined in the chorus.

As with every other current of European thought, romantic conservatism received a dreadful shock in World War I. But it nevertheless rebounded after the War, as the survivors tried to make sense of what had happened to them and to repair the ills of their respective nations. The need to do so was exacerbated by the Depression, and it was from this ferment that the Inklings as well as many other such groups emerged. But just as the cataclysm of Robespierre and Napoleon had called romantic conservatism into being, that of Hitler effectively destroyed it. This was partly because some of its proponents saw alliance with fascism as a quick way to score a victory against a liberal establishment that had previously seemed impregnable, but it was also because the Nazis directly destroyed as much of it as they could. A fitting end-scene, perhaps, of the movement in Germany might be seen in the execution of Count von Stauffenberg, a member of the George Circle, crying "long live secret Germany!" as the firing squad's bullets cut him down. As might be guessed from this swift encapsulation, volumes could be written about this history.

The aftermath of the War saw the world divided between American-sponsored liberal democracy and Soviet-style communism, each equally opposed to romantic conservative views, albeit in different ways and on different fronts. Even so, they managed to survive as a sort of literary mood amongst a number of writers, including, of course, the surviving Inklings and a few of their disciples. The collapse of the Soviet Union did not affect the retreat of romantic conservatism into complete political irrelevancy. Indeed, in the years since, the gradual emergence of the nanny state in the various nations of the West epitomizes everything the romantic conservatives loathed.

Such events as the United States Supreme Court's ruling that the government may seize any private property to give to developers who might pay larger taxes, and Tony Blair's outlawing of hunting in England and Wales, might well give comfort to any remaining fascists. Government management of private ownership of property and the means of production was a cardinal dogma of fascist economic theory, and Hitler's outlawing of hunting with hounds is one of the few bits of Nazi-era legislation to remain on German law books.

In the face of all of this, is romantic conservatism dead? By no means, although it is virtually confined to literary or enthusiast circles — it might be said to have become entirely romantic, in the vulgar sense of being purely theoretical and seemingly unattainable. In Great Britain, such groups as the *Prag* magazine crowd, the circle inspired by the group at Oxford centring around Fr. Aidan Nichols, OP, and the Royal Stuart Society, to name a very few, keep the ideas of romantic conservatism alive. Writing in a publication of the latter, the late Robert F. J. Parsons, OBE, wrote:

> Traditional values are constantly under attack. The media are not exactly governed by their supporters. Even those who profess support, as does Mrs Thatcher with her reference to the merits of "Victorian values," do little in practice to express that profession of faith. Education, Church, home newspapers, television, police, Parliament, are all permeated with a spirit that is fundamentally hostile to the cornerstones of our civilisation either actively or, more often and in many ways more dangerously, passively because either not understanding or not feeling able to summon up the requisite energy to act against heavy odds.[34]

So too, on the continent, such groups as Italy's Identità Europea, the Paneuropa Union, and France's Alliance Royale deal with such ideas, as do various groups advocating single issues, from quality education to traditional Christian liturgy to organic farming to conservation of the built heritage. Groups dedicated to the writings of various such thinkers serve much the same purpose.

---

[34] Robert F. J. Parsons, *The Role of Jacobitism in the Modern World* (Royal Stuart Society, 1986), 39.

Being effectively severed from any chance, as things stand, of having an influence on governance, do the political ideas of the Inklings and their innumerable confreres have any relevance at all today? Certainly. The West faces a number of large and seemingly insuperable problems. European unity, for instance, may be inevitable and perhaps even essential. But what will the shape of that unity be? What about the demographic problem, the "population implosion," in Europe and North America? What about the threat posed by radical Islam, especially in terms of terrorism at home? What is certain is that the current rulership in the "developed" countries has no long-term solutions for any of these problems; it may well be that the romantic conservatives do.[35] An imperial crown would integrate the nations and protect the spheres of its subordinates.

Utopian? Perhaps. But it is couched in terms that each of our three authors would in all likelihood recognise and agree with, as would most of their conservative romantic colleagues. As things stand, it is doubtful that the powers-that-be would ever permit such things. Still and all, a cataclysm gave birth to romantic conservatism, and another eliminated it. It may well be that a third will bring it back.

---

[35] See, for a prime example, the passage from Fr. Aidan Nichols quoted above on p. 16.

CHAPTER 13

Kingship in the Work of the Inklings[1]

An age of fable has ended. The world has gotten old; skepticism is our wisdom. We do not believe in the magic of pedigree, and we expect the son not to take up his father's role.... We have canceled faith, the gold standard of monarchy, as well as "the Pleasure of His Majesty," once the common currency.

—Charles Fenyvesi[2]

A S IS WELL KNOWN, THE RELIGIOUS IDEALS of J.R.R. Tolkien, C.S. Lewis, and Charles Williams were extremely traditional; Roman Catholic in the case of the first named, Anglo-Catholic as regards the second two. Volumes have been written about the effect of this sacramental religiosity on their fantasy writings. Less touched upon have been their political conceptions, specifically in regard to monarchy. But just as their concept of Christianity was medieval (either through conservative Catholicism or via the Anglican "branch theory"), so too was their ideal of governance.

In the course of their writings, they all employed elements of authentic Christian sacral kingship. Their kings are neither the figureheads with which we are familiar in everyday life nor the all-powerful despots the modern mind conjures up when it thinks of the word "king." Rather, they are mythic figures of romance — images, like their prototypes Arthur and Charlemagne, of Christ the King. In all their activities, the

---

[1] This article was originally presented at Mythcon XXII in San Diego, California, on July 26, 1991. The Mythopoeic Society, the annual convener of Mythcon, is dedicated to the study of fantasy literature, particularly the works of the Inklings, as described in the previous chapter. It is important to realise that Tolkien (1892–1973), Lewis (1898–1963), and Williams (1886–1945) have many American fans of both their religious and fictional-fantasy work. Thus, the Inklings might serve to some degree as a means of making monarchist ideas at least comprehensible to the more literate denizens of the world's premier republic.
[2] Fenyvesi, *Splendor in Exile*, 276–77.

Inklings' monarchs conform to the medieval archetypes of king as quasi-priest, judge, warlord, and fount of honour. We will examine in some detail various of the monarchies which they describe, and end with a consideration of their beliefs about the role of monarchy in the real world. It is my view that their political beliefs as expressed in their writings, although vaguer in application than their religious ideas, were nevertheless just as central to the genesis of their work.

ELVEN KINGSHIP

The first example we will look at are the Elvish kings in Tolkien's *The Silmarillion* and *The Lord of the Rings*. They are particularly appropriate for approaching the medieval idea of kingship. During the Middle Ages, the contradiction between the sacred nature of the Crown per se, and the sometimes objectionable activities of various individual monarchs, prompted the evolution of the doctrine of "the king's two bodies." The body political was the Crown in the abstract: guarantor of justice, divine regent, fount of honour. To this aspect of the king was due all the emotion which we today call "patriotism." The Crown in this sense was undying, hence the phrase, "the king is dead—long live the king!" Accordingly, the related saying, "the life of the king is the health of the land," was true of the body political. In a word, the king in this sense was a sort of human flag, in much the same way that the surviving sovereigns of Spain, Scandinavia, the Low Countries, Britain, and the Dominions are today.

The body natural was quite another matter. This was the current incarnation, so to speak, of the Crown. It was this aspect that performed the day-to-day actions of the king. To oppose the Crown itself was treason; but if the wearer of that Crown acted outside or against the law, it was the duty of the subject to join with others to force him—for his own as well as others' sakes—back to the path of law, *á la* Magna Carta. The most basic example of the body natural's imperfection, however, was that it would die, to be replaced by another. The relationship of the two bodies was most plainly put by the accessional phrase just mentioned, but it was clearly symbolised in the Polish royal funeral rite. While the dead king lay in state in Cracow Cathedral, a visored knight representing him outside would fall from his horse, breaking his lance. At the same time, the old ruler's seal was broken. Thus the death of the person and the survival of the Crown were dramatised.

But there is no such distinction with Tolkien's Elvish kings. Whatever their period, the Vanyar's Ingwë, Thingol of Doriath, Gil-Galad of Lindon, Galadriel of Lothlórien, Thranduil of Mirkwood, and their colleagues were deathless. In them, both bodies are united, for being immortal unless killed, they are in fact as well as in aspiration the very archetypes of their realms. They last as long as their lands do, and when they die, their people's nationality passes. As the ruin of the human Crown generally meant the extinction or conquest of the nation, so the actual death of Elvish monarchs generally means the same. So it is that among them we may see the purely theoretical aspects of sacred monarchy given full play.

Firstly, as medieval theory held kingship to be of divine origin, so it is among the Elves in *The Silmarillion*. The first Elvish kings are the leaders of the three kindreds of the Eldar who respond to the Valar's summons. Of these, the primacy of honour is given to Ingwë, head of Vanyar. After his arrival in Valinor, he is "ever held the High King of all the Elves."[3] His position, in other words, is analogous to that of the high king of Ireland over the other kings of that island, or more particularly that of the Holy Roman Emperor over all the other Latin Christian monarchs.

As with these two real-world sovereigns, Ingwë's high kingship is nominal, in the sense that it means little in the day-to-day running of affairs outside his own circle. But lack of "power," the ability to make things happen, is not the same as lack of "authority," the right to indicate what ought to happen. Just as the Holy Roman Emperor and the ardrí were more important for what they were (holders of supreme temporal authority) than for what they actually did (precious little outside their own realms), so too with Ingwë. For a pre-modern people, unused to having every detail of life organised by a central state power, symbol is as important as or even more important than mere "reality." The Elves were nothing if not pre-modern.

---

[3] J. R. R. Tolkien, *The Silmarillion*, ed. Christopher Tolkien (Ballantine Books, 1977), 65.

The kings under Ingwë, like those of Munster, Ulster, Connaught, and Leinster, in the one example, or those of France, Naples, Poland, Scotland, etc., in the other, carry on their reigns with little or no regular counsel or approval given by their overlord; his primacy is strictly of honour, though no less prized for that.

Since both of the king's two bodies are united in Elvish sovereigns due to their relative immortality, it might be wise to point out some of their actions in accordance with the four archetypes of royal authority.

In sacred kingship, the king partakes of the priestly mediating power. Among non-Christian rulers, this is accomplished either by maintaining that the monarch is divine or at least the son of a god (e.g., with ancient Egypt, the Incas, the Dogon); head of the national cult and chief priest (China and Japan); or a sort of regent for divine authority (ancient Israel and the Mesopotamian city-states). Obviously, these categories are not rigid and tend to blend in various cultures. Among Christians, however, the pre-existence of an independent priestly hierarchy in the Church put Christian sacred kingship into a development of the last category. But while primarily divine vicars in the temporal sphere, they were not entirely without a demi-priestly character. Their coronations, which included sacred anointing, were likened to an eighth sacrament; during the ceremony they wore the vestments of a deacon or subdeacon. In some countries they received clerical privileges like drinking from the chalice at Mass or being allowed to touch sacred objects; they were sometimes given other ecclesiastical rights, such as canonries or liturgical roles. For the Elvish kings, there was no need of such symbolic acts. They were indeed the regents of the Valar, an authority given them during the lifetimes of many of their still-living subjects. Hence, the elaborate ritual necessary to show the fact of divine regency in human courts is completely absent in Elvish ones.

The pre-eminent centre of royal authority in medieval monarchs was judicial. The same holds for the Elvish ones. Thingol of Doriath, Galadriel of Lórien, Thranduil of Mirkwood, Turgon of Gondolin, and their kind all exercised this power continually. Like the medieval kings, this was in large degree their major peacetime function: acting as the highest court in the land, an activity still commemorated in Great Britain and the Commonwealth by the Court of King's Bench. But just as law was considered to be an independent living thing, discovered and interpreted but not created by the king, so too with the Elves, as may be seen by Melian's rebukes of Thingol upon certain of his judgements.

Almost as important a role for the medieval king was that of warlord. While standing armies were a creation of later centuries, medieval kings maintained an escort of knights and men-at-arms to defend their court and persons, as with the Knights of the Round Table or Charlemagne's Paladins. If they wished to carry on any greater campaign than defending their own castles, they were forced either to mobilise their barons (often a dangerous move), hire mercenaries (also perilous at times), or else some combination of the two. In Beleriand, the successive high kings of the Ñoldor were forced in similar fashion to summon the forces of other Ñoldorin lords (and other kindreds of Elves also) — with sometimes disastrous results, as at Nírnaeth Arnoediad. But where medieval Europe reserved warfare to the nobles and their retainers (except for the tenantry being called on to defend their homes), a situation which subsisted until the invention of conscription by the French revolutionaries, all able-bodied male Elves were expected to serve. Given the demonic nature of the Morgothian opposition, however, this might be likened to the Crusades, where the services of peasants and townsmen were actively solicited, although not drafted.

The last major archetype to be considered is that of the king as fount of honour. Among European monarchies, the granting of titles, hereditary and otherwise, and of fiefs was complicated by human mortality (resulting in the various ceremonies of homage, entrees, and so forth). The immortal Elvish rulers, on the other hand, simply appointed individuals to offices, needing to replace them only when death in battle (or rarely) treason vacated them. While neither medieval Christendom nor the Elvish lands of Beleriand and the rest of Middle-earth knew the modern state, the former did require, simply because of human limitation and fatigue on the part of the ruler, the Royal Household, whose four parts (chamber, hall, chapel, and stable) eventually grew into the central national administrations with which we are all familiar. Since an Elvish king knew no such limitations, he needed to delegate only simple functions, not decision-making or administrative tasks.

Númenórean kingship, both in the Land of the Star and in exile, was much more like that of medieval Europe, being, indeed, consciously modelled by its author on it. Due to the humanity of the Dúnedain, their kings perforce were graced with the "two bodies." So durable indeed was its body political that not even the treason of Ar-Pharazôn and the inundation of Númenor could destroy it. It passed to the nearest faithful branch, the lords of Andúnië, and continued on the mainland.

Being pre-Christian (and Tolkien's letters reveal a certain apprehension regarding his imaginary world's concordance with salvation history), the Dúnedain monarchy had no equivalent to the Church. Nevertheless, the kings of Númenor, Arnor, and Gondor did have several demi-priestly tasks. Like the Chinese emperor's yearly sacrifice at Peking's Temple of Heaven, the king of Númenor offered the first fruits to Eru at the Meneltarma annually.[4] The account in *Unfinished Tales* of Amon Anwar, the burial place of Elendil, makes one wonder if the king of Gondor did not perform a similar rite there; if he did, would not also his counterpart in Arnor have done so, perhaps at the Barrow-downs? In addition to this, the patronage of the Istari, particularly Gandalf — who himself functions as a sort of pope — is very reminiscent of the medieval kingdoms. His coronation of Aragorn would seem to confirm this, as in real life the primate of each country performed this task, though the pope himself crowned the Holy Roman Emperor. The other semi-priestly power given medieval monarchs was that of healing. While the power of the kings of France and England to cure scrofula ("the king's evil") is well known, the abilities of their colleagues of Denmark and Castile, respectively, to cure epilepsy or exorcise demons is less renowned, as is the belief mentioned in Chapter 7 that the Holy Roman Emperors had some control over weather (hence the German idiom *Kaiserwetter* for a warm, sunny day). This comes dramatically to the fore in *The Return of the King*, when Aragorn proves the

---

4 Tolkien, *The Silmiarillion*, 329.

truth of the old Gondorian proverb, "The hands of the king are the hands of a healer."[5]

The kings of the Dúnedain also have an authority based upon their role as supreme judges. Aragorn exercises this power after his coronation, meting out judgements to nations and individuals alike. But in doing so, he is bound by custom and justice, as when he confirms the grant of their land to the Rohirrim and deprives Beregond of his position in the Guard of the Citadel, sending him to be one of Faramir's retainers instead.

As warlords, the Dúnedain kings and their stewards act exactly as their medieval equivalents did. This is brought out most clearly in the gathering of troops from the outward fiefs to defend Minas Tirith against Sauron's last attack. But "The Tale of Years"[6] could well be a fictionalisation of any account of the military doings of a medieval monarchy.

Similiarly, the Númenórean Crown functions in standard manner as the fount of honour. All the trappings of a medieval royal household are present—steward, great officers of state, and so on. There is the feudal organisation of the country, complete with fiefs and what we would call today a very rudimentary infrastructure; what few central government functions exist, such as road maintenance and lower courts of justice, are farmed out to local magnates and notables. The prince of Dol Amroth, cousin of the steward and foremost nobleman in the realm, functions much as did the dukes of Burgundy in Capetian France. While we are not given much detail about internal administration of such fiefs in Gondor or Arnor, the Shire's organisation—an idealised medieval setting—was probably rather standard, with local government large on ceremony and small in conduct of quotidian affairs.

NARNIAN KINGSHIP

Moving from J. R. R. Tolkien to C. S. Lewis, we will see how Narnian kingship fits into the framework we have established. Unlike Tolkien's Middle-earth, where both the three chiefs of the Eldar and Elros and his descendants have their kingship

---

[5] Tolkien, *The Return of the King*, 169.
[6] Tolkien, Appendix B, 452–72.

bestowed upon them by the Valar, who, after all, are angels rather than deities, the Narnian monarchy is directly established by Aslan, who, as is well known, is simply Christ in that world. The repeated description of Aslan throughout *The Chronicles of Narnia* as the high king over all kings in Narnia is very reminiscent of the medieval idea of the sovereign as the vicar or regent of Christ the King. The oration Aslan gives monarchs-to-be Frank and Helen in *The Magician's Nephew* expresses very well the requirements of Christian kingship as expressed in so many medieval "manuals for princes":

> My children . . . you are to be the first King and Queen of Narnia. . . . You shall rule and name all these creatures, and do justice among them, and protect them from their enemies when enemies arise. And enemies will arise, for there is an evil Witch in this world. . . . Can you rule these creatures kindly and fairly, remembering that they are not slaves like the dumb beasts of the world you were born in, but Talking Beasts and free subjects? . . . And would you bring up your children and grandchildren to do the same? . . . And you wouldn't have favourites either among your own children and grandchildren or among the other creatures, or let any hold another under or use it hardly? . . . And if enemies came against the land (for enemies will arise) and there was war, would you be the first in the charge and the last in the retreat? . . . Then . . . you will have done all that a King should do. Your coronation will be held presently. And you and your children and grandchildren shall be blessed, and some will be Kings of Narnia, and others will be Kings of Archenland which lies yonder over the Southern Mountains.[7]

This sums up both the Narnian and the medieval conception of monarchy. On two subsequent occasions (as we are told in *The Lion, The Witch, and the Wardrobe* and *Prince Caspian*), Aslan renewed the Narnian crown, first with the four children and then with Caspian. When the latter set the Lone Islands to rights in *Voyage of the Dawn Treader,* he incidentally acted just as medieval theologians would have wished him to. Priest (or at least mediator between Aslan and his subjects), judge, and warlord, the ideal king of Narnia also summed up in himself the four major attributes of Christian sacred monarchy.

---

[7] C. S. Lewis, *The Chronicles of Narnia* (HarperCollins, 2001), 81–82.

KINGSHIP IN WILLIAMS

Charles Williams dealt directly with sacral monarchy in both *Taliessin Through Logres* and *The Region of the Summer Stars*. Here too, as one would expect, we see all the details of medieval kingship reproduced — Arthur as priest, judge, warlord, and fount of honour — and overmuch commentary on the obvious would not be useful. But the medieval relation of earthly kingship to divine authority subsists in Williams's modern novelistic settings as well. While praying before the Grail in *War in Heaven*, the duke of the Northern Ridings is "aware of a sense of the adoration of kings."[8] All of the traditions of his Catholic recusant family, loyal alike to pope, emperor, and king, "drew his mind into a vivid consciousness of all the royal and sacerdotal figures of the world adoring before this consecrated shrine. 'Jhesu, Rex et Sacerdos,' he prayed."[9]

MODERN IMPLICATIONS

This is an important transition Williams makes. We no longer live in the Middle Ages. To assist centralising monarchs in taming the diffuse powers of their realms, the Renaissance and the Reformation saw the fourfold Royal Household referred to earlier transmute into the powerful administration of the modern state. After 1789, most of these states in Europe and the Americas saw fit to dispense with the descendants of the sovereigns who had called them into being. In the few nations of former Christendom retaining monarchial heads of state, their roles became severely attenuated. Control over national judiciaries passed from their hands; as the technology of battle "progressed," their warlordship became nominal. Archduke Otto von Habsburg, the son of the last Austrian emperor, believed that "monarchy began to decline when kings no longer fought on the battlefield but set themselves apart and walled themselves in their palaces."[10] Increasingly, they became sorts of "crowned ombudsmen," a fact alluded to by Emperor Franz Joseph of Austria when he defined his role as "to protect my people from their politicians."[11]

---

8 Williams, *War in Heaven*, 135.
9 Williams, 136.
10 Fenyvesi, *Splendor in Exile*, 65.
11 Lukes, *On the Edge*, 17.

Since the World Wars, even this role has faded to a great degree, although flashes of it persist to this day; in Great Britain and the Dominions that share her king, it happened even earlier. But cojointly with this, the monarch's quasi-priestly attributes, which include his role as fount of honour and as living symbol of the nation, have increased in importance. As the body natural has lost importance, the body political has, in a sense, gained. The king of Great Britain and the Commonwealth has little power, when compared with his Tudor ancestors; but his Plantagenet predecessors had little more than he does. It is merely the gathering of power into the hands of the British bureaucracy and cabinet that makes the royal prerogative look so insignificant. Yet, he wields the same authority that medieval English kings did. The question we must answer, then, is how the Inklings looked upon this surviving authority in real life, as opposed to mere historical or literary interest.

Before we answer this question, however, there is one point covered by Williams in *Shadows of Ecstasy* which ought to be touched upon. Medieval sacral monarchy was the product of the mixing of pre-Christian sacred kingship with sacramental Christianity. When that faith spread beyond medieval Christendom's borders and came into contact with non-European sacred kings, the same result occurred. Pacific Christian kings, as those of Hawaii, Samoa, Tonga, Wallis and Futuna, and African ones like the rulers of Kongo, Buganda, Burundi, Bunyoro, Barotse, Swaziland, and Lesotho, all developed what were the obvious beginnings of Christian sacral monarchy.[12] Less well known is that the same process occurred with the Indian caciques of Spanish America, such as Mexico's princes of Tlaxcala or Peru's marquesses of Oropesa. These developments were all derailed by modernisation and independence, but the testimony they give to the psychological resonance of most peoples with the concept of the "holy Crown" is important. One of the still enduring native monarchies that has been to a degree Christianised is that of the Zulu nation, the fictional ruler of which makes an appearance in *Shadows of Ecstasy*, thus allowing Williams to show, in a passage we quoted in the previous

---

[12] See, for a striking example, Claudio Salvucci, "Zairean—or Sarum? The Forgotten Congolese Liturgy," in Peter Kwasniewski, ed., *Is African Catholicism a "Vatican II Success Story"?* (Os Justi Press, 2025), 103–12.

chapter, that the "ecstasy" or charism of kingship transcends national or racial lines in its ability to touch the soul:

> For a few moments royalty — a dark alien royalty — had appeared in the room, imposed upon all of them by the mere intensity of the Zulu chieftain's own strength and conviction. By virtue of that wide reading which both she and her husband loved, she had felt a shadow of it at times; in the superb lines of Marlowe or Shakespeare, in the rolling titles heard on ceremonial occasions at Church or in local celebrations: "The King's Most Excellent Majesty," "His Majesty the King-Emperor," "The Government of His Britannic Majesty."[13]

Williams goes on a few sentences later to describe kingship as "single bliss and sole felicity" and to equate it with poetry.[14]

That Williams was serious in his adherence to monarchy in the world of fact is obvious from Alice Hadfield's observation, which we quoted in the previous chapter:

> Though youthfully a very temporary republican, he slowly created for himself over the years a synthesis in which all men and women were equal and yet different within their hierarchies of excellence and distinction, in which above political equality everyone's distinctness was embodied in the single person of the monarch, as everyone's personal equality and distinctness was held in Christ. He retained his sense of monarchy, hereditary in that it must have a blood link with the long history of England, visible to high and low, free from fashion, choice or vote, apex of an administration free, equal and yet hierarchical in public distinction.[15]

Lewis shared Williams's loyalty; when Merlin in *That Hideous Strength* echoes the revolutionary mentality, urging deposition of the powerless Saxon king because of that very powerlessness, Ransom replies, "I have no wish to overthrow him. He is the king. He was crowned and anointed by the Archbishop. In the order of Logres I may be Pendragon, but in the order of Britain I am the King's man."[16] Whether in Narnia or England, Lewis believed that allegiance was owed to the crowned of God, simply because it was right and the natural order of things.

---

13 Williams, *Shadows of Ecstasy*, 61.
14 Williams, 61.
15 Hadfield, *Charles Williams*, 21.
16 Lewis, *That Hideous Strength*, 289.

What then of Tolkien? He too shared the royalism of his confreres. We saw how Humphrey Carpenter described him as "'right-wing' in that he honoured his monarch and his country and did not believe in the rule of the people . . . because he believed that in the end his fellow-men would not benefit from it."[17] It is difficult for Americans to comprehend, let alone sympathise with, such views. The very birth of our nation involved a rejection of kingship; since 1776, we have ingested republicanism with our mother's apple pie. As Fenyvesi, himself no monarchist, observes, "Republican accountability requires a pursuit of the rational. Citizens bow to the technician whose presumption is efficiency and whose excuse is science. He knows all about systems, and 'functional' is his highest praise."[18] But the royalism of the Inklings appeals as much or more to hearts and souls as to heads. Their essentially religious political orientation is particularly alien to us, given our national dogma of separation of Church and state.

Nevertheless, it is important to realise that they did not and do not stand alone. In their own time and place, their ideas on monarchy were more or less shared by such worthies as Belloc, Chesterton, Kipling, Machen, and of course, T. S. Eliot and Dorothy Sayers. They, in turn, were much inspired by the Young England movement of the nineteenth century, itself the British version of the counterrevolutionary wing of the romantic movement, which had adherents in every country in Europe.

Nor must it be supposed that this ideology is a thing of the past. Despite the overthrow of most European monarchies during the course of the twentieth century, royalist movements and parties survive in every nation on the continent. They became particularly vocal during the 1989 bicentennial of the French Revolution and surfaced with surprising strength in Eastern Europe, and even in the Soviet Union, in the period since. Most astonishing of all, adherents of the imperial family of Brazil mustered enough force there to have a plebiscite on restoration scheduled for 1993. Above mere politics, however, the number of monarchists — like Eugène Ionesco — in the European artistic world remains great.

---

[17] Carpenter, *J. R. R. Tolkien: A Biography*, 132–33.
[18] Fenyvesi, *Splendor in Exile*, 277.

Since the execution of Socrates for monotheism and monarchism, the battle between republicanism and royalism, to which the advent of Christianity offered a new and pervasive twist, has gone on. In one century, monarchies predominate, in another, republics. In an age consecrated no less than that of Pericles's Athens to the downfall of kings, the Inklings chose to be defenders of the Crown. It is well, then, to conclude by giving C. S. Lewis the last word:

> Monarchy can easily be "debunked"; but watch the faces, mark well the accents, of the debunkers. These are the men whose tap-root in Eden has been cut: whom no rumour of the polyphony, the dance, can reach—men to whom pebbles laid in a row are more beautiful than an arch. Yet even if they desire mere equality they cannot reach it. Where men are forbidden to honour a king they honour millionaires, athletes, or film-stars instead: even famous prostitutes or gangsters. For spiritual nature, like bodily nature, will be served; deny it food and it will gobble poison.[19]

---

[19] C. S. Lewis, *Present Concerns: A Compelling Collection of Timely, Journalistic Essays*, ed. Walter Hooper (Harcourt, 1986), 20.

❖ CHAPTER 14 ❖
The Counterrevolution Revisited

HE MONTH OF JUNE, WITH ITS OBSERVANCE of White Rose Day on June 10 and the feast of the Sacred Heart (the Friday following the octave day of Corpus Christi), always reminds me of the Jacobites who observed the first day, and of those heroes—in the Vendée, Tyrol, Italy, Spain, Mexico, and elsewhere—who made the Sacred Heart their symbol and tried to unite their sacrifices in fighting for the right with the sacrifice of Jesus on Calvary. What all these groups had in common was that they were counterrevolutionaries—a term that simply meant that they resisted those who usurped power in their respective countries. But few scholars have attempted to explore the history and message of these thinkers and fighters in a coherent way until Brazilian activist Plinio Corrêa de Oliveira, with his 1959 *Revolução e Contra-Revolução* (in English, *Revolution and Counter-Revolution* [The American Society for the Defense of Tradition, Family and Property, 1993]), and Hungarian Thomas Molnar, with *The Counter-Revolution* (Funk & Wagnalls, 1969).

The first of these writers interpreted Western history since 1518 as a succession of waves of anti-Catholic—indeed, purely evil—revolutions, proceeding through 1789, 1848, 1917, and so on. For his part, Molnar attempted to see why counterrevolutionaries consistently failed, but he also attempted to do something rarely, if ever, done before and infrequently since: to see in the opposition to these revolutions not merely negative naysayers but holders of a more or less coherent worldview among themselves.

The Hungarian scholar divined that a large part of the problem is that revolutions occur only when the rulership has come to doubt its own legitimacy and is reluctant to deal as ruthlessly with its opponents as those opponents were inevitably happy to deal with the old regime and its supporters. Molnar attributes this misfortune to a period of ideological "softening up" in the given society. He also points out that the counter-revolutionaries failed to see that the real enemy was not, in fact, the mobs stirred up against the established order but the middle-class intellectuals who invented and popularised the erroneous notions used to stir them up.

In their works, both writers left out the Anglo-American world, which in the end would generate an endless amount of pro-revolutionary assistance in continental Europe, Latin America, and elsewhere. Part of the reason for this is that "conservatives" in the Anglosphere took great pains to depict the revolutions of 1688 and 1775 as being different from those others. But in truth, their effect would be huge — not least in the Catholic Church, where the American example in partic-ular convinced the Fathers of Vatican II that such liberalism was different in kind, rather than merely in degree, from the kind of anticlerical liberalism with which they were familiar.

In any case, while defence of monarchy was a large part of counterrevolutionary discourse prior to 1918 (successive defeats over the course of the nineteenth century had led most deposed counterrevolutionary monarchs to seek refuge in Austria-Hungary), the fall of the dynasties in 1918 led to the birth of a new sort of counterrevolution, which Molnar describes thus:

> Gradually, the counterrevolutionaries came to the realisa-tion that they were the real revolutionaries, in the sense of the word that is compatible with the reaction to the doctrines of the revolution. Bernanos wrote during this period that to be a reactionary means simply to be alive, because only a corpse does not react anymore — against the maggots teeming on it. This phrase could have been adopted as the counterrevolutionary motto: it vividly painted what the counterrevolutionaries believed their task to be, namely, to become alive inside an agonising, no longer reacting body, the state, invaded by a poison-carrying enemy. The counterrevolutionaries were revolu-tionists insofar as they intended to reactivate this agonis-ing body, not by calling forth a new political party, but by an appeal to the entire nation in the name of *salus populi*. Ernst von Salomon, in his *Der Fragebogen*, written after 1945, formulates the mood of twenty-five years before: "Unless it were possible to recreate a constructive form

of the state, Bolshevism must be the natural heir to the obvious and shameless dissolution of all organic strength by the ideological senselessness of the bourgeois-liberal and social-democrat wizards."[1] This is what was tried almost everywhere in Europe during the twenty-some years separating the two World Wars: Horthy in Hungary, Salazar in Portugal, Piłsudski in Poland, Mussolini in Italy, Franco in Spain, and others, with less success, elsewhere, for example in Germany. Between 1919 and 1933, many young Germans adopted as their ideal Moeller van den Bruck's "conservative revolutionary"; this hero figure survived until 1944 among the youthful members of the anti-Hitler resistance, who hoped to rid their country both of National Socialism and of an imminent bolshevisation.

Crushed between Hitler and Stalin, what was left of this kind of counterrevolutionary was pushed into oblivion in 1968.

So, the question might well be asked: why bother studying the works and efforts of a long line of losers? Well, for one thing, regardless of its opponents, the ongoing revolution described by Corrêa de Oliveira and Molnar has continued into our own time, dissolving anything it touches. The sixteenth century saw a revolt against the Altar, the eighteenth against the Throne, and the twentieth against both; those vanquished, it has set its sights on demolishing reality itself. Everything good — in a word — must go. But our current foes, who would demolish natural law, are still propelled forward by the same dynamic ultimately unleashed at Wittenberg. To combat it, we must look at its roots and re-examine its opponents.

An important thing to remember is that when one phase of the revolution ends, many of its heretofore adherents oppose further movement in that direction. Thus, Edmund Burke, whom Samuel Johnson called "a *bottomless* Whig" at the time of the American War of Independence,[2] was driven somewhat rightward by the events he witnessed, becoming the author of *Reflections on the Revolution in France* (London, 1793). So has it often proved throughout history: even Martin Luther, when serfs claiming him as guru decided to apply private judgement to property issues, felt compelled to write *Against the Murderous,*

---

[1] Ernst von Salomon, *The Answers*, trans. Constantine Fitzgibbon (Putnam, 1954), 250.
[2] James Boswell, *The Life of Samuel Johnson* (Henry Baldwin, 1791), vol. 2, 455.

Thieving Hordes of Peasants. One can only wonder what he would have thought of the French Revolution.

It is time to look at all the many counterrevolutionary writers and movements, from Johann Maier von Eck to Molnar himself. They are a multinational band to be sure, with many hailing from the Europe "beyond the seas": Canada's George Grant and Msgr. Lionel Groulx rub shoulders with Australia's Denys Jackson and Bob Santamaria, Chile's Jaime Eyzaguirre, Sri Lanka's J. P. de Fonseka, and the American Ralph Adams Cram. Nor are all counterrevolutionaries Catholic: England's William Cobbett, the Dutchman Guillaume Groen van Prinsterer, and the Prussian Friedrich Julius Stahl were avid supporters of their countries' respective state churches. Such diverse figures offer wildly varying solutions depending upon their time and place. Yet they do have certain commonalities, which it would be well for moderns facing the same hideous strength to explore — and this is certainly the easiest time in history in which to do so.

The internet, which has brought so much evil into so many lives, may also bring good, if one knows where and how to look. Virtually everything that is in the public domain (and much that is not) is now readily available. Do you wish to explore the writings of Portuguese Integralists, Russian Slavophiles, or Argentine Carlists? You can, so long as you have the names. Do you wish to delve into the many revolts against the French revolutionaries, both at home and in the nations they invaded? At your fingertips! What about the Papal Zouaves, or the Royalists in the Latin American Wars of Independence? Not a problem. Even if you do not read French, German, Spanish, Polish, Russian, or whatever other language a thinker or party about which you are interested wrote in and spoke, there are translation devices that seemingly improve in quality every day. As the revolution has been universal, so has its opposition.

This is an important endeavour, exploring and resurrecting this gallant band, because many counterfeits are on offer. Seemingly every youngster opposed to the current horrors knows something of Evola, which is unfortunate, but they rarely know anything of Attilio Mordini, which is worse. Mere opposition to revolutionary "modernity" is not enough; the opposition of those of its opponents who really had something true, good, and beautiful to offer as an alternative must be put forward. Out of the chaff must be sifted the wheat. Italy's Alleanza Cattolica has made a stab in this direction with its online *Dizionario del Pensiero Forte*, but much, much more must be done in this direction — and not only in Italian.

As the situation across the West heats up, as it shall, this process becomes ever more important. But the figures suggested are not purely of academic interest. In Central Europe, there is something of a coalition of small and conservative states slowly arising. However, this is severely hampered by the mutual hostility of the Magyars and their neighbours. It is difficult for the latter to understand the pain so many Hungarians yet feel over the revolt of the minorities in 1848 and the Trianon Treaty of 1920. But they in turn are often energised by their ancestors' struggles against the Magyarisation policies the Hungarian liberals pursued in the nineteenth and early twentieth centuries, which stemmed from memories of 1848 and in turn led to Trianon. These might be academic questions in other places, but in Central Europe they are very much alive.

The problem with this is that the cultures and attitudes of the Hungarians, Slovakians, Croatians, Romanians — and indeed, the Poles, Ukrainians, Slovenians, and (to this writer's delighted surprise) increasingly the Czechs — have been moulded by very similar religious and cultural attitudes derived from their shared history. If they are to maintain the Christian and sane ethos each of them has enjoyed and is in a sense rediscovering, they must maintain some degree of unity versus a West that would corrupt and an East that would dominate them. It must be pointed out to Hungarians that in 1848, Jelačić and his collaborators were not simply struggling for their own nationalities, and so following Kossuth's example; they were in essence fighting for the Habsburgs and the Holy Crown. But to the Slovaks, Croats, and the rest, it should be pointed out that István Count Széchenyi stood up for their rights as subjects of that same Holy Crown. After 1867, the very Magyarisation policies that would poison their relationship with the Hungarians were stoutly opposed by the Catholic People's Party, led by such as the Zichys and the Eszterházys. Both sides must be reminded that the chances for a peaceful solution between the Habsburgs and the then-Hungarian government were destroyed by the murder of Count von Lamberg by a mob in Budapest. In a word, if these countries are to be spared from becoming either Ireland or Belarus in the next decade, their shared history must be re-examined from a counterrevolutionary viewpoint. The myths that all sides have cherished and that have encouraged each to hate the other must be exploded—both for the sake of objective truth and to allow a decent future for them all. It will be a painful process, but far better than the alternatives.

Nor is Central Europe the only place where this counterrevolutionary re-examination must take place. Conservatives in the Anglosphere need to take a long hard look at 1688 and 1776, myths as foundational to and cherished by us as 1848 is to Central Europe; so too with Germany, Italy, France, and every nation in the West, howsoever corrupt we may have become. This is not in pursuit of some sort of fanciful reconstruction of the current arrangements, but so that we may finally see things as they are. We must rediscover the principles that—in as many forms as there are Western nations—founded each of our countries and the West as a whole. It is a hard task, to be sure, but one that is essential if utter collapse is to be avoided. Otherwise, our descendants shall have to begin to rebuild from utter ruin, even as our fathers did a millennium and a half ago. The more we leave them that is intact, the easier their task shall be.

⊰CHAPTER 15⊱
Postliberalism, Integralism— What Does It All Mean?

AGAINST THE BACKGROUND OF UNREST, unease, and governmental incompetence on both sides of the Atlantic today, a number of relatively new and seemingly allied "-isms" have made their appearance across the Western world. The summer of 2020, with its bizarre combination of dictatorial lockdowns for the law-abiding and license to burn, riot, and steal for those so inclined, was a watershed moment for many. So too was the lockstep endorsement of these measures by the various ecclesiastical establishments—which included depriving their faithful of the sacraments (a measure Catholics who still believe in their efficacy could not help seeing as an intolerable act). While the Canadian, Australian, and New Zealand governments made their citizens virtual prisoners, the electoral overthrow of President Trump—setting aside the question of its authenticity—signalled a triumphant return to power for the Democrats. These latter, having cheered on the rioters during the hot, hot summer of burning love mere months before, found a similar (if much smaller and far less destructive) outbreak on Capitol Hill to be an intolerable attack upon the very foundations of the American republic. Presumably, the burned-out ruins and scores of lost lives in at least a dozen cities across the land were nothing in comparison. Meanwhile, the shrill orgy of attacks on the very foundations of Western culture and all those historical figures who have spread it around the world has continued to echo through learned societies, academia, media, and bureaucracy, all under the ironic name of "woke."

There was some welcome slight relief, of course, in the easing of the Covid restrictions, perhaps best symbolised by the Queen's Platinum Jubilee celebrations (even as those around her coronation in 1953 presaged the end of wartime rationing in Britain). But of course, a new crisis broke out in 2022 with Russia's invasion of Ukraine — an unwelcome revelation that the one major ruler of a world power who employed decent rhetoric, Vladimir Putin, was not above a quick snatch-and-grab. Alas, his fiercest opponents were also often the most furious wavers of the rainbow flag; whilst ordinary folk try to make sense of it all, innocent Ukrainians (and for that matter, Russians) continue to die.

In the face of all this, our certainties regarding conservative and liberal, right and left, and much else are up for grabs. Major corporations, once upon a time seen as bastions of conservatism, or at least anti-socialism, have become the foremost apostles of wokery in their advertising (save in the Near East, where the fat cats are all too aware it would destroy their bottom line). The less said about the current pontificate in this case the better, although it might well have won the approval of Julius III. In the United States, the American civil religion, once a glue that held together all sides of the political spectrum, has been reduced to a quarry of slogans for members of the Republican Party; their woke opponents have turned on it like Unitarians renouncing Calvinism. Woke denunciation of the United States as the most evil nation in history is the flipside of American exceptionalism. Our Western European cousins have seen their various Christian Democratic parties jettison both Christianity and democracy in order to become government employment providers; the British and Canadian Conservatives have undergone a similar transformation. In a word, voters (where votes have any meaning) everywhere outside Central Europe are offered just two choices: hard woke and soft woke.

So it is that the aforementioned alternatives have appeared to fill the ideological gap between disgusting and loathsome. It might well be argued that the current scene offers the *reductio ad absurdum* of a revolution that arguably began in 1517; having successively and successfully defeated Altar, Throne, and family, it has turned its sights on reality itself. Various thinkers for various reasons have begun to mount a coherent response to — and defence against — this hideous strength. They are certainly united in their intelligence and good will. But they are separated by several things. Firstly, even as the revolution has had successive stages over the past six centuries, so too has its resistance: the medieval Guelphs and Ghibellines would no doubt have united against Luther, even as he and St. Ignatius Loyola would have bonded against Robespierre. As each stage of revolt moved on, elements of it that had become "conservative" by decades of custom often formed part of the resistance to the next revolution. Thus, while modern-day opponents of our current upheaval must mine the powerful historical deposit of counterrevolutionary thought for inspiration, that deposit is rife with contradictions: Catholic versus Protestant versus Orthodox; monarchy versus republic; centralism versus localism; free trade versus protection; and on and on.

Moreover, each of these counterrevolutionary thinkers analyses the situation from a different perspective; that is to say, having different national origins, educations, and careers, they have first experienced this world-historical horror in a setting peculiar to them and in a context different from that of many of their colleagues. Some are theologians, others are academics of varying disciplines, still others are politicians, journalists, or economists. In trying to make sense of the current madness, it is easy for anyone to be like the blind men with the elephant: able to correctly describe the part of the animal they are touching, but hard-put to grasp the entirety — and ready to argue with those who describe other parts.

So it is that there have emerged some spirited, and occasionally nasty, disputes within their ranks. Because I know many and respect these folk, I am not going to identify the particular quarrels nor their proponents. But I shall list some of these good people, regardless of the sides they may take in particular internecine squabbles. I shall then go on to consider what the reasons for these quarrels may be. So here we go, in no particular order: Edmund Waldstein, Adrian Vermeule, Patrick Deneen, Thomas Storck, Thomas Crean, Sohrab Ahmari, Larry Chapp, Alan Fimister, Conor Casey, Chad Pecknold, Josh Hammer, Gladden Pappin, Alasdair MacIntyre, John Gray, David Goodhart, Christophe Guilluy, Phillip Blond, Adrian Pabst, Aidan Nichols, Christophe Buffin de Chosal, David Engels, John Milbank, and Matthew Crawford. There are of course many others. Doubtless some listed here would object to being placed with this company. But, as I say, I know and like a number of them, and respect the rest. Nevertheless, let us proceed to see where they agree and where they find grounds for disagreement.

The agreement is actually vast and may be summarised in two words: *common good*. For all of these thinkers, the end of the state is *not*, as in liberalism, simply to allow the greatest number to pursue whatever they wish with a minimum of murder and mayhem toward one another — essentially a negative role for politics. Rather, to the state, or more particularly to government, falls the task of assisting its citizens to achieve the highest mutual good — always keeping in mind that every job should be handled by the lowest possible level (such folk being generally very fond of *subsidiarity*).

Here the question of what constitutes the common good becomes paramount. For most (if not all) of our thinkers, the common good includes not being slaughtered in the womb or in the old age home; a decent standard of living connected to good labour but also not permitting starvation in the streets; a general and uplifting standard of education, culture, and exposure to nature that allows the individual to reach his highest potential; stable families wherein such individuals may be nourished and formed; a network of intermediate bodies that not only assist the individual and the family in their respective quests for the good life, but also elevate the community as a whole; and government that provides sufficient internal and external security of various kinds to permit of these goals being accomplished. So far, there is primarily both accord in the ranks and undying opposition to the current woke elite. But there is disagreement on one important area, that of the highest good: the eternal salvation of the individual.

The reasons for this dispute are historical. At the Last Supper, amongst other acts (such as establishing the Mass and priesthood), Christ united the Davidic kingship to which He was heir with the *communio* of the Church. This was something of which His earliest disciples were keenly aware. When such countries as Armenia, Georgia, and Ethiopia became majority Christian nations, their national identities as well as their monarchies became bound up with their new faith. This same connexion was established by Theodosius the Great over the whole Roman Empire with the Edict of Thessalonica in 380. From this time on, Roman citizenship as well as membership in the Church was conferred by baptism. The theory remained the same in that Empire's succeeding Eastern and Western incarnations; in Constantinople as well as in Aachen, Viscount Bryce's words regarding the Holy Roman Empire, which we quoted back in Chapter 7, were true: "The Holy Roman Church and the Holy Roman Empire are one and the same thing, seen from different sides; and Catholicism, the principle of the universal Christian society, is also Romanism."[1] This "universal Christian society," the *res publica Christiana,* included not only all the Western Catholic nations, but despite 1054, the Eastern Orthodox ones as well, as shown by the Crusades (the schism would not harden into a seeming permanence until 1462, at the behest of the triumphant Turkish sultan).

What all of this meant for each of the polities (they were hardly modern states) in this assemblage was that the notion of the common good, deriving ultimately from Greek, Roman, Jewish, and Christian ideas, was capped by a perceived highest good. It was the duty of the temporal authorities to assist the Church in her spiritual mission of saving the souls of the faithful, who were themselves the only full citizens of the polity, which was the local temporal expression of Christendom. This is why the parish—from Ireland to Russia—was the lowest level of spiritual and temporal government alike, with responsibilities in both spheres. Moreover, as the emperor, kings, dukes, counts, and so on down to the bailiffs and manor lords were responsible for protecting the faithful from external threat, to them also fell the role of protecting their peoples from the internal contagion of heresy. This contagion was seen by most people during the ages of faith to be as vile as Holocaust denial in our society today, and its persecution was popular among the majority. The denizens of every age find certain ideas—or denials of ideas—disgusting and dangerous.

With the Protestant Revolt came a division. Now, large numbers of Christians in each realm were set against the majority and essentially lost their citizenship. It might be pointed out that in Spain, Portugal, and the Italian States, where the

---

[1] Bryce, *The Holy Roman Empire,* 106.

Inquisition monitored not only heresy but morals, the bloody
religious civil wars that convulsed France, Germany, and the
British Isles were avoided. The latter conflicts, which unleashed
horrors in the name of faith, spawned a religious indiffer-
entism; from this came the Enlightenment, and thence the
French and other revolutions, with their horrors in the name
of freedom, for which far more have died than for the name
of God. During the nineteenth and early twentieth centuries
in Europe and Latin America, various groups of Catholics and
Protestants resisted these progressive movements, and from
these groups developed what were variously called conservatives, the right, legitimists, and integralists.

The United States of America, however, were *sui generis*. Initially produced by a civil war among supporters and opponents
of a monarchy itself both Protestant and liberal, they started
their national life without the European or Latin American
equivalent of conservatism. That highly elastic word came to
mean what was elsewhere called liberal, while in time that latter term came to mean folk who elsewhere would be socialists.
A common civic religion was invented, which granted sacred
status to the new country's institutions, and in which all
Americans could participate, while a second civil war created
a partial alternative faith for Southerners. The common dogma
of this religion was the "pursuit of liberty." One remnant of
the states' European origins was a common moral consensus,
which gave the national faith an anchor. This splintered in the
1960s, cutting the civil religion adrift, and in the end leading
us to where we are.

Divisions among the sort of thinkers we have been describing tend to revolve around how each of them puts religion —
and especially Catholicism — in relation to the common good;
to what degree they hold to which adumbration of liberalism;
and what role the American experience plays in their world-
views. These are not small things. But in the interests of amity
and sanity, I would like to point out three important facts to
those concerned with such arguments. First, the most hard-
boiled proponents of a Catholic confessional state are only too
aware that the arrangement they consider ideal was itself the
product of centuries of organic development in places where
the overwhelming number of people professed the faith. Far

from wanting to impose a kind of Catholic sharia upon an unwilling captive population, they are aware that what they want will take the same kind of evangelisation that the great apostles and missionaries of the Church's first thousand years put forth.

Secondly, while the American experiment was certainly riddled with Calvinism, deism, Unitarianism, and Masonry from its inception, it also allowed Catholics the freedom to evangelise. It is our fault that we settled for respectability and getting two nominal members of our Church into the top government job. Had we American Catholics been animated by the same love of country our ancestors had for theirs, we would be living in a very different situation today.

Beyond those considerations, however, I wish to offer a very practical note to consider from Viktor Orbán. This is one of the twelve reasons he offered for his party's success in Hungary:

> Our opponents, the progressive liberals and neo-Marxists, have unlimited unity: they have one another's backs. By contrast, we conservatives are capable of squabbling with one another over the smallest issue. And then we wonder at how our opponents corner us. We do indeed possess intellectual sophistication, and we care about intellectual nuance. But if we want to succeed in politics, we should never look at what we disagree on, but instead look for our common ground.[2]

As it stands, our masters sacrifice our unborn to Moloch, destroy the innocence of those of our children who do survive, and enjoin the profanation of marriage. If our squabbles strengthen them, we are their unwitting partners, despite our best intentions.

---

[2] Viktor Orbán, "Speech by Prime Minister Viktor Orbán at the Opening of CPAC Hungary," *The European Conservative*, May 22, 2022, https://european-conservative.com/articles/commentary/speech-by-prime-minister-viktor-orban-at-the-opening-of-cpac-hungary/.

PART IV

✦✦✦✦✦✦✦✦✦✦✦

Monarchy
Today

⋪CHAPTER 16⋫

Confessions of an American Monarchist

There may be liberty under a right monarchy: there has come a sort of slavery under the democracies of the modern form where a political oligarchy and a money oligarchy, now in alliance, now in conflict, have brought about grave disorder, social chaos, and the negation of the free and the good life, under the forms of a free commonwealth founded on assumptions that are baseless biologically, philosophically, historically, and from the standpoint of plain commonsense.

—Ralph Adams Cram[1]

LTHOUGH IT IS LESS SO NOW, FOR THE BETTER part of my life, the phrase "American monarchist" has been something of a chimæra, like "dehydrated water." The very notion of monarchy was consciously or otherwise held in contempt in my native land. If an American expressed a fondness for the institution, he was obviously spitting on the flag, mom, and apple pie. The absurdity of the idea was underscored by the very success of our great nation, a superpower that stalked the planet. Our very national identity, after all, was founded on a revolution against a monarchy portrayed as tyrannical (cf. Schoolhouse Rock's "No More Kings"). All of our civic holidays—Independence Day, Memorial Day, Washington's Birthday, Veterans Day, Flag Day, Constitution Day, and on and on—celebrated our republican institutions and disparaged what they had replaced. Every morning, schoolchildren swore the Pledge of Allegiance "to the flag, and to the republic for which it stands." As a boy, I certainly partook of all this quite happily.

But while my parents were certainly patriotic — my father was a tail gunner against the Japanese in World War II — their undeniable love of country was nuanced by their backgrounds. Dad was a French Canadian from New Bedford, Massachusetts,

---

[1] Ralph Adams Cram, "Invitation to Monarchy," *The American Mercury* (1936): 486.

whose first language was French (although his radio-actor's English was flawless). He loved the Bourbons who had sent our fathers to the New World, and correspondingly hated the Revolution that had murdered Louis XVI and so many others. The Chouans and the Vendéens were heroes to him, as well as Quebec's own Papal Zouaves and their comrades-in-arms who fought for Bl. Pius IX. Paradoxically, he had a certain fascination with the two Napoleons. Moreover, he had a Scots ancestor who had fought for Bonnie Prince Charlie at Culloden. Hence, he loved Scotland, the Stuarts, and the Jacobites. My mother had a fascination with both the Habsburgs and the Romanoffs, which she duly passed on to me as well.

My early boyhood in the Hudson Valley was marked by family explorations of the colonial heritage of Westchester and Fairfield counties, which gave me an enduring interest in that era. When we moved to Los Angeles, this pastime turned into exploring Southern California's Spanish heritage — its mission and ranchos. For us, Irving and Cooper were supplemented by Zorro and *Ramona*. Moreover, we came to know a great many emigres — White Russians, Central Europeans of various kinds, and Balkan folk. Their love for their respective sovereigns (bearing in mind that many were of the World War I generation) made a huge impression on me.

This era was the '60s and '70s, filled as they were with revolutionary changes in Church and society, all of which I instinctively disliked. My historical outlook was affected by seeing the parallels with the French Revolution and those other movements that had driven from their homelands so many folk whom we knew — even our own American Revolution, which was responsible for the French affair in so many ways. Certainly, the hatred of the Quebec Act expressed by the Founding Fathers did not sit well with me. My studies of the royal saints of the Catholic Church also had an effect.

Another thing that did not escape me was the willingness of the British Isles' Charles I, France's Louis XVI, Russia's Nicholas II, Austria-Hungary's Karl I and IV, and others to sacrifice themselves for their respective peoples. By the same token, Spain's Alfonso XIII, Italy's Umberto II, Belgium's Leopold III, Romania's Michael, and latterly, Greece's Constantine II chose to abdicate rather than visit the horrors of civil war on their subjects, which also made an impact. Finally, the constitutional conflicts of Christian X of Denmark, Gustav V of Sweden, and Britain's Edward VII with "their" governments—where, in each case, the king was so clearly in the right—added their weight. In a word, all of these incidents spelled out very clearly for me the shabbiness of the political class in contrast to the dignity of the monarchs whose power they usurped. Franz Joseph's oft-quoted dictum that his job was to "protect my people from their politicians"[2] made perfect sense to me. Reading such works as Geoffrey Bocca's *Kings Without Thrones: European Monarchy in the Twentieth Century* (Dial Press, 1959) and Walter Curley's *Monarchs in Waiting* (Dodd, Mead & Company, 1973) convinced me that the then-current crop of claimants was far superior to the elected creatures on offer in their various countries.

Certainly, I was unable to find a country that had done well by replacing its monarchy with a republic, even among countries with former rulers under whom I would not have enjoyed living (such as the Qing emperors or the Ottoman sultans). Commonwealth Realms that deposed the Queen inevitably degenerated into banana republics, while the overthrow during this period of Prince Sihanouk of Cambodia, the king of Afghanistan, the king of Laos, and the emperor of Ethiopia were unmitigated disasters for those countries and for the United States. It was the sleazy ill-treatment of the king of Greece during the 1975 referendum campaign that pushed me into declaring myself a monarchist, much to the shock of most of my teenaged friends.

Of course, there are monarchies and there are monarchies, ranging from Saudi Arabia to Monaco. In my college years, I studied the various Christian theorists of monarchy: de Maistre, Chateaubriand, von Kuehnelt-Leddihn, Molnar, Maurras, Donoso Cortés, Figgis, Stahl, Belloc, Chesterton, and many, many more. I also carefully examined the manifestos of the Cavaliers and Jacobites, the French Legitimists, Spanish Carlists, and Portuguese Miguelists, and so became aware of certain points. The first was that the so-called "absolute monarchs" and "enlightened despots" of the sixteenth, seventeenth, and eighteenth centuries—while still better than much of what replaced

---

[2] Lukes, *On the Edge*, 17.

them, and not nearly so absolute as the current regimes (none of them could have legalised abortion or changed the nature of marriage, for example) — were themselves in a real sense corruptors of a better system that they had inherited. That system was the "medieval synthesis," a "mixed government" of king and estates. With this in mind, the nineteenth century featured conflicts between adherents of "traditional" monarchy — such as the aforementioned Legitimists, Carlists, etc. — and "liberal" monarchists, who wanted a figurehead king.

While certain that even such "crowned republics" were superior in their way to what would replace them, I came to realise that their opponents had been seeking a modern, updated version of the medieval synthesis. This would incorporate the new realities brought about by the Industrial Revolution: the rise of an urban proletariat, disaffected from the traditions of Church, state, and culture, that emerged as the largest single challenge to the internal peace of the Western nations in the nineteenth century. In a word, they were looking at the same issues as Catholic and other Christian social theorists of the time.

From all of this, I teased out five common points, as discussed in the opening chapter, which have since been the core of my own monarchism:

> 1. The Altar: the confessional state, wherein the Church acts as the animating principle of society, and confers legitimacy and authority upon the king via the coronation and other ceremonies of state.

> 2. The Throne: a monarchy whose God-given authority guides the use of his power, which is sufficient to defend his subjects from each other and from foreign foes.

> 3. Subsidiarity: local liberties, provincial rights, and the ability of the lesser levels of governance to deal with their own affairs, under the sovereign's authority.

> 4. Solidarity: class cooperation rather than conflict, as the various social classes are seen as members of one family, with the monarch as father (this has been described as corporatism, solidarism, distributism, guild socialism, and various other titles, generally dealing with one particular aspect).

> 5. *The res publica Christiana*, the *Reichsidee, Abendland,* Christendom: the idea that all Christian monarchies somehow belong to a single commonwealth.

All of this made sense of European — and even Latin American and Commonwealth — history, so that one could see quite clearly how modern liberalism, national socialism, fascism per se, and communism were all branches of a single tree. It even provided an understanding of Bonapartism and Napoleon's two unacknowledged heirs: Bismarck's Germany and Cavour's Italy. But it had one major flaw: it had no real reference to American history or contemporary politics. Or did it?

I had joined the International Monarchist League in 1979. Founded in 1943, the League was created to avoid the mistakes of monarchical abolition in 1918, which, as Churchill observed, had paved the way for the second world conflict. In its way, the League attempted to give unity to monarchists, to defend monarchy where it still existed, and to work for restorations where it had been abolished. But little of this applied to the United States. What relevance, then, did we American members have?

History gave an answer. Once our lower 48 states were consolidated and Alaska bought from Russia, we began the climb to world power status, which we achieved in the 1890s. The deep antimonarchical prejudice that infects us was at the bottom of our annexing both the Kingdom of Hawaii and the Paramountcy of Samoa. It also fueled our war with Spain in 1898 — arguably the most unjust of many unjust wars — which garnered us Puerto Rico, Guam, and the Philippines, and doomed Cuba to decades of chaos and misrule. This prejudice guided Woodrow Wilson in insisting on the ejection of the Habsburgs, Hohenzollerns, Wittelsbachs, Wettins, and so on. As I noted earlier, Churchill pithily commented on this move: "This war would never have come unless, under American and modernising pressure, we had driven the Habsburgs out of Austria and Hungary and the Hohenzollerns out of Germany. By making these vacuums we gave the opening for the Hitlerite monster to crawl out of its sewer on to the vacant thrones."[3]

Unfortunately, this lesson was not learned by FDR. Despite the archduke's valuable services to the Allied cause and his adherents' resistance struggle against the occupiers, the US backed Stalin's occupation of Central Europe against Otto von Habsburg's vision of a Danubian Federation; we supported

---

[3] Winston S. Churchill, *The Second World War: Triumph and Tragedy* (Houghton Mifflin Company, 1953), 750.

Tito against King Peter II of Yugoslavia; and we helped rig the 1946 referendum against Umberto II in Italy. Of course, over the coming two decades, we did all we could to support the rebels attacking our European Allies in their colonies, often in concert with our supposed Soviet enemies. We assisted in the overthrow of the kings of Egypt, Iraq, Yemen, and Libya, and counselled Diệm in South Vietnam to depose Bảo Đại (though, to be fair, we were complicit in Diem's murder some years later). We also played a greater or lesser part in all the overthrows in my time that were mentioned earlier.

If any of this activity had ever brought the United States any kind of benefit, that might be something—but it never has. Nor, despite the hopes of many of us, did that bipartisan policy cease after the fall of the Soviet Union. This was particularly sad, for many dreamt of restorations not only in Central Europe and the Balkans, but in Russia herself. Alas, it was not to be. President Bush vetoed restorations in Romania and Bulgaria in 1992. When it was pointed out to Secretary of State Albright that the monarchists were the largest opposition to the Milošević government, whom we were bombing, and that we should, therefore, back the monarchists, she airily replied, "We don't do kings."[4] Bush Jr. would have his special emissary very publicly forbid Afghanistan's Loya Jirga from restoring its king, thereby guaranteeing an eventual defeat.

Apart from unsuccessfully attempting to get our foreign policy elite to cease doing these costly things, was there any other point to American monarchism? I have long said that if you want to hate the United States, study the history of our foreign policy; but if you wish to love us, take a long road trip through our country. Certainly, the kneejerk hatred of monarchy that characterises so much of our culture had led our leaders over the course of more than a century to make decisions that would cost untold amounts of blood and treasure, both foreign and American. The proper role, then, of an American monarchist—apart from supporting monarchy's retention or restoration overseas—was to show the price that we had paid for continually attacking it in foreign lands, in the hope of introducing a strain of sanity into American foreign

---

[4] Colby Cosh, "Crowns and Chaos in the Middle East," *Maclean's*, January 22, 2012, https://macleans.ca/uncategorized/crowns-and-chaos-in-the-middle-east/.

policy. But monarchy had little relevance to our internal conditions — at least, that was how it seemed to me in the 1990s.

The other American monarchists whom I encountered in those days generally fit into one of four categories: (1) Anglophiles, who simply believed that British institutions were better than our own; (2) philosophical monarchists, who, without loyalty to a specific dynasty or nation, felt that some form of monarchy was the superior form of government; (3) religious monarchists, who believe that it was the form of government best suited to their religion, whether Catholic, Orthodox, Anglican, Lutheran, Muslim, Buddhist, or Hindu; and (4) emigres or their descendants who retained some lingering loyalty to their ancestral monarchs. For my part, I was and am a mixture of the last three, much as I respected Queen Elizabeth II and especially the then Prince of Wales (now King Charles III). Having studied his writings and efforts closely, I responded to the various criticisms continually levelled at him due to the scandals of those days by remarking that "he is still far better than the majority of the trash I've been asked to vote for or against." That usually silenced the argument. But I was too aware of the damage done to the British monarchy — both by the defeat of the Jacobites and by the Loyalist side in our Revolution — to see in it an ideal.

Nevertheless, as the years went by, and the American civic religion so deeply rooted in veneration of our republican institutions began to decay, I looked again at what relevance monarchy might have to the country I loved so much, and for whose future I feared (and fear). Certain things almost immediately began to emerge, the more I studied and thought.

There is only a single American republican tradition — albeit with its Confederate regional variant as a sort of Shia response to Yankee Sunnism (hence the presence of Washington on a horse on the Confederate State of America's seal). Born in 1776, it has given birth to Wokeism as Calvinism gave birth to Unitarianism. But our colonial roots, laid by different monarchies, are extremely varied. Twelve of our original thirteen states were founded under the House of Stuart (albeit with Dutch and Swedish settlements annexed). From the diverse elements of that founding came the Episcopal, Congregational (and Unitarian), Presbyterian, Lutheran, Reformed, Methodist, and Baptist denominations that have dominated so much of our religious history. Thanks to both King Charles I and King Charles II, we Catholics have English colonial footholds in Maryland, Pennsylvania, and Kentucky.

From those foundations also came our common law, and the sheriffs, mayors, notaries, coroners, and all the rest of county and local government that we inherited from our English and British kings. Moreover, the division into effective and ceremonial sides of government (king versus prime minister; Lords versus Commons; sheriffs and lords lieutenant versus county council chairmen; and lord mayors, lord provosts, provosts, and mayors versus chairmen of town, city, and borough councils) did not occur on our shores. In most states, rather than being a ceremonial figure as in modern Britain, the sheriff is as powerful a figure as ever his medieval predecessors were. Quite a number of our National Guard and militia units were founded under the king, which is why the first so-named body claims to be the oldest part of the federal government, with 1636 as its founding year — 140 years before the Declaration of Independence. From the kings' efforts also came various local ethnic groups, from New England's Swamp Yankees and Boston Brahmins to the Conchs of the Florida Keys. Folklorists from the British Isles have rejoiced in the traditions they have found preserved among them.

But predating all of that were the Spanish foundations — starting in 1567 — in Florida, Texas, New Mexico, Colorado, Arizona, and of course, California. The most obvious gift of the Most Catholic Kings of Spain were the local expressions of the Catholic Church, the missions and presidios they built in various places, and the descendants of their colonists and their various folkways. But in addition, land law in the southwestern states comes directly to us from Spain. Puerto Rico, Guam, and the Northern Marianas are even more steeped in these Iberian foundations.

Their Most Christian Majesties Henri IV, Louis XIV, and Louis XV of France also contributed a great deal to what would become the United States. As Mexico City was the centre from which Spanish influence came to us, so was Quebec for the French. But the Mississippi and Ohio Rivers were the means whereby the French settled the centre of the country. Most of

the area was overwhelmed by American and European immigrants after independence, but isolated islands of Francophonie
from that time still exist in Michigan, Wisconsin, Illinois, Indi-
ana, Missouri, Arkansas, Mississippi, and Alabama. Louisiana
bears most strongly the marks of the French — not only in the
language still spoken and the culture enjoyed by Creoles and
Cajuns, but in the civil law based upon the Code Napoleon
(criminal law is common law as in the other states), and in
having civil "parishes" rather than counties.

This heritage survives among us in a thousand unacknowledged ways, from the fragments of "the King's Highway"
(Charleston to Boston) and "El Camino Real" in California,
remains of much longer royal roads of colonial days; to the
"prothonotaries" of the Maryland, Pennsylvania, and Delaware
courts; to the king's bench jurisdiction or king's bench power,
which is the extraordinary jurisdiction of an individual state's
highest court over its inferior courts, in some of the states
of the union. Indeed, the very concept of the "peace," which
justices thereof may bind miscreants to keep, or punish them
for disturbing, is in origin "the king's peace." The eleven Indian
pueblos of New Mexico stand in a feudal relationship with
the presidency of the United States, as symbolised by canes of
office issued by President Lincoln for each of their governors to
wield for his year in office. This was transferred directly from
the king of Spain (they also retain the canes he sent, centuries
ago). Colonial-era churches treasure whatever royal charters,
communion vessels, or the like that they received from their
respective sovereigns many years ago.

In a word, for all our republican zeal, our foundations are
monarchical. Nor did this influence end after independence.
Thousands of immigrants came to America from Europe in
the nineteenth and early twentieth centuries. Their former
rulers did not lose interest in them. The Habsburgs founded
400 Catholic parishes throughout the United States and funded
300 missionaries, including St. John Neumann. Many an Orthodox church in the United States boasts gifts given by the tsar,
as a goodly number of Lutheran and Reformed parishes and
schools received similar tokens from the Scandinavian monarchs and the Prussian king (later the German Kaiser). Today,
many ethnic institutions maintain relationships with their

respective ancestral crowned heads. Alaska and the Virgin Islands treasure various presents, from tsars in the first case and Danish kings in the second.

Despite the *cultus* surrounding the Revolution, there was a lack of American "conservatism" in the European and Latin American sense, something which our neighbours to the north and south did have, with certain repercussions on our side of the border. Both the Jacobites and the influx of American Loyalists to Canada gave a particular flavour to Canadian High or "Red" Toryism — to a great degree lacking even in the current British Conservative Party. Its paladins included Bishop Strachan and the "Family Compact" in earlier days, and George Farthing, Stephen Leacock, and the illustrious George Grant closer to our time. The French Canadians had their own strain, as demonstrated by such Bishops as Laflèche and Bourget, and François Trudel, in earlier days; and, more latterly, Msgr. Lionel Groulx and Maurice Duplessis. These would find followers among the French in New England and to a smaller extent in Louisiana. In Mexico, conservatism was expressed as defence of the Catholic faith and the country's Spanish identity against various regimes supported by the United States. Sinarquismo, an interwar expression of it, found adherents in America's Southwest — not least the redoubtable Pedro Villaseñor of Los Angeles.

In the early twenty-teens, all of these random facts began to align in my mind. In a sense, there is indeed a "royal America," but it is as varied as the peoples that make up the country itself. As the civic religion continued to decline — after a great post 9/11 gasp — I began to wonder how an American monarchy might have dealt with the two great dramas in our national history: the settling of the frontier and the status of the Indians on the one hand, and the abolition of slavery and resulting racial issues on the other.

:: :: ::

We may take as our point of departure the following statement from the *Associazione Culturale Identità Europea*, which we first saw in Chapter 1:

> By encouraging a EUROPEAN IDENTITY we do not intend to promote a "western culture" which absorbs and dissolves all diversities in a leveling attempt. On the contrary,

> our aim is to enlarge this identity beyond the European
> boundaries, thus recovering that large part of our conti-
> nent "outside Europe"—from Argentina to Canada and
> from South Africa to Australia—which looks at the old
> continent not as a distant ancestor but as a real homeland.[5]

In Latin America, after the shock of the conquest, Spanish
colonial administration saw the erection of two (eventually
four) viceroyalties, which in law was the equal of the kingdoms
of Spain. But they were further divided according to whether
an area was mostly Spanish and Mestizo or Indian into the
republic of the Spanish and the republic of the Indians. This
latter category encompassed autonomous territories ranging
in size from the New Mexican pueblos to the Principality of
Tlaxcala, ruled by its native princes. All of these autonomies
were suppressed by the nascent Latin American republics in the
nineteenth century. The French coexistence with their Indian
allies was proverbial, as was the British Crown's encouragement
of their settlers' rapacity against them. But with the treaty
of 1763 giving Canada to Britain, the Crown was as obligated
to defend its new Indian subjects' rights as it was those of
its new French-Canadian subjects. This was the origin of the
Proclamation of 1763 and the Quebec Act, neither of which
was popular amongst the oligarchies of the thirteen colonies,
thereby helping to cause the American Revolution. In contrast
to the settling of the American West—with the exception of
the Riel Rebellions—the consolidation of Western Canada was
relatively peaceful and equitable. Even those rebellions were
not against Queen Victoria: Riel himself led the Metis in the
name of the queen.

As far as slavery went, the Black Codes of the French and
Spanish required far more humane treatment of the slaves than
that which prevailed in the British American colonies. Even
there, however, during the Revolution, the king emancipated
those slaves who joined the Loyalists—hence the presence of
their descendants not only in Canada, but in Sierra Leone and
the Bahamas. Emancipation by the British, French, Spanish,
Dutch, Danish, and Brazilian monarchs was gradual and far
easier than in the United States. As a result, racial relations in

---

[5] "Manifesto of European Identity."

those countries, although not without difficulties, have been nothing as severe as we have had.

All of these historical considerations, alongside the increasing fragmentation leading up to the election of 2016, caused me to think along several different lines. One was the idea of building an American patriotism rooted in the United States as it really is, rather than dependent upon the dying civic religion. The second was an exploration of monarchy in the abstract. The result was my first (and, so far, only) attempt at a novel: *Star-Spangled Crown*. Set in a relatively close future, its conceit was an already established and functioning American monarchy, through which I was able to look at all of the aspects of Americana we have discussed here. Although I highly doubt that anything remotely like what is described in the book shall ever happen, it proved an interesting exercise in stimulating thought and debate.

The subsequent Trump and Biden administrations, the transformation of the European Union into a secularising superstate, the growing claims of Vladimir Putin to be the defender of "Christian values" while America and Europe appeared to be competing to make his claims credible, the rise of Viktor Orbán and other voices in Central Europe as seemingly lone voices of sanity, and at last the war in Ukraine pushed me along as they did everyone else. Moving to Europe in 2018 also helped crystallise my thinking about America, Europe, and monarchy, as did writing a biography of Bl. Emperor Karl. I became convinced that the answer to America's spiritual and cultural — and so political — ills lay in the mother continent, and there, in the lands of the former Habsburg empire.

From the time that I was in high school, I corresponded with Archduke Otto von Habsburg, and together with all the reading I described earlier, he was a leading influence on my thought. Standing as he did between two worlds — the *ancien régime* as exemplified by Austria-Hungary, and the post-World War II Europe of Christian Democracy, the Soviet menace, and the European Union — he had a wealth of wisdom from which to draw. He was a great one for maintaining ultimate principles while attempting to apply them effectively in the present, yet always remaining mindful that this present would soon pass away and be replaced.

Of the five European conservative points we considered above (Altar, Throne, subsidiarity, solidarity, and Christendom), restoration of Altar and Throne would never be permitted by either the Soviets or Americans, and the Catholic hierarchy itself tacitly abandoned the first after Vatican II. Surviving European states accordingly wrapped up subsidiarity and solidarity in vague "Christian values," and attempted to retool Christendom into what would become the European Union. Rather than pursuing a Habsburg-led Danubian Federation—which notion, originated by Franz Ferdinand, had been espoused by Bl. Karl, Zita during her "regency," Otto himself before and during World War II, and even Churchill—the archduke threw himself into creating a European Union that would incarnate the spirit if not the form of the Holy Empire. This was a vision which I came to share, while hoping that better times for Church and state might come.

Unfortunately, when that day seemed to arrive in the form of the fall of the Soviet Bloc, many such dreams were ultimately dashed—not least by the action of my government in vetoing restoration in the Balkans, as previously mentioned. Both the United States government and the EU itself slowly transformed over the following decades into machines for imposing infanticide, perversion, and latterly euthanasia on their own peoples, the newly freed Central European countries, and the Third World. Having died in 2011, the archduke was spared the sight of much of this. Two years later, Benedict XVI, who had shown such vision and wisdom in his pontificate, resigned the papacy and was replaced with a very different sort of pontiff.

Meanwhile, Vladimir Putin had been presenting himself as the defender of Christian values against the hideous strength rising in the West. Indeed, the current cold war between the United States and Russia stems from the reaction of President Obama in 2012 to Putin's anti-homosexual proselytisation law—long before the problems in Syria and Ukraine. At that time, given the way in which the Grand Duchess Maria Vladimirovna was allowed to travel about her homeland and decorate various government officials with dynastic orders, the suspicion rose that Putin favoured restoration as a way of reinvigorating Russia. These hopes reached their apogee in 2015, when Vladimir Petrov, deputy of the Russian Legislative

Assembly for the Leningrad Region, proposed as much; because he was a member of Putin's party, it was widely thought this showed Putin's approval for the idea. But that was as far as it went. The reemergence with official approval, since the Ukraine war began in 2022, of red flags and statues of Lenin and Stalin leads one to believe that Putin no longer favours restoration, if he ever did.

In the meantime, Orbán's Hungary — and Poland, until the recent change in government — have appeared as islands of sanity in a world gone increasingly mad. Alongside common-sense measures in defence of marriage, family, and public morality — and the reining in of their chief opponents, the judiciary and the media — the Orbán government returned the name of the country to its pre-communist title, restored the old royal names and officials for counties, began the rebuilding of the Royal Palace in Budapest, and employed two senior Habsburgs as ambassadors. There were echoes elsewhere in the neighbourhood, as similar social measures began to appear here and there in Slovakia, Croatia, and Slovenia. Czechia dropped "republic" from its name and rebuilt the Habsburg Marian column in Prague. In, with, and under all of these movements, the *cultus* of the newly beatified Emperor-King Karl spread. One began to hope that perhaps something approaching the old Habsburg-led Danubian Federation might emerge. Perhaps such a grouping could resist the blandishments of both Putin and Soros, and one day act as a catalyst for the emergence of the kind of Europe for which Otto and his collaborators had worked so hard and diligently.

In 2018, I moved to Austria to begin studying for an advanced degree in Catholic theology. I had visited a number of parts of Europe over the years and met with Monarchists in many parts of Europe on their home turfs. Certainly, both in America and Europe, I had partaken of the culture of remembrance — the beatification of Emperor-King Karl in Rome, and veneration of his relics at a number of shrines; attendance at molebens in honour of Nicholas II; the wreath laying at King Charles I's statue in Trafalgar Square and the Mass following at the Banqueting House; requiems for Louis XVI; the changing of the Guard of Honour at the Savoy Tombs in the Pantheon; and more of the like. But living in Europe would be quite different.

There were the annual audience reenactment in honour of Bl. Karl and Zita at Brandys in Czechia, where reenactment units are reviewed by a senior member of the Imperial House (and the similar Kaiserparade in Korneuburg); the annual requiem for Otto in the Kapuzinerkirche in Vienna, where he rests among his fathers; and the monarchist student fraternities in Austria, with their singing of the imperial anthem at every function. These and a great many other such functions showed at once a deep monarchist sentiment that lies near the surface of a great many people — not just for the Habsburgs in Central Europe, but for both of the branches of the House of Bourbon in France, for Duarte in Portugal, and for a number of others. But, of course, sentiment is not the same as a burning desire for change, although it does imply a hope of one kind or another.

Beyond that, my travels from Ireland to Ukraine showed how well deep Europe — that continent of innumerable local heritages, ways of life, and customs — still survives. The observation of the feasts of the Church year, the many church shrines, the local museums, the old castles and manors in which the old families still dwell or have returned, the local guilds and organisations, reenactment units, and so much else that are the common heritage, both built and intangible, of all Europeans, together reflect the Church and state under which they were slowly accumulated. The natural environment combines with these to form the ineffable landscapes that make up the continent.

My Catholic theological studies reinforced my belief in Christ, His Church, and His sacraments as the means of salvation and escape from the trap of the fall of man. But I learned a few things of strictly political importance. Chief of these was Christ's union, at the Last Supper, of the Davidic kingship to which He was rightful heir with the nascent *communio* of the Church — as a result of which Christian monarchy was seen as a participation in the kingship of Christ. This was symbolised by His washing of the Apostles' feet — a reenactment of which became a key element of the Maundy Thursday ceremonies at every Catholic court in Europe. Practised by the monarchs of Austria-Hungary and Bavaria until 1918 and Spain until 1931, the sole remnant — *sans* actual footwashing — is King Charles

III's annual distribution of "Maundy Money." This tradition began with a law enacted by Theodosius the Great in 380, when baptism became entrance into Roman citizenship as well as into the Church.

From that time, the Empire — East and West — along with the various kingdoms that grew up on her soil and those that followed in formerly barbarian lands, were seen as the "matter" of the Christian body, of which the Church was the "form" or soul. This was why Muslims, Jews, and heretics could not be full members of the body politic. After the Protestant Revolt, this mentality would be turned against those who held on to Catholicism after forms of Protestantism became the established churches in various countries. Of course, while accepted in theory by virtually everyone, adventures such as the split between Rome and Constantinople, the Guelph and Ghibelline feuds, and the investiture controversies in various countries centred on practical application of these ideas to specific contemporary issues. But these were not ideological as such. Ideology emerged with Martin Luther's revolt.

Nevertheless, as I have written elsewhere in these pages, it also became obvious to me that Catholicism, Orthodoxy, and the state churches of Northern Europe had each retained an awareness of certain important elements of that *res publica Christiana*. We Catholics were certainly aware of the necessity of an independent religious leader for Christendom — the pope; we also remembered well that the Church in each country must not only be independent but attempt to shape the countries in which it finds itself. This reality is encompassed in the devotions to the Sacred Heart, the kingship of Christ, and the queenship of Mary, and symbolised by national consecrations thereto. The Orthodox, despite the Russian Revolution in 1917, retain in their liturgy a clear ideal of the place of the imperium and monarchy in the Christian state. Despite the doctrinal problems attendant upon becoming governmental departments, the Protestant state churches of Northern Europe at least hold on more or less to the position in government and society once held by Christianity — albeit lost to the Catholics and Orthodox via many violent revolutions, and now through the passage of time virtually forgotten by them.

Looking at all of this, I came to agree with Fr. Aidan Nichols's call for a renewed monarchy and empire to "ensoul" the EU, as it were.[6] In short, a Christian, imperial, and free European monarchy made up of constituent monarchies is what he has in mind—and ultimately, this is the vision I have come to hold.

But in all of this, what of the land of the stars and stripes, my homeland? Where, in such a vision, do America and the other settler lands fit? In days of yore, the Americas, Australia, New Zealand, and various parts of Asia and Africa received the most adventurous, cantankerous, eccentric, or just bizarre elements of the European population. Whether as initial pioneers or later immigrants, they were the folk who, to a lesser or greater degree, did not fit in. Those who stayed behind were either content with their lot or not terribly adventurous. Ironically, although the outgoers had to deal initially with indigenous resistance, with the hardships of a far less civilised environment, and in many places with ongoing racial issues, they were spared the horrors that befell their more sedentary cousins in the mother continent in the form of the two World Wars and—for half of them—life in the Soviet Bloc. For all that, as Otto von Habsburg once remarked, "Europe really extends from San Francisco to Vladivostok."

This reality was for long obscured by distance, but globalisation is a fact of life today. It struck me a couple of years ago, having flown from Austria to the United States and back twice within a week and a half, that for my fathers, one trip either way was usually a life sentence. Thanks to the speed of travel and the internet, the two sundered halves of the Christian European people interact more and ever more. The evil effects of that reality are all about us, from Antifa burgeoning in the United States to Black Lives Matter chapters arising in Europe. But it is also true in a more positive sense. More and more young Americans are discovering the untapped riches of European Christian and conservative thought; more and more young Europeans are discovering the energy and organisational ability endemic to the former colonials. Together, despite the darkness of the hour, what may they not accomplish?

At 63, I have far more yesterdays than tomorrows. But if history has taught me anything, it is that, normally,

---

[6] See the passage quoted above on p. 16.

accomplishment of any great task can take a number of lifetimes. I am content to spend whatever time I have left in
helping today's young people accomplish the realisation of
the ideals we have been examining in this chapter, knowing
that I am unlikely to see the results. But by the same token,
Lenin, of all people, was quite correct when he said, "There are
decades where nothing happens; and there are weeks where
decades happen." On that note, I shall leave the last word to
Archduke Otto:

> Sometimes, like the Jewish people of the Old Testament,
> we think of everything in an overly earthy way. They
> were waiting for the Messiah as a king in the political
> sense, and we believe that the empire should be expressed
> in the forms known in history. In reality, however, the
> Christian empire is more the spirit of solidarity, the *pax
> Christi* idea, the practical implementation of gospel prin-
> ciples, the cooperation of free peoples who acknowledge
> the kingdom of Christ.[7]

---

[7] Gergely Fejérdy, "Politics in Light of the Eucharist – Otto von Habsburg at
the International Eucharistic Congresses," Otto von Hapsburg Foundation,
September 7, 2021, https://habsburgottoalapitvany.hu/en/politics-in-light-of-
the-eucharist-otto-von-habsburg-at-the-international-eucharistic-congresses/.

CHAPTER 17

The Only Love That Dare Not Speak Its Name

T HE DEATH OF QUEEN ELIZABETH II AND THE accession and coronation of King Charles III—and, to some degree, the death of Constantine II of Greece— once again sparked some popular interest in the world's oldest institution (although not, as we are assured by wags, the oldest profession). The recent publication of three excellent and very different books, dealing with very different aspects of monarchy—*The Habsburg Way: 7 Rules for Turbulent Times*, by Archduke Eduard von Habsburg (Sophia Institute Press, 2023); *Jacobitism in Britain and the United States, 1880–1910*, by Michael J. Connolly (McGill-Queen's University Press, 2023); and *The Enduring Crown Commonwealth: The Past, Present, and Future of the UK-Canada-ANZ Alliance and Why It Matters*, by Michael J. Smith and Stephen Klimczuk-Massion (Rowman & Littlefield, 2023)—are indications that, although continually attacked, monarchy is not merely fascinating for moderns but continues to be objectively important.

The first book I mentioned not only chronicles how one of Europe's most venerable dynasties managed to stay in power for so long, but how any family might use some of its skills for its own success. The second book explores how a group of late-nineteenth-century intellectuals on both sides of the Atlantic used a supposedly dead and irrelevant ideology to trenchantly critique modernity, in ways that remain relevant today. The final work shows how the British monarchy remains key to effectively animating a power-grouping that for the authors is essential if Great Britain, Canada, Australia, and New Zealand are to survive in the long run. These extremely varied topics are themselves indicative of the complex nature of monarchy.

Indeed, monarchy itself is not so easy to define. Mention the word, and the modern mind—fresh from being ordered to its room in masks by our freely elected masters, whilst the same

impose their racial, gender, and hormonal views on a more
or less unwilling society—immediately exclaims "tyranny!"
Images of Nero, Henry VIII, and a wildly distorted George III
are summoned up before said mind, subjected to an obligatory
two minutes of hatred, and then once again sent triumphantly
back to the mental recesses from whence they came. That task
accomplished, one is able to return to the weary world one
actually inhabits, feeling that at least one is "free."

And yet, there are still people who openly call themselves
monarchists. If the "M" word is uttered, the malefactor's hearers
often reply, "So, you want to be a lord or something? If we had
a monarchy again, you'd be nothing!" My favourite response
to this was made by an American lady living in Germany, who
answered, "What makes you think I'm something *now*? Do
you think the chancellor cares if you or I live or die?" There
was no answer to that. At any rate, let us put that argument
aside, as well as those who do indeed look for titles or orders
of knighthood as social accessories, and concentrate on those
who are serious about holding this unpopular view.

Of course, there are as many kinds of monarchists as there are
monarchies. This runs quite a gamut. Bhutan is a kingdom to
be sure—and as a Buddhist state was almost a theocracy—until
the king opted to create a parliament and surrender a great deal
of his power to it. Thailand and Cambodia are also Buddhist
monarchies; while the king has little political power, without
him, in both cases, the country would collapse into factionalism.
Japan's emperor is also severely reined in by his politicians, but
still is so sufficient an incarnation of the national spirit as to be
essential to the powers that be. The Muslim rulers range from
true absolutists, as in Saudi Arabia, Kuwait, Qatar, Bahrain,
Oman, and the seven United Arab Emirs, to the more Western-
style kings of Malaysia, Morocco, and Jordan. The king of Tonga
bears the distinction of being the world's only Methodist monarch; in Africa, Lesotho's king is a devout Catholic, while his
colleague in Eswatini is Christian of some sort but polygamous.
Throughout Africa, Indonesia, India, and Pakistan there are
various traditional sub-national monarchies that have differing
relationships with their respective colonially-created national
governments, although the princes in the latter two states,
having joined either India or Pakistan in their independence in

return for pensions and recognition of their titles and privileges, were defrauded of them by both governments in the 1970s.

But it is the European monarchies that interest most monarchists in the Western world. King Charles III, of course, presides over fifteen Commonwealth Realms, including Great Britain on a figurehead basis of sorts, as do his colleagues in Spain, Scandinavia, and Benelux. The princes of Monaco and Liechtenstein, oddly enough, have the most actual power over their subjects. Monarchists in those countries are dedicated either to maintaining the status quo or extending their monarch's powers in order to restrain the political classes to some degree, however slightly. The Carlists in Spain, Latin America, and the Philippines are a special case, which will be explained presently.

In the rest of Europe, of course, monarchists are interested in restoration, which—prior to the establishment of the Soviet-American dyarchy after 1945 that made it impossible—was a basic plank in the manifestos of groups or parties that considered themselves conservative or "of the right." Today, the situation in Portugal is fairly straightforward. The accepted heir, Dom Duarte, is actually the descendant of the older dispossessed Miguelist line, which lost the nineteenth-century civil war to the junior liberal branch—that branch's last member, King Manuel II, recognised Duarte's father as his heir. Moreover, Portugal has a body of monarchist thought of its own, Integralismo Lusitano, which puts forward the traditional, anti-liberal notion of Altar-and-Throne, subsidiarity-and-solidarity monarchy. Closely bound up as well with orthodox Catholicism, most Portuguese monarchists are part of the monarchist Causa Real party, which has branches throughout the country.

France, however, paints the opposite picture. The country's first problem is the daddy of all dynastic disputes, between the legitimist heir, *de jure* Louis XX, the duke of Anjou, and the Orleanist claimant, *de jure* Jean IV, the count of Paris. Although the legitimists have historically been the more traditionally minded, both heirs have come out in recent years against gay marriage and adoption, in favour of the Yellow Vests, and, basically, in favour of all that right-thinking Frenchmen believe. Both have a number of organisations that favour their respective claims. Then there are organisations, like the Alliance Royale, that believe the succession is a question to be settled

after restoration. It is also fair to say that there are monarchists of one sort or another in most Catholic conservative
organisations in France. Every year, around the anniversary
of the murder of Louis XVI on January 21, there are Masses for
him throughout the country. In these, both the underlying
unity and the visible disunity of French royalism is displayed.

Germany is a complicated case, because in 1918, in addition to
the Hohenzollern German emperor and Prussian king, there were
kings of Bavaria, Saxony, and Württemberg, and a host of grand
dukes, dukes, and princes who retained some autonomy under
the 1871 constitution and who were all deposed in 1918. Moreover,
the Kingdom of Hanover, the Electorate of Hessen-Kassel, and
the Duchy of Nassau — annexed by Prussia in 1866 — all had and
have partisans of their restoration. Despite the best attempts of
the current German establishment to associate monarchists with
the Nazis, the dirty little secret is that most of the resistance to
Hitler came from monarchists of one kind or another — a pattern
also true of Habsburg adherents in Austria.

Indeed, that latter factoid is one the Austrian establishment
wishes would go away, so the memory of the resistance in that
country is virtually forgotten by schools and the like, as is the
collaboration with the Nazis by socialist hero Karl Renner. At
any rate, monarchists in Austria, Hungary, Czechia, Slovakia,
Slovenia, and Croatia, while united in support of the Habsburgs,
are divided by questions of personality, policy, and operation.
But the consensus among them seems to be that a future confederation of states under the dynasty is the route to go. Such
a union would be strong enough, its adherents hope, to stave
off absorption by East or West. Poland, too, has a monarchist
movement comprised of several organisations — none of which
is committed to a dynasty, given the unique nature of Polish
monarchical history.

French, German, and Central European monarchism seems
positively stable compared to Italian royalist contingents.
The first division is between those who remain loyal to the
House of Savoy as the kings of Italy between 1870 and 1946.
An institution with liberal roots, its last king, Umberto II,
was nevertheless a devout Catholic and the last lay owner of
the Shroud of Turin. There is, however, a dynastic dispute
between Umberto's grandson Emanuele Filiberto of Savoy

and Aimone, the Duke of Aosta—and each has organisations committed to his cause. Emmanuel Filberto has no sons, and despite his attempt to make his daughter his heir, by Salic law Aimone will inherit one day. Simultaneously, the adherents of the countries annexed by Sardinia in the Risorgimento also remain loyal to the dynasties of Bourbon-Parma, Austria-Este, Habsburg-Tuscany, Habsburg-Lorraine (for Lombardy and Venetia), and of course, Bourbon of the Two Sicilies (which has a dynastic dispute of its own). Then there are such as the disciples of Attilio Mordini, who are neo-Ghibellines, looking to resurrect some sort of Holy Empire.

Despite the dynastic squabbles of members of the Romanoff family—the Grand Duchess Maria Vladimirovna seems fairly well-placed—it looked as though Putin was actively toying with the idea of a restoration a decade ago. Those times have passed, however, and any such future looks as far away as it did in 1988. The marriage of her son, the Grand Duke George, to an Italian non-royal has not helped.

Ironically, it is in the formerly communist Balkans that the royals are doing best. The Serbian, Romanian (despite yet another dynastic issue), Bulgarian, and Albanian royals all live in one or more of their old palaces. Despite the senior Mr. Bush's vetoing of restorations in Romania and Bulgaria, they are all playing a higher role in national life than one could have imagined thirty years ago. In Greece, in the wake of the recent death of Constantine II, Crown Prince Pavlos has returned with his family to live in their homeland.

Despite the extinction of the older line of the Spanish Bourbons and issues with the current head of the House of Bourbon-Parma, the Carlists soldier on under the leadership of his childless uncle, Prince Sixtus Henry. They still call for the party's traditional vision of the Spanish monarchy, rather than the crowned republic of today, presided over by Felipe VI.

All of which having been said, one might wonder: What could attract anyone to monarchism today? Surely it has been defeated, once and for all? Not by a long shot. There is, of course, the romantic appeal of monarchy, which should not be forgotten. As Charles Fenyvesi wrote back in 1978: "I am a monarchist when the sun goes down, and the scarlets and golds give way to an egalitarian darkness. It is a setting that inspires me to dismiss the insistent present and wander backward—to reflect, to revise, perhaps to regret. It is a time to remember a waltz, a quatrain of long ago, and to recall a lost kingdom."[1] Hence the popularity of Anthony Hope's *The Prisoner of Zenda* (New York, 1894) once, and *The Lord of the Rings* now.

But pleasant as such Ruritanian yearnings are—and monarchy evokes them as no other form of government can—they are far from enough to warrant political ideas, poorer though we would be without them. No, most of the conservative or counterrevolutionary ideas of Europe, from 1815 to 1945, are anchored deeply in monarchy. Ignoring it and its religious roots, you are left with what we have; a sterile "Christian democracy" that is now neither conservative nor counterrevolutionary. Without Altar and Throne, subsidiarity and solidarity have nothing concrete to hang on, and it would be better if this were realised sooner rather than later.

This leads to perhaps the most powerful roots the institution has in the souls of its believers: religion. For Christian monarchy, at its best, was always seen as participation in the kingship of Christ; and while there have been atheist monarchists, like Bolingbroke or Lovecraft, they are a small minority. Indeed, in recent years, the beatifications of Bl. Karl of Austria and Bl. Maria Cristina of Savoy, as well as the opening of the causes for the Servants of God Empress Zita (Karl's consort), King Francis II of the Two Sicilies, Queen Elena of Italy, and Madame Élisabeth, sister of Louis XVI and murdered like her brother—among others—has led to many devout people giving monarchy another look. There has been a similar reconsideration in other Christian denominations: the continuing veneration of Charles I among Anglicans and Ordinariate Catholics, and of the final tsar and other martyred members of his family among the Orthodox.

It may be argued that among many living royals, standards of behaviour are not as high as they were among their sainted ancestors. But often enough—considering what our free and democratic society offers us—*we* do not live up to the standards of their ancestors' subjects. Perhaps if we do the one, they shall do the other.

---

[1] Fenyvesi, *Splendor in Exile*, 275.

⊰ CHAPTER 18 ⊱
What Is Legitimism?

"**L**EGITIMISM**" IS A VERY CURIOUS WORD THAT
pops up in history. It has to do with questions fought—
politically or militarily—in many countries over the
past few centuries. Considering that it deals with the issue
of legitimacy—legitimate rule—it might actually have some
interest for Americans, especially given the contested character
of the 2020 presidential election.

Legitimism is a fairly recent phenomenon. On the surface, it would appear to mean nothing more than loyalty
to a particular royal line, even after its deposition by pre-
sumed usurpers. But there is more to it than that. Certainly,
before the sixteenth century there had been succession disputes, which pitted adherents of one branch of a royal family
against another; the most famous of these were the Hundred
Years' War between the closely related English and French
ruling lines, and the War of the Roses pitting the former's
York and Lancaster branches against one another. But despite
the strange paradoxes of those conflicts — Richard III's ultimate recognition of Henry VI's sanctity, and the French
opposition to the latter being led by St. Joan of Arc — the
combatants in these conflicts had identical views regarding
Church and state, the role of the monarch, and various other
issues that would, in addition to genealogical issues, animate
the future legitimists.

Closer to the legitimist vision were the various groups in
different European countries that arose to combat the Protestant Revolt — the Pilgrimage of Grace and the risings in the
west and north of England, similar risings in Scandinavia,
the Catholic Leagues in Germany, France, the Netherlands,
Switzerland, and the like. Their actions were in defence not
only of the Catholic religion but of the entire social order
that went with it — often against the sovereigns who were at
the head of the nation, but with no idea of replacing them
and theirs with some other clan.

All of these conflicts — the God-given hereditary right of a particular family to the rule of a given country, the religious requirements of that family, and its obligation to uphold the traditional rights, privileges, and obligations of all its subjects — probably first came together during what was once called the English Civil War. Now more accurately and poetically described as "The Wars of the Three Kingdoms," it pitted the Cavaliers of Charles I against Cromwell's Roundheads. While none of his opponents questioned Charles's heirship to his crown, they did dispute his right to rule on account of a number of issues that would animate future legitimists. Charles stood for what he conceived to be the ancient constitution of the Church of England: maintenance of bishops and eventual reunion with Rome. Against the centralizing desires of Cromwell, the king wanted to maintain the traditional governance of Ireland, Scotland, and England, and the autonomous institutions of the north and west of England. Further, he wished to prevent the enclosures, which were disrupting the lives of farmers across the country. As a result, the bulk of the royalists were Catholics and High Anglicans from the Celtic fringe and the north and west of England. Moreover, if they were defeated militarily, they certainly had the better of it in the literary and theological spheres, as shown by the Cavalier poets and the Caroline Divines.

But the classic legitimist mode was yet to be created; that would occur with the overthrow of Charles's son, James VII (of Scotland) and II (of England) in the so-called "Glorious Revolution" of 1688. His and his descendants' supporters, dubbed "Jacobites" (after *Jacobus*, Latin for James), established what has been the legitimist standard ever since. For the Jacobites, it was not simply that the Stuarts had a divinely ordained right to the throne as against the Orange and then Hanoverian usurpers. The Stuarts also stood up for religious traditionalism (Catholic and High Anglican), local liberties (in this case, opposition to the union of English and Scots — and later Irish — parliaments and governments), and maintenance of local ways of life. As with Charles I's Cavalier supporters, the Jacobites tended to come from the Celtic fringe and the north and west of England.

The transplanting of Britain across the sea was affected by these ongoing dynastic struggles: the last battle of the Wars of the Three Kingdoms took place in Maryland, and James II's overthrow saw the takeover of Maryland by the Protestants and the collapse of the Dominion of New England. The defeat of the Jacobite cause in 1746 prompted flocks of pro-Stuart Scots to settle in upstate New York and backcountry North Carolina. As tensions rose in the thirteen colonies during the countdown to the revolution, most Loyalist and rebel controversialists alike tried to justify themselves in terms of the 1688 settlement. But as Eric Nelson documents in *The Royalist Revolution*, a significant number of anti-government pamphleteers attempted to show that the king alone had the right to make laws for his American colonies, as the Stuart kings had authorised their settlement without reference to Parliament. But most of the actual Jacobites here rallied to the king's standard — with results similar to those of Culloden.

The French allies of the rebels in that revolution were bankrupted by their intervention — which had its effect in France when the government had neither cash nor credit for dealing with the Great Hunger of 1788. The resulting crisis led to the calling of the Estates General and the French Revolution. As with the Wars of the Three Kingdoms, the king and his supporters battled unsuccessfully for the old order of Church and state against bloodthirsty rebels. Once more, the king's men were concentrated outside the centre of the realm — Celtic Brittany, Normandy, and the Vendée in the West; and Lyon, the Midi, and Provence in the South. Here too, there was a restoration, with Louis XVIII playing the role of Charles II and Charles X that of James II. With Charles deposed in 1830 and replaced by his cousin, Louis Philippe, we see the origin of the word "legitimism" as a party name. Those who supported the usurper were called "Orleanists," after the branch of the Bourbons from which he had sprung. "Legitimist" was used to describe the supporters of the exiled Charles X and his grandson, Henri V.

For the most part, the Legitimists believed that the restoration had not gone far enough; amongst other things, they believed that it had failed to undo the centralisation imposed by the revolutionaries, failed to restore the ancient provinces with their rights, and failed to return the Church entirely to its proper place at the head of society. The Orleanists, of course, held the opposite of all of these things; as with the Stuarts and the Hanoverians, the dynastic dispute would be bound up with an ideological one. As the Industrial Revolution did its work in France and across Europe, the sympathies of Henri and his supporters were with the workers, while those of the Orleanists were committed to the wealthy factory owners.

Four years before Charles X was driven from his throne in 1830, a similar process was underway in Portugal. When John VI of Portugal died, his older (and more liberal) son, Pedro, had been emperor of Brazil since 1822. He sent his daughter — called Maria II — to reign, although she was a child. His younger brother, Miguel, now claimed the throne for himself, saying that Pedro had forfeited the throne for himself and his descendants by becoming emperor of Brazil. But as with the British Isles and France, there was a lot more involved than the dynastic issue. Miguel's supporters wanted a traditional monarchy, with the Church as the dominant social factor, local liberties against a centralising state, and so forth. Here also, peripheral areas were the strongholds of Miguelist strength — especially Portugal's extreme north and south. However, the liberals, led by a returned Pedro, were eventually victorious in 1834. They dispossessed the religious orders and settled Pedro and his descendants on a liberalized throne that would last until 1910.

The year prior to Pedro's victory in Portugal saw the death of Ferdinand VII of Spain. He had attempted to alter the law of succession of the Bourbons of Spain, so that his daughter Isabella would inherit the throne, rather than his brother, Carlos. The predictable result was another civil war, pitting the Carlists — as Carlos V's supporters were called — against the liberal supporters of Isabel II. The Carlist beliefs could be summed up in four words: *Dios, patria, fueros, rey* — "God, Country, Provincial Rights, King."[1] Once again, we see defended the traditional role of the Church, the old constitution of the country, local liberties, and an effective monarch. In opposition, the triumphant liberals secularised all monastic properties.

---

[1] See Miguel Ayuso Torres, "Spanish Carlism: An Introduction," *Catholicism. org*, January 27, 2016, https://catholicism.org/spanish-carlism-an-introduction.html; Eleonore Villarrubia, "Dios, Patria, Fueros, y Rey: The Story of the Spanish Carlistas," *Catholicism.org*, May 17, 2010, https://catholicism.org/dios-patria-fueros-y-rey-the-story-of-the-spanish-carlistas.html.

In 1831, Charles Felix, last male member of the House of Savoy, kings of Sardinia, died. He was succeeded by his much-distrusted distant cousin, Charles Albert. Liberally inclined (as witnessed by his abandoning of the Maundy Thursday foot-washing ceremony), the new king schemed to depose all his brother monarchs on the Italian peninsula — including the pope — and establish a unified and centralised liberal monarchy. Because of his role in the 1848 rebellions, he was deposed and replaced by his son, Victor Emmanuel II. Assisted by his wily prime minister, Count Cavour, over the next eleven years, through a combination of warfare and diplomacy, Victor Emmanuel would succeed in driving the Austrian emperor from his Kingdom of Lombardy-Venetia, other branches of the Habsburgs from Tuscany and Modena, the Bourbons from Parma and the Two Sicilies, and Bl. Pope Pius IX from the Papal States (he withdrew into what is now the Vatican). When the smoke had cleared in 1870, Italy was united, centralised, and anticlerical. But the adherents of the deposed rulers were called Legitimists; for another decade, the supporters of the exiled Neapolitan Bourbons carried on guerilla warfare. Starting in 1860, thousands of young men came to fight for the pope in the Pontifical Zouaves, which became a sort of Legitimist Foreign Legion.[2] After the final defeat in Rome, the Zouaves returned to their various homelands, spurring devotion to the Sacred Heart and Catholic Action wherever they had come from. One other result of the Risorgimento was the emigration of millions of Italians to the United States, Canada, Argentina, Australia, and elsewhere, in order to avoid both the heavy taxation and the conscription the new regime favoured.

The 1860s also saw our second civil war. The merits or otherwise of North and South aside, Europeans tended to view the conflict in terms of their own experience. For many liberals, the Union was seen as the force of light, seeking to liberate the enslaved. But to many legitimists, the Confederates seemed to be fighting for the same cause of local liberties that they were in their own countries. Thus, foreign volunteers

---

[2] See Eleonore Villarrubia, "The Pope's Legion: The Multinational Fighting Force That Defended the Vatican," *Catholicism.org*, December 23, 2008, https://catholicism.org/the-popes-legion-the-multinational-fighting-force-that-defended-the-vatican-book-review.html.

to the two armies often (although not always) divided into ideological streams.

When the American war had ended, the third great centralising struggle began. The 1848 revolutions in Germany had led to the establishment of an all-German parliament in Frankfurt, which in turn was divided into factions. Some wished for a loosely united Reich headed by the emperor of Austria, which would include some or all of his domains; others wanted a smaller, non-Austrian centralised nation with the king of Prussia at the head. But while this latter was favoured by the majority, it foundered on the legitimism of the then Prussian king, Frederick William IV, who held that, as it had been in the Holy Roman Empire, the role belonged to the Habsburgs. The parliament dissolved in 1850. A decade later, however, Frederick William was dead. His younger brother, the new King William I, followed his chancellor Bismarck, who led him and Prussia into a series of wars that resulted in expelling the Habsburgs from Germany, annexing several independent principalities and a kingdom (Hanover), and creating a new united German Empire in 1871. Its non-Prussian states were cowed, although their sovereigns remained nominally at the helm. Interestingly enough, it was Ludwig von Windthorst, a leading proponent of the exiled House of Hanover in the new German Reichstag, who was instrumental in founding the Catholic Centre Party. Also worthy of note is that it was to Austria that the exiled French, Spanish Carlist, Parmesan, and Neapolitan Bourbons, the Miguelist Braganzas, and the dispossessed Italian and German princes made their way. In a very real sense, Austria became legitimism's last refuge.

Two years after France's defeat in the Franco-Prussian War, Henri V, called the count of Chambord, was presented with the chance to regain his throne. In the end, he refused to accept it, because the government insisted on the retention of the tricolour — the banner of the Revolution, accepted by Louis Philippe — as the French flag. On the surface, his insistence on returning to the white flag of the Bourbon monarchy seemed like pointless intransigence. In reality, the flag question was merely symbolic. Henri did not want to be a liberal monarch as his cousin had been — superior only in his bloodline. When he died childless in 1883, he had reconciled with his Orleans cousin, and most of his followers recognised the duke of Orleans as Philippe VII. But the Carlist heir claimed the throne as a senior descendant of Louis XIV and a small minority of French royalists — the *Blancs d'Espagne* — accepted them. For the remainder, though, the indignity of accepting an Orleans as "its" claimant was sweetened by his taking on most of Henri's programme regarding the place of the Church in public life, revival of the historic provinces, regard for the plight of industrial workers, and the like. These ideas were codified by such thinkers as René de la Tour du Pin and Charles Maurras.

Ironically, the late nineteenth century saw a brief reflowering of legitimism in the country that not only first saw the birth of liberal monarchy, but under Queen Victoria was its greatest exemplar: the British Empire. As it happened, a noble convert to Catholicism, Bertram Ashburnham, 5th Earl of Ashburnham, became the chief Carlist agent in his native Britain, gathering funds and recruits for the cause. Inspired by his experiences with the Spanish, he sought to do something similar for his own country. Thus, in 1886, he cofounded the Order of the White Rose (OWR), which began the neo-Jacobite revival. To it and its later offshoots, such as the Legitimist Jacobite League of Great Britain and Ireland, flocked a great many artists and writers (including Catholic converts and Anglo-Catholics) on the one hand, and Irish, Scots, Welsh, and Cornish nationalists on the other. At the same time (and with the involvement of many of the Anglicans who were involved with neo-Jacobitism) there arose two groups concerned with reviving the *cultus* of Charles I in the Church of England: the Society of King Charles the Martyr (SKCM) and the Royal Martyr Church Union. The Order of the White Rose cast its net as far as the United States, where noted architect Ralph Adams Cram and socialite Isabella Stewart Gardner enthusiastically joined both the OWR and the SKCM (the latter's palatial home, now the museum that bears her name, was used by both for meetings). While neither official governmental disfavour nor disapproval by many Catholic authorities (excepting the neo-Jacobitism of such clerics as Fr. Adrian Fortescue) dampened their enthusiasm, there was one difficulty that came to a head in 1914. The Stuart claims had by this time descended upon Crown Prince Rupert of Bavaria, who was an officer in the German Army.

Three years before the First World War began, the second in line to the Austro-Hungarian thrones, Bl. Charles of Austria, had married Servant of God Zita of Bourbon-Parma.[3] Closely related as she was to Henri V and Carlist claimants, her father was the Sardinian-deposed duke of Parma, while her mother was the daughter of Portugal's Prince Miguel of Braganza. In a word, if the bridegroom epitomised the legitimism of Central Europe, the bride summed up all that of the West. As we know, Bl. Charles ascended the throne in 1916 and tried unsuccessfully to end the war and federalise the Empire. Sent off into Swiss exile, the Imperial couple tried twice unsuccessfully to regain the Hungarian throne in 1921, encountering stiff resistance from Admiral Horthy, the regent. From that time on, those Hungarians who favoured the return of the Habsburgs were called Legitimists.

In the meantime, the liberal line of the kings of Portugal had been overthrown in 1910. Since Manuel II had no heirs, he reconciled with the Miguelist branch of the family. At the same time, a group of Portuguese writers and intellectuals, influenced both by Maurras's work in France and the traditions of Miguelismo, originated a traditionalist Catholic monarchist school of thought they dubbed Integralismo Lusitano. Now, integralism, as our friends at Wikipedia inform us, is "the principle that the Catholic faith should be the basis of public law and public policy within civil society, wherever the preponderance of Catholics within that society makes this possible."[4] In recent years, integralism in general has undergone an upsurge in Catholic circles. While not all integralists were or are legitimists, the vast majority of legitimists were or are integralists — and this was particularly true of the Portuguese.

The Carlists in Spain had fought and lost three civil wars over the course of the nineteenth century and waged political struggle afterwards. In 1936, two things happened: the last of their heirs died and appointed Prince Xavier of Bourbon-Parma (brother of Empress Zita) as his regent; and the Spanish Civil

---

[3] For more on this holy couple, see Charles A. Coulombe, *Blessed Charles of Austria: A Holy Emperor and His Legacy* (TAN Books, 2020); Gary Potter, "Blessed Emperor Karl I of Austria and Empress Zita," *Catholicism.org*, October 25, 2004, https://catholicism.org/karl-hapsburg.html.
[4] "Integralism," Wikimedia Foundation, last modified January 20, 2025, 20:08 (UTC), https://en.wikipedia.org/wiki/Integralism.

War broke out. In the coalition that Franco assembled to fight the communists, the Carlists played a particularly notable part. But their joint victory won little for their cause, save freedom from Moscow.

During and after World War II, legitimists faced the same dilemma that was offered to the European right in general — collaboration with the Axis in hopes of gaining part of their own agenda, and sharing the ensuing ruin — or else resistance to them, forcing alliance with liberals, communists, and socialists. Then would follow the left claiming the credit (which was extremely grotesque in countries like Austria, where the socialists openly collaborated with Hitler and many Habsburg loyalists were martyred) and complete political irrelevance after the 1960s. In France, the respective activities of the Spanish-based Legitimist and the French-based Orleanist heirs led to a re-emergence of active Legitimism in France in the 1980s.

Today, there are small bands of legitimists in each of their former realms. What they lack in size, they often make up for in terms of division over either matters of outwardly obscure principle or else personality disputes. Adding to this fractiousness is the sad reality that for many of its adherents, legitimism is more of a sentiment than an actual cause. One might be forgiven for thinking that their ideas are irrelevant for their own countries' politics, let alone those of these United States.

But a great deal has happened in recent years — and doubtless much more shall. The locking up of much of the world's population in the wake of Covid and concomitant shutting down of their economies by "their" elected governments; the 2020 American presidential election, where at least half the population shall always firmly believe the incumbent president stole the election; and the truth made apparent through the Covid lockdowns that the Church has no real independence from the state but exists at its sufferance — which fact does not bother much of the Church hierarchy; all these have revealed an unpleasant truth. By forcing its subjects to wear masks, the leadership removed its mask as well. We live in a post-democratic age, awaiting whatever great reset those who matter decide upon for us. Of course, most of us (save the Irish) were not consulted when those same masters altered the definition of human to exclude the unborn and the elderly infirm, or of marriage, to include what our fathers regarded as perversion and to abolish its indissolubility.

Considering the high calibre of so many of the legitimist writers and theorists, and the heroism of their officers and soldiers, we should look more closely at the tenets these disparate groups held in common. After all, in a world that is groaning with lack of true vision among its leaders, it will be helpful to review those ideas that inspired such greatness. In essence, they may be broken down to five — allowing for the national and historical differences between them. In many ways, they speak to the attempts of the legitimists to update the core of medieval monarchy to whatever "modern age" they were living in. Here they are:

1. *Altar.* The Catholic Church must be the animating philosophy of society — defining the ethos and the rules whereby the body politic exists and conferring legitimacy and authority upon the sovereign via coronation and similar rites. The Church must guide education and social welfare, and her institutions must be supported by the state.

2. *Throne.* The monarch must have effective executive power — as, say, the president of the United States does — although limited by certain factors. As fount of honour and justice, he must ensure that his subjects are well governed, and he must assist the Church in her mission. Above all, foreign and military policy must be his specific sphere. In addition, he is patron of learning and of the arts and sciences.

3. *Local liberties.* The bulk of governing must be done at the lowest level possible. Only what cannot be done at the village or town level should be done by the county; only what the county cannot accomplish should go to the province; and only what is truly beyond the provincial authorities should come to the notice of the king's ministers. Local identities as expressed in art, folklore, and the like should be encouraged as strongly as possible. The more modern term for this is "subsidiarity."

4. *Corporatism.* The economic and social life of the country should be organised in such a way as to encourage class collaboration and strengthen ties across the class divides. The medieval guilds were an example of this. Rich and poor should see themselves as members of one national family. This is today referred to as "solidarity."

5. *Christendom*. The idea that all such states form part of a loose supranational polity hearkens back to the ideas of the *res publica Christiana*, the Holy Empire, and so on. Member nations were seen to have certain common interests, such as the security of the Holy See and of Christians in the Holy Land and mission countries.

Granted, all these ideas are a long way from the here and now. But back in 1936, forty years after joining the Order of the White Rose, Ralph Adams Cram, contemplating the failure of democracy during the Depression, the rise of dictators in most of Europe, and the New Deal in America, wrote an important article in *The American Mercury*:

> Medieval political theory was based on three firm foundation stones. One: that the object of government was to insure justice. Two: that society, from the household up, must find its focus in one man—father, count, duke, king, emperor—and in this solitary individual, society, in its several unitary forms, incarnates itself and achieves its dynamic symbol. Three: that all authority came from God; that therefore a king ruled by divine right, but this divine right gave no authority to rule evilly or unjustly.[5]

It was with this concept in his mind that he ended the article thusly (and some of these words we have seen earlier):

> And so, after this interlude of well-meant but futile democracy of the modern sort, we should do well to return to the old kingship. Not that of the Renaissance autocracies, which was the debasement of sovereignty, but to the elder sort under which a real democracy was not only possible but well assured. There may be liberty under a right monarchy: there has come a sort of slavery under the democracies of the modern form where a political oligarchy and a money oligarchy, now in alliance, now in conflict, have brought about grave disorder, social chaos, and the negation of the free and the good life, under the forms of a free commonwealth founded on assumptions that are baseless biologically, philosophically, historically, and from the standpoint of plain commonsense.[6]

Certainly, the problems Cram saw with democracy are far worse in a post-democracy. But applying legitimist schemes

---

[5] Cram, "Invitation to Monarchy," 483.
[6] Cram, 486.

to these United States immediately raises all sorts of issues. What is important to remember is that the old order to which legitimists were hearkening only ever existed in small areas of our country: southern Louisiana, northern New Mexico, and certain other fortunate places. In itself, it was not a conscious creation but the result of the centuries-long process of the faith transforming the pagan cultures of the mother continent into Christendom.

What, then, are we to do in the current climate? In the immediate — survive. Keep our faith and ourselves alive and intact through whatever storms the next decades bring us. They shall pass, leaving whatever wreckage they may leave. After that, we must strive to build upon whatever bits and pieces of the old order survive in our corner of the world, from the commons and town meetings of New England — however attenuated they may be — to the California missions. We must maintain local customs and observances, and whatever else is left to us from before. But holding on to these old bones must be combined with evangelising all men and women we can. Only then may such bones live, and our country attain whatever vocation God desires for it.

CHAPTER 19

The Aragorn Option

All that is gold does not glitter,
Not all those who wander are lost;
The old that is strong does not wither,
Deep roots are not reached by the frost.
From the ashes a fire shall be woken,
A light from the shadows shall spring;
Renewed shall be blade that was broken,
The crownless again shall be king.

—J. R. R. Tolkien[1]

HEN NEW YEAR'S DAY ROLLS AROUND, we are far from done with Christmas and its magic. Indeed, the twelve days land us on the Epiphany—the day of the Three Kings—and the season continues more or less merrily along until Candlemas on February 2. It is one of the few things remaining in our society that the vast majority of people can still find common rejoicing in—however obscure its origins and meaning may have been made by the dominant circles in that society. One is still reminded that "the King of Kings salvation brings," even as—in America, anyway—the Christmas decorations are stripped away in stores and replaced with St. Valentine's Day hearts. The immense varieties of Christmas customs in the various nations and regions of the world at once underline the distinctiveness of each and yet their union in observing the birth of our Saviour in their own particular ways. It really can be no surprise that in assembling the twenty-one volumes of *The Enchanted World* (Time-Life Books, 1984–1987), a sort of encyclopaedia of global folklore, its editors gave Christmas its own book—the only holiday to get one.

This enchanted time, dedicated to the birth of a king at once heavenly and earthly, has a great many monarchical overtones, not least because of Christ's royal status. The Three Kings who visited him are enshrined in Cologne's cathedral;

---

[1] Tolkien, *The Fellowship of the Ring*, 231.

their secondary place of veneration is their longtime shrine at
Milan's Sant' Eustorgio Basilica. Indeed, the Epiphany itself has
been a feast much loved by royalty. As Dom Guéranger puts it,

> The race of Emperors like Julian and Valens was to be fol-
> lowed by Monarchs who would bend their knee before this
> Babe of Bethlehem, and offer him the homage of orthodox
> faith and devoted hearts. Theodosius, Charlemagne, our
> own Alfred the Great and Edward the Confessor, Stephen
> of Hungary, the Emperor Henry II, Ferdinand of Castile,
> Louis IX of France, are examples of Kings who had a spe-
> cial devotion to the Feast of the Epiphany. Their ambition
> was to go in company with the Magi to the feet of the
> Divine Infant, and offer him their gifts. At the English
> Court the custom is still retained, and the reigning Sov-
> ereign offers an ingot of gold as a tribute of homage to
> Jesus the King of Kings: the ingot is afterwards redeemed
> by a certain sum of money.[2]

Even today, the sending of the three gifts to the Chapel Royal
to be blessed is as much a part of King Charles III's observances
as his Christmas speech and the trip to Sandringham church.

The latter part of January presents the anniversary of Louis
XVI's murder on January 21, the feast of Bl. Charlemagne on January 28, and, for Anglicans, the murder of Charles I on January
30, which are reminders of both the triumph and tragedy of
Christian monarchy. Here we see Charlemagne, father of Europe
and first Holy Roman Emperor, sandwiched between two men
who died for the very ideal of kingship; the triumphant Frank
exhibited a leadership deriving its authority from God and the
Church, wielded according to traditional laws, and in itself con-
tradicting the kind of leadership—grasping, ignorant, cowardly,
and bloodthirsty—that dominates the world today.

The romantic impulse is to look back at the monarchs of
yore, such as those cited by Dom Guéranger, and reflect on
how many, from Britain's King Arthur to Charlemagne to
Portugal's King Sebastian, are seen in the folklore of their
peoples as being ready to return in messianic fashion when
most needed by their erstwhile subjects. No less an author
than J. R. R. Tolkien made such a return or restoration key
to the plot of *The Lord of the Rings*. Aragorn, for so long the

---

[2] Prosper Guéranger, OSB, *The Liturgical Year*, trans. Laurence Shepherd (Newman Press, 1951), vol. 3, "Christmas: Book 2," 113–14.

wandering heir to the glorious throne in the style of Bonnie Prince Charlie, wins at last and, in a Charlemagne-like style, begins the restoration of a world wrecked by evil. It is a vision that has been acted out several times in history and is deeply rooted in the human psyche. Looking at the moral and mental midgets in charge of things today, one could hardly be blamed for wanting such a thing in our time.

At this point, one might look at our current royals—whether presiding over crowned republics or else attempting to live in a tragic zone caught between their ancestral roles and their forceful exile from public life—or at their heroic forebears and declare that the sons have fallen far from their fathers, as might be said of much of the nobility of many countries. However, this prescinds from a number of realities. Reigning royals have been trained to believe that the political oligarchy is the voice of the people, just as the voice of the people is that of God. For one of these to go so far as to cross "his" government would be unthinkable, especially as the majority of "his" subjects would probably believe the politicians' views of events, as happened in Sweden in 1914 and Denmark in 1920. As for those out of governmental office, the fates of Louis XVI, Charles I, Nicholas II, and Bl. Karl cannot help but remind them of the price of a failed attempt at recovering the throne. Even if, as with Bonnie Prince Charlie, they emerged with their lives whole and intact, they might lose all that they have, often painstakingly built up in their private lives. And for what?

The sad truth is that, as with the British Isles in 1660, France in 1815, and Spain in 1975, restorations are a tricky business and rarely survive for very long. Then, as James II and Charles X found out, there lies the long road back into exile. With Spain, of course, the monarchy has held on so far, but today its socialist prime minister is happy to exchange the pardon of ongoing treason in return for power. Why would any sane person want to go that route?

To be sure, the entire power structure is stacked against any monarch who would either regain his ancestral lands or else preside over them, as the president does over our United States. Is it not entirely impractical, a species of LARPing, to imagine—let alone hope—that we might ever be ruled by something better than what we have?

Perhaps. But Christmas is the season of miracles and of hope for things not usually granted. In every European country there is certainly a good deal of monarchist sentiment, sometimes because of particular rational arguments, sometimes out of deference to tradition, and often due to both. Whether one belongs to an outright monarchist group, observes the various reenactments of older and possibly better times, is a regular communicant at a church that still has concrete signs of long-term royal patronage, is part of an organisation founded under imperial or royal aegis, has served in a military unit created under such conditions, or whatever the case may be, there is a large body of sentiment out there in favour of the Throne. But the trick is transforming that sentiment into a cause believed in by a creative and intense minority. That transformation would seem to require the intense interest of the heir to the Throne.

The problem, however, is that so many monarchists are indeed dreamers and romantics rather than seekers after titles and knighthoods. As opposed to the current leadership, which, however disgusting it may be, is nevertheless entrenched in power, monarchists often seem unrealistic—sometimes to the point of insanity—even to those whose cause they espouse. To take command of such material and attempt a true change of system with it would require an incredible amount of heroism from the respective heir. While heroism is indeed a wonderful thing, we have no right to demand it of anyone save ourselves. God alone has the right to ask any heir to try to play the role of Aragorn; we may not.

And yet, as Soros and Putin circle the globe like punch-drunk fighters, the spectre of nuclear war looms. How long things can go on this way is not a question that can be answered; that it is impossible to continue indefinitely is certain. If nothing better occurs to supplant the current system, it will collapse, and something else shall arise from it. It is impossible to forecast from the current cast of players what it might be and what part any struggle between native Europeans and Muslims might play on the European stage. In all likelihood, however, it will feature some sort of despotism.

In 1920, Hilaire Belloc foretold that Britain, having lost its aristocracy, would either descend into anarchy or regain an effective monarchy:

> But if in the alternative Monarchy comes, it may come
> in any one of a thousand ways — through the unexpected
> development of a new institution, or of an old institution,
> or through the resurrection of a dead institution.
>
> It may come (and that would be the best way, because
> the most continuous) through the return to power of what
> is now the Hereditary House. Or it may come through an
> elective machinery. Or it may come through the accidental
> popularity of one man in some important crisis of the
> commonwealth: or in any other way.[3]

Now, Belloc was speaking here of Britain alone, and his idea
of monarchy encompassed such self-made men as Bonaparte
and Cromwell. But beyond continuity, there is another reason
why the current heirs throughout Europe would be better candidates for rulers than the sort of self-made men who have so
often succeeded them. Their diffidence toward their positions
reminds us that those who passionately want to rule are very
often the least fit to do so.

If one or all the heirs from Portugal to Russia were to pull
themselves together and devise some means for taking power
from the faltering hands of its current holders, they would need
subjects as brave and heroic as they themselves would have to
be for such a venture to succeed. In a word, their peoples — or
at least a sufficient percentage of them — would have to be
worthy of having decent rulership. That is to say, we would
have to be willing to match them in terms of self-sacrifice for
the common good if we wanted them to do so. That willingness,
that worthiness, might be a tremendous fantasy.

But it may not be. History does not flow only in one direction but along many paths. The monarchy of the future would
not be a repeat of what has gone before, but it would retain
or restore elements of it. Monarchy is as much a part of the
European soul as is Christianity; one might see a new Europe as
a federation of kingdoms under an empire. Each realm would
combine subsidiarity in internal affairs with a king who has
sufficient power to prevent his subjects from exploiting, rob-
bing, or murdering each other. At the apex of this new Europe
would be an actual wearer of Charlemagne's crown, a son of
the double eagle, charged with maintaining the peace, order,

---

[3] Hilaire Belloc, *The House of Commons and Monarchy* (George Allen & Unwin, 1920), 188.

and justice of this new Christendom. As Karl von Habsburg
has written,

> The principle of the "Reichsidee" cannot be translated.
> Today I cannot talk to a French person about the *idée
> impériale* because for him it is Napoleon. I can't talk to
> an Englishman about the *imperial idea* because he imme-
> diately thinks of some Maharajas. One has to treat the
> concept in the German sense of the Reich-idea, namely,
> as a supranational legal order that applies to all citizens.[4]

Of course, all of this may indeed be the purest fantasy, and we
may be doomed to follow along the route of ruin and decay
delineated by our current leadership. But in the latter weeks
of the Christmas season, we would do well to remember two
things. First, the anniversaries of Louis XVI, Bl. Charlemagne,
and Charles I offer a great deal for meditating on what rulers
can and ought to be. Second, regardless of whether or not
any earthly monarchies are restored, the king whose birth we
are celebrating shall return. On that day of wrath, may all of
us — commoner or noble, Royal or journalist — be able to loyally
hail Him, who is our judge as well as king.

---

[4] Karl von Habsburg, "Europa, die Freiheit und die Geopolitik," June 14, 2019,
http://bit.ly/4iVOu4v; translation mine.

CHAPTER 20
After the Crowning

> There is an evil which I have seen under the sun, as an error which proceedeth from the ruler: Folly is set in great dignity, and the rich sit in low place. I have seen servants upon horses, and princes walking as servants upon the earth.
>
> Ecclesiastes 10:5–7 (KJV)

AS ALL THE WORLD KNOWS, CHARLES, THIRD of the name, of the United Kingdom of Great Britain and Northern Ireland, Canada, Australia, New Zealand, and of his other realms and territories, was crowned king May 6, 2023. Oceans of commentary—pro and con, and ranging from the insightful to the idiotic—poured forth before and after the event, and shall continue to do so. Having closely followed the career of the former prince of Wales for over three decades, this writer feels compelled to throw in his own two cents—not merely about the coronation itself but about what it might mean for monarchy in the Commonwealth and across Europe.

For decades, it was very fashionable to denigrate the former prince of Wales as anything from a moron to a weirdo; the breakup of his marriage with Princess Diana and his relationship with Camilla were additionally used to attack him by press lord Rupert Murdoch (himself no paragon of marital virtue). As against this tide of calumny and detraction were the actual things the prince said and did in pursuit of his goals. These were well expressed in a letter he wrote to Tom Shebbeare, director of the Prince's Trust, on January 21, 1993:

> I have no "political" agenda—only a desire to see people achieve their potential; to be decently housed in a decent, civilised environment that respects the cultural and vernacular character of the nation; to see this country's real talents (especially inventiveness and engineering skills) put to best use in the *best* interests of the country and the world (at present they are being disgracefully wasted

through lack of co-ordination and strategic thinking); to
retain and value the infrastructure and cultural integrity
of rural communities (where they still exist) because of the
vital role they play in the very *framework* of the nation and
the care and management of the countryside; to value and
nurture the highest standards of military integrity and
professionalism, as displayed by our armed forces, because
of the role they play as an insurance scheme in case of
disaster; and to value and retain our uniquely special
broadcasting standards which are renowned throughout
the world.

The final point is that I have always wanted to roll back
some of the more ludicrous frontiers of the 60s in terms
of education, architecture, art, music, and literature, not
to mention agriculture!

Having read this through, no wonder they want to
destroy me, or get rid of me...![1]

He has continued to push this agenda in the decades since,
and this writer cannot help but wonder how His Majesty will
attempt to forward it within the constitutional restraints every
British monarch has had to work within since 1688 — and even
more since 1783. In that year, the American Revolution not only
created a new country but shattered George III's attempts at
constitutional reform. The victory of the rebels in the colonies
and the Whig oligarchs at home resulted in a situation aptly
summed up by historian Eric Nelson in a quotation we saw in
Chapter 1, that henceforth "on one side of the Atlantic, there
would be kings without monarchy; on the other, monarchy
without kings."[2] It is this situation that Charles III has inherited from his mother.

The coronation itself, despite certain elements this writer
could have done without, was by and large a reaffirmation
of the values that Christian monarchy has always stood for.
After taking the oath, the king offered a prayer of his own
composition:

God of compassion and mercy whose Son was sent not to
be served but to serve, give grace that I may find in thy
service perfect freedom and in that freedom knowledge
of thy truth. Grant that I may be a blessing to all thy

[1] Jonathan Dimbleby, *The Prince of Wales: A Biography* (Little, Brown & Co.,
1994), 493–94.
[2] Nelson, *The Royalist Revolution*, 232.

children, of every faith and conviction, that together we may discover the ways of gentleness and be led into the paths of peace. Through Jesus Christ our Lord. Amen.[3]

Altogether, it struck me as I watched on television that it would be difficult — taking together the sentiments expressed in letter and prayer — to find an individual in public life with more benevolent intentions toward his peoples.

Following this, the archbishop of Canterbury bestowed the sword of offering upon the king with these words:

> With this sword do justice, stop the growth of iniquity, protect the holy Church of God and all people of good-will, help and defend widows and orphans, restore the things that are gone to decay, maintain the things that are restored, punish and reform what is amiss, and confirm what is in good order: that doing these things you may be glorious in all virtue; and so faithfully serve our Lord Jesus Christ in this life, that you may reign for ever with him in the life which is to come. Amen.[4]

I could not help but ponder how much better off the king's subjects would be if their new sovereign really had the power to do all these things. It also struck me how closely this formula resembled that uttered by the archbishop of Esztergom when he gave the sword to Bl. Karl at his 1916 coronation in Budapest:

> Accept this sword through the hands of bishops, who unworthy, yet consecrated by the authority of the holy apostles, impart it to you by divine ordinance for the defense of the faith of the holy Church and remember the words of the psalmist, who prophesied, saying, "Gird yourself with your sword upon your thigh, O most mighty one," that by it you may exercise equity, powerfully destroying the growth of iniquity, and protect the holy Church of God and his faithful people. Pursue false Christians, no less than the unfaithful, help and defend widows and orphans, restore those things which have fallen into decay and maintain those things thus restored, avenge injustice and confirm good dispositions, that doing this, you may be glorious in the triumph of justice and may reign forever with the Savior of the world,

---

[3] "The Authorised Liturgy for the Coronation Rite of His Majesty King Charles III," The Church of England, May 6, 2023, https://www.royal.uk/sites/default/files/documents/2023-05/23-24132%20Coronation%20Liturgy_05%20May_0.pdf.
[4] "The Authorised Liturgy," *The Church of England*.

whose image you bear, who with the Father and the Holy
Spirit, lives and reigns, forever and ever. Amen.[5]

The similarity between the two formulae comes from the fact
that both rites are of Catholic origin, and each reflects what
medieval Catholics demanded of and hoped for from their
monarchs.

But these words were said to Bl. Emperor-King Karl I of
Austria-Hungary with some realistic hope that he might actually be able to achieve these high goals; we, living a century
later, know that treason by so many of his subjects, betrayal by
his German allies, and the implacable opposition of Woodrow
Wilson would doom his attempts to do so. When Canterbury's
archbishop uttered them to Charles III of Great Britain and
Northern Ireland and his other Realms and Territories, it was
not and could not be so. Bl. Karl's predecessor, Franz Joseph,
memorably described the duty rendered upon him by his coronation as an obligation "to protect my people from their politicians."[6] Where Karl tried with might and main to do this—and
in the end lost his life by so doing—it is unthinkable that the
new king should do so, whether in London, Ottawa, Canberra,
Wellington, or any of his other capitals. The politicians and
their masters, that is to say, Parliament, are sovereign, and he
and his have reigned solely at their sufferance for centuries.
These chains are the more insufferable when comparing His
Majesty's qualities to those of the vast majority of his mother's
prime ministers. Save for a few exceptions (Churchill, Thatcher,
Diefenbaker, and Menzies, perhaps), Charles III towers above
them in terms of personal qualities and—as the notorious
"black spider" memos showed—caring for the average subject.

But it would be unfair to blame only the British and Commonwealth political oligarchs. Every constitutional monarchy
in Europe—Spain, Norway, Denmark, Sweden, the Netherlands,
Belgium, and Luxembourg—offers similar patterns. Sooner or
later, the monarchs lost their powers to protect their peoples
from elected officials who claimed loyalty to both sovereign
and people, but in reality served neither. Gustav V of Sweden
clashed with his government over the 1914 Courtyard Speech;

---

[5] Coulombe, *Blessed Charles of Austria*, 151–52.
[6] Lukes, *On the Edge*, 17.

Denmark's Christian X in the Easter Crisis of 1920; Belgian King Baudouin I over the abortion issue in 1990, and most recently Luxembourg's Grand Duke Henri with his "Christian" Democratic prime minister on euthanasia. Each of these ended in defeat for the monarch involved, and so was hailed as a victory for "democracy."

In each case, it was the monarch who was, objectively speaking, right, and "his" government wrong. The gradual and continual erosion of what are called the reserve powers in these monarchies correlate with the growth of democracy. In reality, this means the removal of any restraint whatsoever on those who have learned to manipulate the electoral process and the citizenry it supposedly serves. In executive republics, the presidential veto is a constant threat that helps to ensure that legislation is likelier to serve the populace, but it is wielded for political considerations. If the royal assent was not a given but something which could be won only by proving to the sovereign that the measure was worthwhile, the quality of legislation would improve wildly.

Looking at those countries in Europe that have lost their monarchies, one sees two realities. The first—apart from those who died for their people, such as Charles I, Louis XVI, Nicholas II, and Bl. Karl himself—is the long line of monarchs who chose exile over allowing bloody civil wars to be waged on their behalf. Such were France's Charles X, Sweden-Norway's Oscar II, Portugal's Manuel II, Spain's Alfonso XIII, Italy's Umberto II, Romania's Michael, Belgium's Leopold III, and most recently, Greece's Constantine II. Of course, it might seem to some that such conflict might have been better than what eventuated in those countries afterwards. While a professional in political life might make such a calculation, it is much harder for someone trained from birth to think of his subjects as his children. Certainly, the bloodshed in the Wars of the Three Kingdoms, the Jacobite risings, the counterrevolutions across Europe from 1789 to 1815, the counterrevolutions of 1848, and the Miguelist and Carlist wars might give pause to those in whose cause such blood might once again be shed.

This leads to the second consideration. Many of today's European royals do not have the purest lifestyles—something their opponents gleefully point out, even though they are often in favour of far deeper vices. I would be the last to defend such aberrations. Truly, if you compare the current crop to the many saints among their ancestors, most are certainly found wanting.

But that would be an unfair comparison. Far more realistic is how they stack up against the current crop of politicos feeding at the public tough in our various countries — those who locked us in our rooms, masked us, and threatened us with the law if we refused dangerous vaccinations. Both claimants to the French throne — the Legitimist duke of Anjou and the Orleanist count of Paris — sided with the Yellow Vests and were against same-sex "marriage." Can anyone deny that either would be a huge improvement in the Elysée Palace over Macron? Much the same could be said about the current claimants in comparison with the resident of any presidential palace across the continent, from Lisbon to Moscow. Even Budapest cannot be seen in isolation from Vienna, Prague, Ljubljana, Bratislava, and Zagreb. Restoration would be Orbán's crowning achievement, so to speak.

A much sadder comparison, of course, would be that of the subjects of the great monarchs of the past with their latter-day descendants, that is to say, our own precious selves. Our fathers built the great countries of Europe alongside the ancestors of today's royals; but the words of Moeller van den Broeck haunt me: "Germany ceased to have kings when the Germans ceased to be a kingly people." Such could be said of any nation in Europe or any of her daughter nations across the seas. Let us pray and work to deserve better than the rulers we now have. As Charles III is the first king since 1685 to be anointed with chrism that Catholics and Orthodox believe to be valid, let us pray that he is able to live up to the proud words of the coronation. And let us be ready to support him in the inevitable conflict with the oligarchs if he does so.

✦CHAPTER 21✦

Hailing the Chiefs

$\mathbb{T}$ HE AMERICAN CIVIC RELIGION HAS A WHOLE
year's worth of lesser and greater feasts on its parali-
turgical calendar: Flag Day, Independence Day, Memorial Day, Labor Day, Loyalty Day, Constitution Day, Four Chaplains Day, Thanksgiving Day, and quite a number more. But
the Monday nearest February 22—often called Presidents' Day,
but still legally Washington's birthday—points up a particularly
American custom: the semi-deification of our past presidents
(at least by their supporters). Their birthplaces are treasured
as shrines, the more recent have libraries and museums to
which their remaining faithful may make pilgrimage, and their
memorials and monuments—especially the favoured few in
Washington, DC—are important temples of the national faith.

February has two important presidential birthdays in addition to George Washington's: Abraham Lincoln's and Ronald Reagan's. On January 30, death day of the martyred King
Charles I, we also have Franklin D. Roosevelt's natal day. Arguably, this quartet are the most important of our presidential
band (although cases can certainly be made for Thomas Jefferson and Theodore Roosevelt, as Mount Rushmore attests, as well
as Woodrow Wilson and JFK). As the National Park Service's
website tells us in its introduction to the presidential sites:

> American presidents seem bigger than life. But many
> were just ordinary citizens who found themselves in the
> right place at the right time. They had the right ideas
> and qualities to become president of the United States.
> The National Park Service preserves the journeys that
> influenced these leaders and protects the experiences that
> have grown our nation. Discover the places and stories of
> presidents—before, during, and after their time in office.[1]

As might be supposed, the White House, as the centre of this
most awesome of all earthly institutions, stands as the focal

---

[1] "Presidents: Hail to the Chief," National Park Service, accessed February 6,
2025, https://www.nps.gov/subjects/presidents/index.htm.

point of veneration. Just as with Buckingham Palace, the Palais d'Élysée, the Kremlin, or any other residence of heads of state and government, the White House is the venue for the various rituals of the government's ceremonial year. Here, the chief executive receives the letters of credence of new ambassadors, pardons two Thanksgiving turkeys, lights the National Christmas Tree, and presides over the annual Easter Egg Roll. To St. Matthew's Cathedral will he go with the justices of the Supreme Court for the annual Red Mass, occasionally to St. John's in Lafayette Square (the "Church of the Presidents") for worship, and to the Washington Hilton for the yearly National Prayer Breakfast. He issues proclamations for various observances and presides over ceremonies of national mourning and prayer at the Episcopalian National Cathedral. Memorial Day finds the commander in chief delivering an address at the remembrance ceremonies at Arlington National Cemetery. At the equally venerable US Capitol, the president delivers the State of the Union address; unlike the speeches from the thrones made by the British king and his Commonwealth viceroys, it really does represent the president's views.

As might be expected, the presidential inauguration is as impressive an event as Yankee ingenuity can devise, with the solemn swearing in of the president by the chief justice serving as merely the centrepiece of a number of ceremonies, ranging from church services to gala balls and an enormous parade. Moreover, where British coronations are literally a once-in-a-lifetime event, we Americans enjoy this sort of thing every four years. Impressive as a president's entrance into history is, so too is his departure therefrom via state funeral. No one who has seen the riderless horse and the caisson, nor the lying in state, nor the funeral (in the past few years at the National Cathedral) cannot fail to be impressed by it all.

To be sure, as it has evolved, the American presidency has become important to far many more than those ruled directly by it. In the words of the Miller Center for its study at the University of Virginia:

> The U. S. presidency includes a small and select group of individuals who have led what is now the most important country in the world, humankind's most powerful military force, and a government that employs millions — and on whom many millions more depend.

> From this one office issue forth the critical decisions
> that affect countless lives around the world and shape
> the course of history. Only this small club of leaders, and
> those closest to them, could truly understand the power
> of the presidency and what it means to wield it.[2]

As might well be understood, this thoroughly American
product is the envy of the political class across the planet.
Throughout Latin America, Africa, Russia, and even France
(since the birth of the Fifth Republic in 1958), executive presidencies of all creeds and colours have striven to imitate the
success of George Washington's legacy. From Buenos Aires'
Casa Rosada to Pretoria's Mahlamba Ndlopfu, mediocre figures in presidential sashes strut and fret their hour upon
the stage and then are heard no more. But whilst they do so,
they enjoy their perks, reward their friends, and punish their
enemies as they choose.

But in most of Europe and in those Commonwealth republics that have not shifted to the executive model, a much
different style of presidency prevails — one that manages to
have the defects of both executive presidencies and constitutional monarchies, without the benefits of either. On the
one hand, instead of being either directly elected or brought
to power through a coup, as are most executive presidents,
such a chief of state is generally chosen by one or both houses
of the country's parliament. In practise, this means that the
presidential residence becomes a sort of retirement home
for used-up politicians. His Excellency has very little power,
instead fulfilling the ceremonial roles required by the chief-
ship of state — opening parliament, awarding decorations,
encouraging the arts and sciences, dedicating plaques, and
the like. In all of this, he functions much like the remaining constitutional monarchs in Europe, Japan, and elsewhere.
Indeed, he often lives in one or two of the old imperial or royal
residences, surrounded by guards whose unit lineages claim
descent from those that formerly guarded the Lord's anointed,
and whose uniforms often hearken back to that time.

The problem with such folk is that, at the end of the day,
they are not monarchs. As the creation of one or another

---

[2] "About The Miller Center: Who We Are," University of Virginia, February 6,
2025, https://millercenter.org/about/who-we-are.

political party, they are not living representatives of the
nation's history and heritage, as are even the most powerless
of crowned figureheads. Such figures cannot serve as "living
flags," let alone constitutional guarantors. As Charles Fenyvesi
put it, "Regardless of his personal imperfections, a monarch
represents the majesty of history. He is an heir — a link in a
chain that leads to the Middle Ages that in turn connects to
antiquity and beyond, to the beginning of measured time when
the first hero slew the dragon of disorder and established the
rule of law."[3] This imbues them with authority.[4]

In those favoured nations that still boast figures nominally
at the helm, the truth is that the course is set by the same sort
of politicos who misrule the vast majority of republics, with
little or no regard for the wisdom of monarchical authority.
Did the king of Belgium refuse to assent to abortion? Depose
him for a day. Would the grand duke of Luxembourg not sign
a euthanasia bill? Strip him of the power to obstruct the will
of the current pigs at the governmental trough. Despite the
overwhelming political power they wield, however, the political
class in the remaining monarchies cannot help but gaze long-
ingly at the top spot that is out of their reach; whenever possible, they chip away at royal symbols and chew the remaining
bits of royal prerogative, all in hope of one day quietly doing
away with the dreaded thing altogether and taking what they
conceive to be their rightful place in the sun. Pathetic as this
dynamic may be in countries with a resident monarch, it is
all the more so in Commonwealth Realms. In each of these, a
large chunk of the political establishment (often enough in
both the "liberal" and "conservative" parties) is committed
to making the transition from stable monarchy to banana
republic — as seen most recently in Barbados.

So is there any alternative to these bleak vistas? Well, this
writer would not favour violent revolution — even those as
world-shattering and government-shaking as the Reuss plot
and the January 6 insurrection, which the rulership in both
Germany and the United States were mightily triggered by.
Yet even peaceful change would be resisted by those who have

---

[3] Fenyvesi, *Splendor in Exile*, 278–79.
[4] On the distinction between authority and power, see Chapter 4 and the
passage from Fr. Aidan Nichols on p. 16.

wielded their power to shut down the world's economies, lock their subjects down in their homes, and cover them with masks.

But change might come if a great many people begin to realise two important facts. The first is that the sort of democracy most of us have been taught to believe in — if not a heresy, as Lord Percy of Newcastle maintained[5] — is certainly a myth. The political classes, while certainly possessing talents the rest of us do not, are no more representative of "the people" than the actors and athletes the people pay to entertain them. As such, giving them the complete control they currently wield is, as P. J. O'Rourke once famously observed, "like giving whiskey and car keys to teenage boys."[6]

But another myth, held as widely on the right as on the left, is that the majority of the people at any given moment are virtuous, and if properly informed will do the right thing. The truth is that people are by nature fallen and reflect the society in which they dwell. When abortion was imposed upon the United States by the Supreme Court in 1973, the vast majority of Americans thought abortion was murder, albeit not so deeply as to do much about it. But decades of World War I and II veterans being replaced on the voter rolls by products of an ever-decaying educational and entertainment system has brought us to a situation wherein the majority of pro-abortion state constitutional amendments proposed in the 2020 and 2024 elections were adopted.

One might say that what is needed for equitable governance is a monarch combining the party-free national rootedness of the sovereigns of Britain, Scandinavia, Spain, and Benelux with the ability to defend his people from foreign foes, politicians, and each other. Restricted by a notional belief that he would fry in hell forever if he misruled, and hedged about with local and institutional liberties, such a paragon might well have a better chance of ruling justly than any of the various substitutes on offer today.

It may well be so. But if one looks at the various monarchs — from Charles I of the Three Kingdoms in 1649 to Charles I (and

---

[5] See Lord Percy of Newcastle, *The Heresy of Democracy: A Study in the History of Government* (Eyre & Spottiswoode, 1954).

[6] P. J. O'Rourke, *Parliament of Whores: A Lone Humorist Attempts to Explain the Entire U. S. Government* (Atlantic Monthly Press, 1991), xviii.

IV and III) of Austria-Hungary in 1922 — who offered to risk life and limb to defend their subjects from rapacious and cruel oligarchies, one is forced to stop and think. It is not merely that their various causes went down in defeat; it is that the descendants of those for whom they fought, suffered, and died continue to think of these tragedies as *progress*. Perhaps we must first renew our minds in the truth before we can deserve better.

CHAPTER 22

Wanted:
Real Leadership

HERE IS ACROSS THE PLANET TODAY A REAL shortage more dire than that of food and fuel, and a worse evil than inflation or unemployment. It is in fact a dearth of real, authentic leadership. Now, that might seem paradoxical, given that recent years have seen most of the world's population forced to do its masters' bidding, pushed towards masks and injections in most places (but away from the traditional Mass by the Catholic Church's leadership), and driven into war by the rulership in Russia and Ukraine. Certainly, the myth of democracy has never appeared more mythic than now. But to understand what we need, we must really comprehend what we have.

The first thing we must understand is that every human society that has ever existed has been made up of the rulers and the ruled. The former are always a minority and the latter a majority. To recall what was argued in earlier chapters, every society has a state Church, an established faith, an animating philosophy which—religious or not—gives the rulers their legitimacy and authority and sets the rules whereby the members of the given society play the game (or pretend to). The state may well be separated from *my* Church, but some body of belief fulfills the role, and the state cannot be separated from it.

A basic problem with our Western systems is that they deny these two omnipresent realities. This has the unfortunate effect of making the rulership irresponsible, in both the constitutional and popular senses of that word. In the Middle Ages, authority— the right to say what ought to be done—was concentrated in Church and king. Power was diffuse. With us, it is the opposite; power—the ability to make things happen—is concentrated, and authority is diffused among a semi-mythical electorate.

Given this unpleasant reality, it is no surprise that power is wielded today in an authoritarian manner. But what makes modern leadership interesting is that, regardless of its nationality (or, in the case of the Church, lack thereof), and in, with, and under its democratic cloak of semi-invisibility, it always shares three major characteristics to a greater or lesser degree. Each of these qualities deserves a proper look.

The first is, to be blunt, evil. I mean that our leaders tend to have no regard for truth, goodness, or beauty, but only the pursuit of power. The laws of God and man are utterly meaningless to them, save when those laws are convenient weapons to use against opposition (which generally means those of us who *do* respect such laws). The violation of these laws is no hindrance; even the blood of the innocent — whether unborn, ill, religious minorities, refugees, or elderly — does not stir their compassion. Indeed, our leaders can be quite bloodthirsty. Although they enjoy talking about compassion and all sorts of other virtues, they do not exhibit even basic kindness in their decisions.

One sure sign of evil is the twisting and confusing of virtue and vice. For such as our leaders, human beings have no value save as sources of money or blood in war. Because leadership is a good given to man by God, it is no surprise to find that, in time, evil leadership becomes the negation of that gift.

The second characteristic of our current elites is insanity. Now, I do not mean they believe themselves to be Napoleon or some other such delusion. But for a dominant set, insanity means that the visions in their heads are more real to them than not only the welfare of their subjects (being evil, that is not an issue) but their own self-interest. For example, for the Nazis, implementing their genocidal racial policies on the Eastern Front was more important than defeating the Soviet Union. Today, for many American political leaders, it is more important to have women in combat than to win battles. In the Church, hierarchs attack whatever element of the Body that shows growth; in local communities, mayors or city councilmen defund the police.

The third of this unholy trinity is stupidity. By this, I do not mean a mere vulgar insult. No, stupidity is the marriage of two other elements, by no means wonderful by themselves but lethal when combined: ignorance and arrogance. The ignorant person who is humble may learn; the brilliant but arrogant man can be annoying, but at least has some justification. The stupid man in charge knows little of what his office requires, and cares even less, because he believes that he is always right. He does not even pretend to make sense, simply wielding his power to force his hapless subjects into line—regardless of the result.

In any ruling set, at least to my eye, these vices come in order: evil comes first, followed by insanity, and last of all, stupidity—which, like the pale horse, brings Hades in its wake (Rev 6:8). These three qualities tend to reinforce each other over time, dragging the masters and their minions ever further down. Stupidity is probably the hardest of these three vices to live under. With evil, if a citizen can understand how his rulers are bent, he can work around their wickedness; with insanity, all he needs to do is to figure out the path of the mania and plan accordingly. But stupidity is wild and unpredictable. It can literally do anything; sometimes it even errs in favour of the good.

Of course, as earlier noted, evil leadership is no leadership at all. Neither is insane or stupid leadership. So let us look at their opposite qualities, which in fact define real, true leadership. The first of these, of course, is goodness. A good leader—that is, a real leader—is devoted to a cause above and beyond himself and his own comforts and desires. He is willing to sacrifice himself for his God, his country, his belief—and for those he leads, who are as precious to him as the cause which motivates him. Indeed, the well-being of both ruler and ruled are bound up together. The good leader believes that his own eternity may well depend upon how he tries to fulfill his responsibilities to his subjects.

The good leader is sane. What does that mean? It means he strives to see things as they are, not as he would wish them to be. If he truly feels his views can improve the world around him, he never leaves out of his reckoning the realities of divine and human nature. He ever strives to make his judgements conform to objective reality and is willing to surrender preconceived notions, particularly if they get in the way of his higher goal.

Lastly, he is intelligent. Humble enough to know when he does not know, he seeks to learn ever more about the situation he is dealing with. He can never learn enough about it. Such a leader will employ every means at his command to acquire ever more knowledge. He is not too proud to consult others.

Moreover, he tries to know his opponents as they are, rather than simply demonise them. If he can find points of contact, or at least understand the other side's motivations, he will. At the end of the day, while resolute to follow a course of action, he is not too proud to admit that he may be wrong. As a result of his humility, this leader is able to reason clearly and act decisively. As with their negations, these qualities feed into one another. Goodness will spark sanity, and in turn they together shall result in intelligence.

One might well ask at this point why our dominant classes have ceased to produce decent leaders. There are any number of reasons. The World Wars knocked the stuffing out of Europe's pride in itself and in its accomplishments, both as a culture and on a national basis. Then there is the decline of belief in God and the growth of functional universalism amongst the Catholic hierarchy, with the attendant implosion of that body's very *raison d'être,* at least in the minds of those who govern her. The rise of technology has helped spread among the masses — from which, ironically, a chunk of the rulership is regularly recruited in any society — a cult of comfort rather than sacrifice, which in turn is reflected in those in charge. The unbridled pursuit of our own comfort leads to indifference to the pains of others, and at last a sort of unthinking cruelty: this is how abortion has been sold. Of course, the very concept of leadership itself has been knocked about, with egalitarianism proclaimed as our birthright, as all the while real liberty continually shrinks and power is increasingly concentrated offstage, as it were.

The vast majority of those who dictate for us the course of our lives fall into the vicious set of qualities. Yet there is great virtue in turning our attention more and more toward the virtuous set rather than focusing solely on the vicious. Any culture or group ruled by vice is doomed unless and until the corresponding virtues make their appearance, so we must keep our eyes open for any such folk who emerge in the current wrack. Of course, most of us are mixed creatures, but when we see any scrap of these virtues in our fellow men, we should support them to the best of our ability. Moreover, we should try to cultivate goodness, sanity, and intelligence in ourselves.

Indeed, there is another quality we should try to add to the other three: initiative. Wherever we are, and whatever condition we find ourselves in, if there is something we can do to improve the immediate situation, we should. It is an old maxim of leaders in clubs and associations that if someone has a bright idea for a new effort, as soon as the leaders give him the opportunity to form a committee and do it himself, he usually disappears. Let us be different; let us come up with ideas that we ourselves are willing to carry out.

So let us begin again. Let us look first at the great epitome of leadership, Christ Himself, the great king who did not hesitate to lay His life down for His friends. We must venerate the great saints of civil authority — Bl. Charlemagne, St. Louis, St. Nuno Álvares Pereira, Bl. Charles of Austria, and the many other great saints who have been leaders as well. Let us look at the great leaders of the past for inspiration, bearing in mind that they need not have been perfect. George Washington voluntarily gave up complete control of the newly independent colonies and returned to his farm, an action which George III had earlier prased by saying, "If he did he would be the greatest man in the world."[1] Despite their flaws, many twentieth-century leaders presented these virtuous leadership qualities: Charles de Gaulle preserved France's independence against the best efforts of both FDR and Lyndon B. Johnson; Churchill held firm during the war; and Chiang Kai-Shek kept his flag flying into exile. Francisco Franco, despite what happened after his time, managed to unite the fractured Spanish right sufficiently to defeat the communists. One could multiply such examples by both time and place.

Moreover, we must inculcate such veneration on the one hand and admiration on the other into our young — at home, and in any schools we have influence upon. We must try to recapture the spirit of chivalry, which has always been the foundation of leadership in the Christian West. Whatever occupation we find ourselves in — fatherhood, mentorship, management, military, religious, or whatever — let us strive mightily to be good, sane, and intelligent. The great lack of our day is leadership; may God send it to us soon!

---

[1] Joseph Farington, *The Farington Diary*, ed. James Greig (George H. Doran Company, 1923), vol. 1, 278.

CHAPTER 23

A New Charter for the Nobility

You who seek the knightly order
Must begin your life anew;
Watch and pray you most devoutly,
Pride and wicked sin eschew;

Protect the Church, the child, the widow,
Strongly guard the people too;
Valor, loyalty and virtue
From a worthy knight are due.

—Eustache Deschamps, "The Knightly Code"[1]

LTHOUGH MY EUROPEAN READERS MAY WELL not have the same difficulty, many Americans tend to have a hard time distinguishing between (or even defining) royalty, nobility, aristocracy, gentry, patricians, and knights. Royalty refers to sovereign houses—families that have ruled supreme in various countries. In most countries, this has been a fairly straightforward affair. But in Germany and Italy, thanks to the vagaries of history, and despite a readily identifiable family of Emperors—the Habsburgs—there were a dizzying number of kingdoms, principalities, grand duchies, duchies, and so on. In the days before World War I, when royals married exclusively other royals (if they wished to retain their rights to the Crown for themselves or their children), these lesser princely houses were still "marriageable." This was not the case for scions of the lower nobility.

The titled nobility—princes, dukes, marquesses, counts or earls (an English title the feminine version of which, however, was still "countess"), viscounts, and barons—were a varied lot in 1914. The exact precedence varied from place to place. Moreover, the British system was very different from the continental because it was set up, in a sense, to end the nobility. From

---

[1] Thomas Walsh, *The Catholic Anthology* (The Macmillan Company, 1927), 95.

Portugal to Russia, all members of a titled noble family inherited the title. But in the British Isles, it was only the oldest son. His brother and sister would be "Lord John Smith" and "Lady Jane Smith"—hence the fictional Lord Peter Wimsey's older brother being the equally fictional duke of Denver. Their children in turn would be referred to as "the Honourable John Smith," as with P. G. Wodehouse's creation, the Hon. Bertram Wilberforce Wooster.

British or continental, however, there was a great distinction between noble families of medieval creation—*noblesse de l'épée*, in French usage—who had served the sovereigns as warriors in the many wars of feudal times and in the Crusades, as opposed to the *noblesse de la robe*, who had emerged in the seventeenth century as civil servants attending the growth of the modern state, officers in the more modern military service, and latterly as captains of industry and commerce.

The untitled gentry of the countryside and the patricians of various cities across Europe were seen as part of the aristocracy alongside the titled nobility. The gentry were the manor lords of song and story, and their medieval ancestors were often knights; when these were driven off the battlefield by gunpowder, one sort of knighthood became an honour bestowed at the discretion of the king—often for a price. Many such gentry escaped paying the cost of such an honour, which led to the custom in English of calling such a landowner "squire"—in the Middle Ages, this was the title of a candidate for knighthood who had not yet received the accolade. The gentry, like the nobility, held family coats of arms—this was what made one a "gentleman." In time, the behaviour one hoped would go with such an exalted parentage came to be called "gentlemanly." The original class were called "lords of the manor" in England and "barons" in Scotland; nevertheless, these titles did not admit them to the House of Lords in England or the Parliament in Scotland. The patricians, the urban equivalent of the gentry, were to be found in the great trading cities of Europe, where they were often members of either merchant or noble guilds. From that lofty spot, they looked down their noses at the titled nobility, who had their titles thanks to a sovereign's gift. The patricians prized their independence.

Knights came in many different varieties. Originally, knighthood could be bestowed by any other knight, a bishop, or a sovereign; but in time, the latter claimed to be the sole owner of that power. Nevertheless, the great independent orders of knighthood—the Templars, Hospitallers (later Malta), Teutonic Knights, etc.—retained their independence after the fall of Jerusalem, although the first of these suffered a terrible suppression. Then followed the knights of the royal orders, such as Britain's Garter, France's St. Esprit, and Burgundy's, Austria's, and Spain's Order of the Golden Fleece. There were also hereditary knighthoods granted, along with the British equivalent, the Baronets.

The nobility and knights were considered one class or estate in medieval society, with the churchmen being another, and commoners (which, depending on the country, often included the gentry and the patricians) being the third. In some places, the commons were divided, and there were four rather than three estates. But many were the pictures in the Middle Ages that depicted priest, knight, and peasant, each with a phrase indicating its respective position in the collective order: "I defend all," by the knight; "I bless all," by the priest; and "I feed all," by the peasant.

As the Middle Ages wore on, representatives of these estates took on ever more responsibility; if their emperor or king needed extra money, they would be convoked and asked to fund whatever difficulty had arisen. In England, the abbots and bishops ("lords spiritual") and titled nobility ("lords temporal") were brought together in one House of Lords. The House of Commons arose from the joint gatherings of the representatives of the boroughs with landowners from the various counties—the "knights of the shire." These developments were paralleled across Europe, with nobility and knights sitting in what became upper houses throughout the continent. Alongside the monarchs and the Church, the nobility became the great patrons of art, music, and dance, even as they pioneered hunting and dotted the countryside from Portugal and Ireland to Russia with their great houses and castles. But these arrangements would totter and fall.

The Protestant Revolt ushered in a series of internecine struggles, the ferocity of which bred an indifference toward Christianity among many of the educated. In turn, the resulting "Enlightenment" ushered in a horrific series of revolutions, the equally cruel ferocity of which was aimed especially at the Church, the monarchies, and the aristocracy. Even in countries relatively untouched by these conflicts, the nineteenth-century shift in so many countries from agriculture to industry eroded—and, in many cases, destroyed—the basis of the nobility's power. The two World Wars, the rise of the cult of equality, the fall of most of the European monarchies, and the reluctance to grant hereditary titles (only the kings of Spain and Belgium continue to grant them, as did the popes up to and including Benedict XVI) threatened the relevance and even the very existence of the nobility. In the communist countries and Austria (thanks to the ever-ridiculous Karl Renner), use of noble titles was made a crime. The head of the House of Habsburg was prosecuted for this by the Austrian courts in 2018.[2] With a virtual end to accessions to their titled state, the nobility of Europe have become a closed caste and far more exclusive than they were in days of yore. A few have become part of the faceless elite that presently dominates government, media, and business. Quite a number struggle to maintain historic houses and properties that they have held on to or regained. Across Europe, there are a large number of national and local nobility associations, many of which are part of the continent-wide umbrella group called the European Commission of the Nobility (CILANE); these organise various social and educational events. Those who still have houses or land are often members of societies belonging to the European Landowners' Association and the European Historic Houses Association, though there are, of course, many non-noble members of these groups. Many others retain only the name and title, often in the Americas or Australia, whence their fathers fled the calamities earlier mentioned.

Aside from fighting absurd Austrian laws, what is the point of the European nobility today? This very question was posed by a devout and politically active young nobleman from an old and distinguished family. I have given a good deal of thought to the question he asked of me, even though it is a daunting

---

[2] See "Karl Habsburg-Lothringen," Wikimedia Foundation, last modified January 22, 2025, 01:47 (UTC), https://de.wikipedia.org/wiki/Karl_Habsburg-Lothringen#Habsburgs_Verhältnis_zum_Habsburgergesetz_und_zum_Adelsaufhebungsgesetz.

question, since I am not a noble myself. As with most things, we must begin with first principles. For the nobility, that must be chivalry: service to God, Church, monarch, those less fortunate, and the weak. That service, paradoxically, also means exercising leadership—a leadership rooted in self-sacrifice.

Indeed, the world today is suffocating for lack of such leadership. Masters we have aplenty in Church and state, but not leaders who are willing to sacrifice their own pleasures and profits for the sake of their own souls and those of the people committed to their care. Obviously, one need not be an aristocrat to try to be such a leader; but it is far easier for those who have generations of such an ethos in their ancestry. Most of us are where we are by accident of birth, which is why one sees so many "dynasties" in the entertainment industry and media. Our inclinations and upbringing often point us in one direction or another. How much truer can this be for those whose fathers did great things for their fellow men?

Of course, decades of constant noble-bashing in education and media across the globe have left their mark, and many young noblemen are rather diffident toward acting as members of their state. Use of titles is ridiculed as snobbery or worse (unlike such things as the Academy Awards, or the mere acquisition of wealth). Indeed, boasting of a title is often evidence that the title is not authentic. But a thick skin is important to develop—not least because hatred of the nobility so often masks a hatred of all things elevated.

Many of the nobility carry on in quiet—and very often extremely local—areas of service, helping to conserve local heritage and the environment. Where this is the case, it is a precious patrimony, both for the nobleman and his neighbours. If one finds oneself heir to such efforts, they must be taken on gladly, as part of a life's vocation. We non-nobles must do our best to encourage them in what are often lonely and thankless tasks.

But what of the national and international scene, where their fathers once cut such figures in the Church, military, diplomatic corps, and government? Today, coming from a noble family can often be a disadvantage. Here is where one must cultivate, first of all, a renewed sense of personal mission, built upon the strong foundations of faith, chivalry, and the sense of *noblesse oblige* that shaped one's ancestors — as well as that thick skin and a desire to work with fellow members of the nobility. Being imbued with a deep and driving sense of purpose is essential if one is to avoid the malaise that today affects so many in those leadership positions.

For the rest of us, if any such leaders in those fields arise, we need to support them, as opposed to supporting the dreary folk who usually seek our votes, donations, or both. We must try to free ourselves of the anti-aristocratic prejudices we have been spoon-fed since childhood. Who will be more likely to give us better leadership at either the local or national levels: career politicians and bureaucrats for whom we are mere cows to be milked, or scions of families with names that are as much a part of the history of our town or country as the rocks and buildings? Surely this goes double for members of formerly ruling families.

The sad truth is that, just as many of today's nobility are not the men their fathers were, so also with us commoners. The clansmen who rose in the Jacobite rebellions, the peasants that fought the Revolution in the Vendée and Tyrol, and the White Guards in Russia were all as much steeped in their religion and national traditions as the titled heroes who led them. But today, the vast majority of us are cut off to a great degree from those traditions; few of us even have a useful trade. If we want the aristocrats to live up to their best traditions, surely we must live up to ours. For the past two and a half centuries, demagogues have made "equality" an almost religious dogma. But if we would have a true equality, let it be based not upon pulling down to the lowest level those remaining descendants of the nobility. Rather, let us show our own mettle by trying to live up to the knightly code that made their fathers noble *in deed*.

✦CHAPTER 24✦
Nostalgia, Revival, and Restoration

NOSTALGIA

Nostalgia is one of the most powerful emotions in the human psyche, not least because change—so often for the worse—is one of the most powerful realities we all face. Some of this change, be it political, cultural, or religious, is specific to whatever era we live in. But much of it is quite literally perennial. The cycle of seasons and holidays, of months, of days of the week—even of hours of the day, as immortalised in the Divine Office—is the backdrop against which we live out our lives. The difference between these lives of ours and the eternally recurring observances in them is that the former are winding down. Birth, childhood, youth, middle age, senescence, and death are the waystations on the one-way trip toward the four last things we are all taking, and from which—until doomsday—there is no return (unless God allows us to come back briefly from purgatory to ask for prayers and Masses,[1] or we reach heaven and later appear on this earth to help the faithful). No amount of money, wisdom, honour, or renown—or their respective opposites—can alter this reality. No matter how deeply or intensely we love, our families and friends, like ourselves, shall depart this world, and each lasting relationship we have must end in death—theirs or ours. As Hebrews 13:14 puts it, "We have not here an abiding city."

To this dark reality, there are several reactions. One may try to live as virtuous a life as possible, in order to secure a happy eternity; or he might say with the Epicureans, "eat, drink, and be happy, for tomorrow we die!" But just as both saints and sinners share human nature, so too do they share basic emotions. And one clear emotion, common to most of humanity when faced with the transitory nature of things

---

[1] See André Marie, "Rome's Purgatory Museum: A November Pilgrimage," *Catholicism.org*, November 15, 2008, https://catholicism.org/ad-rem-no-90.html.

and the horror of adverse change, is longing for the eternal, the unchanging—be it religion, literature, or sport. Another is to seek refuge in the past—that is, nostalgia.

On a recent trip with friends to New England, I drove through the town of Newton, Massachusetts. The houses of the section we were in, with their different styles and myriad of May flowers, evoked something in me.[2] I could not figure out what it was until one of my companions said, "you can cut the nostalgia with a knife!" Indeed, you could have. To be sure, nostalgia is a potent force. In today's fractured TV scene, it powers whole "classic television" networks like MeTV, COZI TV, and Antenna TV, which allow you to curl up in front of your set and enjoy your favourite programmes from whichever of the past seven decades was your own golden childhood and youth. YouTube allows you to find videos of the songs from "your era," and there are always professional sports, classic cars, and old movies to send you back to that special time.

If you should like something a bit more "live-action" to take you even further elsewhen, fear not! The Art Deco Societies, the Renaissance Pleasure Faires and the Revels, or the Society for Creative Anachronism all await your pleasure. You might join a military reenactment unit, take part in one of the few remaining symphonic outdoor dramas, join a live action role-playing group, or volunteer at a living history museum. Too frothy for you? Not to worry; you can take part in serious historical preservation of our built heritage, or else join societies dedicated to the study of such figures as Sir William Wallace, Owain Glendower, or Richard III. Too remote in time? You can join similar groups studying the life of Churchill, or chronicle the New Deal and all its works and pomps.[3] There are the wide range of presidential homes and libraries you can throw yourself into, to live again the reign of whomever you consider to have been America's brightest and best. If that is too far removed from you, you might qualify for one of the hereditary societies and so be able to celebrate your worshipful fathers' great contributions to our land.

---

[2] For a sampling of the neighborhood, see "Upper Falls Historic District Funding Program," The Newton Upper Falls Historic District, City of Newton, June 30, 1978, https://web.archive.org/web/20150717071252/http://www.newtonma.gov/civicax/filebank/documents/45557.

[3] See *Living New Deal*, accessed February 6, 2025, https://livingnewdeal.org/.

Nor need nostalgia be purely personal; it can be political too. For Britons who miss the Conservative Party, there is the Monday Club; if they are Jacobites, they could join the Royal Stuart Society. The French have Legitimist, Orleanist, and Bonapartist heirs, as well as the Action Française and the Alliance Royale, to name a couple of monarchist groups. There are still Spanish Carlists and Portuguese royalists, and the Habsburgs retain devotees in Austria, Hungary, Czechia, and the rest of their former Empire. Italy is awash with political nostalgia; Umberto II, the last king, still has many fans, as do his son and nephew, who are competing for the empty throne. There are those who would see a Catholic and united Italy, and those who would undo the Risorgimento — restoring the Kingdom of the Two Sicilies (under either the Calabria or the Castro branch of the Sovereign House), the Grand Duchy of Tuscany (with its own Habsburgs), the Duchies of Parma and Modena, the Lombard-Venetian Kingdom — even, to some degree anyway, the Papal States. Germany is even more complex, since some of its monarchists favour the united Empire, but Prussia, Bavaria, Saxony, Hanover, and all the other states retain their claimants. Russia's heiress has her adherents; Poland has monarchists but no heir. The Greek, Bulgarian, Romanian, Serbian, and Albanian royals live once more in their native lands, carry out official duties, and are awaiting what may come. Japan's Nippon Kaigi ("Japan Conference") would like to return to the pre-war constitution — among other things, strengthening the position of the emperor, restoring state patronage of Shinto, and regaining the right to wage war — and the current prime minister, Shigeru Ishiba, is a member. But don't think such political nostalgia overseas is restricted to monarchists. Far from it! Mussolini, de Gaulle, Pétain, Schuman, Franco, Adenauer, Salazar, De Gasperi, the Peróns, von Stauffenberg and his companions, Dollfuss, von Moltke, Hammarskjöld, and Pinochet all have their advocates today, as do Mexico's Sinarquistas and Brazil's Integralistas. Some might gasp at my bracketing these folk together; but it is not about whether they agreed among themselves or whether this writer likes them or not. It is that they all lived quite a while ago and yet retain impassioned adherents who believe that the views of their heroes would be of use today.

And so it is here in our own country, where such political nostalgia is also rampant — and never more than now. The Federalist Society and the Constitution Party would like to return to the nation's foundational documents (the American Solidarity Party would add Catholic social teaching to them); the League of the South and the Abbeville Institute wish to resurrect the "Lost Cause" of the Confederacy. There remain fans of Huey Long and Fr. Charles Coughlin, while the Orange Order in the US and the Ancient Order of Hibernians continue to filter our political present through the Irish past. Nor is the politics of nostalgia confined to American conservatives; the modern left consciously or otherwise longs for a reincarnation of the New Deal. Similarly, the American Federation of Labor and Congress of Industrial Organizations (AFL-CIO), the Grange, the National Association of Manufacturers, and the National Association for the Advancement of Colored People (NAACP) are all fuelled by dreams of their respective glorious pasts — pasts that featured successes through appeals to common principles rarely held today, at least by those in power. There is also nonpartisan political nostalgia to enjoy: the Benevolent and Protective Order of Elks, the American Legion, the Veterans of Foreign Wars (VFW), the Knights of Columbus, and so many others promote loyalty and patriotism — to the country of my childhood, of those principles mentioned above, not the land desecrated by *Roe v. Wade* for so many bloody decades, whose masters finally broke the will of the Boy Scout leadership. Don't get me wrong; I do not disapprove of the nostalgia generated by all of the above organisations, and I am proud to belong to a few of them. But the fact remains that they all look to some aspect of the past to make sense of the present and generate hope for the future — rather than accepting what we have (such as it is) on its own terms.

REVIVALS

Whatever its object and ideology, political nostalgia sees solutions to today's problems in the work of past figures or movements. They may or may not be correct, but usually such nostalgia remains the property of a dedicated few, while politics stumbles along in whatever groove the great and the powerful wish it to. In culture and the arts, however, "revivals" tend to be rather more successful and have more influence on day-to-day life. On the New England trip earlier referenced, my path took me through the towns of Deerfield and Stockbridge, Massachusetts (the latter featuring the über-nostalgic Norman Rockwell Museum), and Litchfield, Connecticut — prime examples of the colonial revival movement that gripped the country in varying degrees from the American centennial of 1876 to World War II, and echoes even today. In addition to the current layout of those towns, it brought us such reconstructions as Colonial Williamsburg, Old Sturbridge Village, and a host of other "living history museums" — to say nothing of innumerable "ye olde" bars and taverns, either real or imitations. It was at once an architectural style and a social movement, the latter countering the perceived corruption and disruption of the "Gilded Age" with the supposed virtue and patriotism of the colonial and revolutionary eras. The basic notion also spawned a number of regional "revival" styles: Dutch, French, Spanish, Mission, Monterey, and Santa Fe — to say nothing of that revival named for Queen Anne, who, so far as I can see, had no more to do with it than she did with Blackbeard's ship (though American Catholics should always be grateful to her memory for her intervention on our behalf in Maryland).

But the colonial and accompanying revivals were only the most recent and American versions of another perennial trend in human history. Through the arts and crafts movement, the colonial revival was connected with the Gothic revival that emerged from romanticism's revolt against the dead but revolution-bloodied hand of the neoclassical Enlightenment. Not just in architecture and aesthetics, but in life as well, it posed the seeming unity and peace of the Middle Ages against the horrors the continent had just witnessed (and which, as it turned out, were asleep but not dead). Three Englishmen — Augustus Pugin, John Ruskin with his Guild of St. George, and William Morris — called upon their countrymen to return to the ways of their fathers; this message also came to America, where Ralph Adams Cram was its foremost practitioner. In its wake were such allied movements as the pre-Raphaelites, the Celtic revival, and Merry England; on the continent were many varieties of romantic nationalism, calling upon the members of various long-suppressed nationalities to regain the glory of their ancestors. This was often accompanied by the compiling of or even invention of national epics, ranging from the *Mabinogion* to the *Kalevala*.

Yet the neoclassicism of the Enlightenment was, in the minds of its practitioners, an attempt to push past the bloodshed of the religious wars following the Protestant Revolt and the supposed medieval barbarism to the order and harmony of the Greeks and Romans. It, too, was a revival, in much the same spirit as that of the Renaissance and the humanists — who, however, remained committed to Catholicism; their enemy was the horror and disorder brought on by the Black Plague and the civil wars in England, France, Germany, and Italy, to say nothing of the Great Schism. What all of these attempts at revival had in common — as do the ideas of the political nostalgics touched upon earlier — is the notion of a golden age. If only we could simply do this or that in the manner of whichever paragons we choose, the golden age would return, and the king in the mountain (be he Arthur, Charlemagne, or someone else) would waken, ushering in a new Camelot — or at least, that is what our unexamined emotions might tell us.

There is another use of revival, and that is specifically amongst American evangelicals. Historically, this can refer specifically to three "Great Awakenings" — the first in the early eighteenth, the second in the late eighteenth and early nineteenth, and the third in the late nineteenth and early twentieth centuries; these produced such famous figures as Jonathan Edwards, Dwight Moody, and Billy Graham. But in, with, and under these events there is the "spirit of revival" — an uplifting of fervour among Christians that will result in conversions of those outside the flock. On one occasion I found myself at a luncheon, where I was placed at a tableful of evangelical ministers. They were discussing the prospects of such a revival in the area we were in. All nodded sagely that they thought it was possible. At first glance, such goings-on may seem utterly unconnected to the kinds of revival we have been looking at. But they are not. For what evangelicals are seeking, in their unhistorical way, is a revival of the early Church. Their lack of history not only makes it hard for them to see what that early Church was like, but often causes them to quarrel over the nature of pristine Christianity — as, for example, whether the first Christians had the gift of tongues in the sense that Pentecostals mean it. Nevertheless, it does represent an attempt to return to a golden age, of sorts.

RESTORATIONS

When revolutions occur, those who fight them are often divided as to what they are fighting for; it is rarely simply a return to the status quo. Most often, theorists on the counter-revolutionary side ponder what went wrong — for something must have, or things would not have gone as they did. So it was for Joseph de Maistre and Louis de Bonald in the wake of the French Revolution, and for Joseph Galloway in the wake of the American. It is rare that they get the chance to put Humpty-Dumpty back together again. Even if they manage to do so, restoration rarely works, as we saw with Mary Tudor's attempt to restore England to communion with Rome forever. In eerie emulation of each other, England's Charles I and France's Louis XVI were beheaded; their "reasonable" successors, Charles II and Louis XVIII, were able to manage reigning alongside the forces that were to some degree responsible for their predecessors' murder — they had to be. But *their* successors, James II and Charles X, were unable to, and they were replaced by the more malleable William of Orange and Louis Philippe. Try as one might, in political life, what has been broken cannot be simply fixed. Both of those periods in English and French history are called the "Restoration" — and it is that idea we must look at, for it is really "restoration" that both revival and nostalgia hope to bring about. What would happen should they succeed?

Alas, moments in life and in history are like dishes; they may be broken and repaired, but the break always remains, however well the pieces are glued together. Napoleon, having come to power as the incarnation of the Revolution, decided that what was needed in Europe was the restoration of the Carolingian Empire — he would be the new Charlemagne. But, for all that, he forced the then Holy Roman Emperor, Francis II, to abdicate the imperial throne, and tried to emulate Justinian in promulgating his own code of law. His Empire first fell short and then fell to pieces. Abraham Lincoln sought to restore the Union by launching the bloodiest conflict this country had ever been engaged in, and he succeeded in reconquering the South.

But he could not restore the United States as it had been — the states that produced writers such as Irving, Hawthorne, Cooper, and Poe; the poet Longfellow; the composer Foster; and statesmen such as Webster, Clay, and Calhoun. Instead, there was (rather than *were*) the United States as it would be until FDR — a unified country to be sure, with many benefits, but not the nation Abe had set out to restore. Emperor Meiji's "restoration" in Japan looked very little like that country's pre-Tokugawa past. Chiang Kai-Shek, after determining that China had to regain some continuity with her religious and cultural past (as Napoleon had done regarding France), ceased to be a revolutionary in 1928. A Methodist himself, he believed that some melding of Western technology, Christianity, and Confucian philosophy was necessary to save his country, which was then beset by both Moscow and Tokyo. When the Japanese offered the last emperor of China, Puyi, the rulership of Manchuria in 1931, Chiang offered the emperor restoration of some of his former prerogatives. Puyi did not believe Chiang — in no small part because he had not punished the soldiers who looted the imperial tombs. So Puyi presided over the disastrous "restoration" of Manchukuo, while Chiang attempted to create a form of Confucianism that could guide a state without an emperor, whose position was key to Confucian concepts. As it happened, he lost the mainland in the Chinese Civil War but was able to try out his notions on Taiwan, where they were quite successful. While the Confucian temples in Taipei and Tainan continue to be supported by the government, the Taiwan of today is far from what Chiang envisioned.

YEARNING FOR THE AGE TO COME

What, then, can we learn from this collection of failed fantasies? That nostalgia, revival, and restoration are pointless exercises in futility? By no means! Humanly speaking, they most often fail to accomplish their goal of returning to the golden age. But it is an attempt that must be made in the face of an arrogant "modernity," even though what is called "modern" and what opposes it are at once both mutable and perennial, as Orson Welles once elegantly explained.[4] Beyond

---

[4] Tim2muntU, "Orson Welles on Falstaff," posted January 6, 2013, YouTube,

that, while they may not restore some fancied Camelot, they very often produce worthwhile things of their own, as the beautiful buildings created worldwide by the various architectural revivals show.

This, however, is all on the natural level. But a desire to restore the past can do more; it can, if a person is of good will, lead him to contemplate what transcends all ages. The yearning for the Latin Mass—if it is done purely because "that's what we had when I was a kid"—is indeed an exercise in nostalgia. But if it is instead a desire to transcend the immediate, to enter into communion with the eternal and unchanging Blessed Sacrament, as it was at the Last Supper and Calvary, and upon all the world's altars, past, present, and to come—well, that is something different. For many of us, that first step made for nostalgia's sake is a necessary one; we often can approach the higher things only through the medium of the lesser.

So, too, with all of the attempts at concretizing nostalgia we have looked at in this chapter. Even a devotee of Mussolini may discover Bl. Ildefonso Schuster; or a Protestant seeking revival might just discover the Holy Ghost working in the Catholic Church. Both the nostalgic's search for the perfect past (his own or someone else's) and the revivalist's quest for a golden age are really unconscious yearnings for heaven, the "land of the living," the "realms of endless day." The Church's footprints are all over every aspect of life, art, culture, and history, ready to lead the good-willed thither.

---

https://web.archive.org/web/20190512141501/https://www.youtube.com/watch?v=zHyKbnw734Y.

⁍ ENVOI ⁌

NOW WE ARE COME TO THE END OF OUR TRAVels together. I can only hope that these essays, originally written at very different times during my life and career, have helped you form your own views in these matters. My opinions regarding monarchy have changed little over the years; if anything, the events I have witnessed in the world have confirmed me in them. But I shall take my leave of you with one of my favourite endings to one of my favourite books—Sir Thomas Malory in *Le Morte d'Arthur* (London, 1485), suitably altered to our circumstances:

HERE IS THE END OF THE BOOK OF THE Compleat Monarchist. I pray you all, gentlemen and gentlewomen that read this book of Monarchy, from the beginning to the ending, pray for me while I am alive, that God send me good deliverance, and when I am dead, I pray you all pray for my soul. For this book was ended the third year of the reign of King Charles the Third, by Charles Coulombe, gentleman, as Jesu help him for his great might, as he is the servant of Jesu both day and night.

◆ ◆
◆

⤛BIBLIOGRAPHY⤜

WORKS CITED

"About The Miller Center: Who We Are." University of Virginia, February 6, 2025, https://millercenter.org/about/who-we-are.

André Marie. "Rome's Purgatory Museum: A November Pilgrimage." *Catholicism.org*, November 15, 2008, https://catholicism.org/ad-rem-no-90.html.

Anonymous [Valentin Tomberg]. *Meditations on the Tarot: A Journey into Christian Hermeticism*. Translated by Robert Powell. Jeremy P. Tarcher/Penguin, 2002.

"The Authorised Liturgy for the Coronation Rite of His Majesty King Charles III." The Church of England, May 6, 2023, www.royal.uk/sites/default/files/documents/2023-05/23-24132%20Coronation%20Liturgy_05%20May_0.pdf.

Ayuso Torres, Miguel. "Spanish Carlism: An Introduction." *Catholicism.org*, January 27, 2016, https://catholicism.org/spanish-carlism-an-introduction.html.

Babcock, C. Merton, ed. *Henry Wadsworth Longfellow: Selected Poems*. Peter Pauper Press, 1982.

Baltimore Catechism II. TAN Books, 2010.

Belloc, Hilaire. *Europe and the Faith*. Paulist Press, 1921.

——. *The House of Commons and Monarchy*. George Allen & Unwin, 1920.

Benedict XVI. "Address of His Holiness Benedict XVI to the Roman Curia Offering Them His Christmas Greetings." December 22, 2005, www.vatican.va/content/benedict-xvi/en/speeches/2005/december/documents/hf_ben_xvi_spe_20051222_roman-curia.html.

——. "Full text of Benedict XVI's recent, rare, and lengthy interview." *Catholic News Agency*, March 17, 2016, www.catholicnewsagency.com/news/33591/full-text-of-benedict-xvis-recent-rare-and-lengthy-interview.

——. "Homily for the Mass of Possession of the Chair of the Bishop of Rome," May 7, 2005.

Berthe, Augustine. *Garcia Moreno*. Translated by Lady Herbert. Dolorosa Press, 2006.

Bilmanis, Alfred. *A History of Latvia*. Princeton University Press, 1951.

Boswell, James. *The Life of Samuel Johnson*. Henry Baldwin, 1791.

Bryce, James. *The Holy Roman Empire*. Macmillan Company, 1913.

Carpenter, Humphrey. *The Inklings: C. S. Lewis, J. R. R. Tolkien, Charles Williams, and Their Friends*. Houghton Mifflin, 1979.

——. *J. R. R. Tolkien: A Biography*. Houghton Mifflin, 2000.

——, ed. *The Letters of J. R. R. Tolkien*. Houghton Mifflin, 1981.

Caudron, André. "La Tour du Pin Chambly, René, marquis de la Charce." *Le Maitron*, March 30, 2010, https://maitron.fr/spip.php?article82173.

Cazamian, Louis. *The Social Novel in England 1830–1850*. Translated by Martin Fido. Routledge & Kegan Paul, 1973.

Chase, Allan. *Falange: The Axis Secret Army in the Americas*. G. P. Putnam's Sons, 1943.

Chateaubriand, François-René de. *The Genius of Christianity: Or, the Spirit and Beauty of the Christian Religion* (Baltimore, 1856).

Churchill, Winston S. *The Second World War: Triumph and Tragedy*. Houghton Mifflin Company, 1953.

Cosh, Colby. "Crowns and Chaos in the Middle East." *Maclean's*, January 22, 2012, https://macleans.ca/uncategorized/crowns-and-chaos-in-the-middle-east/.

Coulombe, Charles A. *Blessed Charles of Austria: A Holy Emperor and His Legacy*. TAN Books, 2020.

Cram, Ralph Adams. "Invitation to Monarchy." *The American Mercury* (1936): 479–86.

Crumbaugh, Justin and Nil Santiánez, eds. *Spanish Fascist Writing*. Translated by María Soledad Barbón, et al. University of Toronto Press, 2021.

Curry, Patrick. *Defending Middle-Earth: Tolkien, Myth and Modernity*. St. Martin's Press, 1997.

Davis, Michael Warren. "Why I'm a Monarchist." *The Imaginative Conservative*, March 13, 2014, https://theimaginativeconservative.org/2014/03/im-monarchist.html.

de Leonardis, Massimo. "Monarchism in Italy." *Royal Stuart Review* 8, no. 1 (1990).

de Maistre, Joseph. *Lettres d'un royaliste savoisien a ses compatriotes*. H. Pelagaud fils et Roblot, 1793.

de Mattei, Roberto. "The *Ralliement* of Leo XIII: A Pastoral Experience that Moved Away from Doctrine." *Rorate Caeli*, March 19, 2015, https://rorate-caeli.blogspot.com/2015/03/the-ralliement-ofleo-xiii-pastoral.html.

Derrick, Michael. *The Portugal of Salazar*. Campion Books, 1939.

Dickens, Charles. *The Chimes*. Baker & Taylor Company, 1908.

Dimbleby, Jonathan. *The Prince of Wales: A Biography*. Little, Brown & Co., 1994.

Disraeli, Benjamin. *Coningsby*. London, 1844.

"Empire." *Encyclopaedia Britannica: A Dictionary of Arts, Sciences, Literature and General Information*. Volume 9, pp. 347–56. Cambridge University Press, 1910.

Ederer, Rupert J., ed. *The Social Teachings of Wilhelm Emmanuel von Ketteler: Bishop of Mainz (1811–1877)*. University Press of America, 1981.

Epstein, Klaus. *The Genesis of German Conservatism*. Princeton University Press, 1966.

Farington, Joseph. *The Farington Diary*. Edited by James Greig. George H. Doran Company, 1923.

Fejérdy, Gergely. "Politics in Light of the Eucharist—Otto von Habsburg at the International Eucharistic Congresses." Otto von Hapsburg Foundation, September 7, 2021, https://habsburgottoalapitvany.hu/en/politics-in-light-ofthe-eucharist-otto-von-habsburg-at-the-international-eucharistic-congresses/.

Fenyvesi, Charles. *Splendor in Exile: The Ex-Majesties of Europe*. New Republic Books, 1979.

Fimister, Alan. *The Iron Sceptre of the Son of Man: Romanitas as a Note of the Church*. Os Justi Press, 2023.

Freeman, Elizabeth, ed. *The Traditionalist's Anthology*. Farnham Printing Company, 1986.

Frier, Bruce W., ed. *The Codex of Justinian*. Translated by Fred H. Blume. Cambridge University Press, 2016.

Gautier, Léon. *Chivalry*. London, 1891.

"Grundsätze." Paneuropa. Accessed February 6, 2025, www.paneuropa.at/philosophie/grundsaetze/.

Guéranger, Prosper. *The Liturgical Year*. Translated by Laurence Shepherd. Newman Press, 1949–52.

Hadfield, Alice Mary. *Charles Williams: An Exploration of His Life and Work*. Oxford University Press, 1983.

Higgins, Colin. *Harold and Maude*. Avon Books, 1971.

Hoffmann, Peter. *The History of the German Resistance, 1933–1945*. MIT Press, 1977.

Hunter, Ryan. "Why I am a Monarchist." *Orthodox in the District*, November 3, 2015, https://ryanphunter.wordpress.com/2015/11/03/why-i-am-a-monarchist/.

John Paul II. "Beatification of Five Servants of God," October 3, 2024, www.vatican.va/content/john-paul-ii/en/homilies/2004/documents/hf_jp-ii_hom_20041003_beatifications.html.

Karl von Habsburg. "Europa, die Freiheit und die Geopolitik." June 14, 2019, http://bit.ly/4iVOu4v.

Kovács, Elisabeth. "Kaiser und König Karl I. (IV.) und die Bischöfe der Österreichisch-ungarischen Monarchie (1916–1922)." *Mitteilungen des Instituts für Österreichische Geschichtsforschung* 109 (2001): 154–72.

Lewis, C. S. *The Chronicles of Narnia*. HarperCollins, 2001.

——. *Of This and Other Worlds*. Fount, 2000.

——. *Present Concerns: A Compelling Collection of Timely, Journalistic Essays*. Edited by Walter Hooper. Harcourt, 1986.

——. *That Hideous Strength*. Scribner, 1996.

Lovecraft, H. P. *Collected Essays*. Edited by S. T. Joshi. Hippocampus Press, 2005.

——. *The Dreams in the Witch House and Other Weird Stories*. Edited by S. T. Joshi. Penguin Books, 2004.

Lukes, Igor. *On the Edge of the Cold War: American Diplomats and Spies in Postwar Prague*. Oxford University Press, 2012.

Luttwak, Edward N. *The Grand Strategy of the Byzantine Empire*. Belknap Press, 2009.

MacKay, Charles. *The Cavalier Songs and Ballads of England from 1642 to 1684*. London, 1863.

"Manifesto of European Identity." Identità Europea, April 19, 1997, https://web.archive.org/web/20230512023113/http://www.identitaeuropea.it/?page_id=862.

Manners, John. *England's Trust, and Other Poems*. London, 1841.

Médaille, John. "Why I am a Monarchist." *Front Porch Republic*, November 29, 2010, www.frontporchrepublic.com/2010/11/why-i-am-a-monarchist/.

Miller, Walter M., Jr. *A Canticle for Leibowitz*. J. B. Lippincott Company, 1960.

Moynihan, Martin, trans. *Letters: C. S. Lewis—Don Giovanni Calabria*. Servant Books, 1988.

Muret, Charlotte Touzalin. *French Royalist Doctrines Since the Revolution*. Columbia University Press, 1933.

Nelson, Eric. *The Royalist Revolution: Monarchy and the American Founding*. Harvard University Press, 2014.

Nichols, Aidan. *Christendom Awake: On Re-Energizing the Church in Culture*. William B. Eerdmans, 1999.

Novalis. *Philosophical Writings*. Translated by Margaret Mahony Stoljar. State University of New York Press, 1997.

Oldmeadow, Ernest. *A Layman's Christian Year*. Burns, Oates & Washbourne, 1938.

Orbán, Viktor. "Speech by Prime Minister Viktor Orbán at the Opening of CPAC Hungary." *The European Conservative*, May 22, 2022, https://europeanconservative.com/articles/commentary/speech-by-prime-minister-viktororban-at-the-opening-of-cpac-hungary/.

O'Rourke, P. J. *Parliament of Whores: A Lone Humorist Attempts to Explain the Entire U. S. Government*. Atlantic Monthly Press, 1991.

Parsons, Robert F. J. *The Role of Jacobitism in the Modern World*. Royal Stuart Society, 1986.

Pearce, Joseph. *Literary Converts: Spiritual Inspiration in an Age of Unbelief*. Ignatius Press, 1999.

Percy, Lord Eustace. *The Heresy of Democracy: A Study in the History of Government*. Eyre & Spottiswoode, 1954.

Potter, Gary. "Blessed Emperor Karl I of Austria and Empress Zita." *Catholicism.org*, October 25, 2004, https://catholicism.org/karlhapsburg.html.

——. *In Reaction*. Neumann Press, 1991.

"Presidents: Hail to the Chief." National Park Service. Accessed February 6, 2025, www.nps.gov/subjects/presidents/index.htm.

"The Principal Proclamation." The Royal Household, September 10, 2022, www.royal.uk/principal-proclamation.

Rogger, Hans. *The European Right: A Historical Profile*. University of California Press, 1965.

Salomon, Ernst von. *The Answers*. Translated by Constantine Fitzgibbon. Putnam, 1954.

Salvucci, Claudio. "Zairean — or Sarum? The Forgotten Congolese Liturgy." In Peter Kwasniewski, ed., *Is African Catholicism a "Vatican II Success Story"?*, 103–12. Os Justi Press, 2025.

Schmid, Cecil. "Kurt Schuschnigg und die 'österreichische Identität': Verortung einer Österreich-Ideologie zwischen zweitem deutschen Staat, Reichsgedanken und österreichischer Sendung." Master's thesis, University of Vienna, 2021, https://doi.org/10.25365/thesis.66145.

Shaw, Joseph, ed. *A Defence of Monarchy: Catholics under a Protestant King*. Angelico Press, 2023.

——. "Medievalism, from Ruskin to Tolkien." In Joseph Shaw, ed., *The Latin Mass and the Intellectuals*, 272–81. Arouca Press, 2023.

Sibley, Agnes. *Charles Williams*. Twayne Publishers, 1982.

Solovyev, Vladimir. *Russia and the Universal Church*. Translated by Herbert Rees. Geoffrey Bles, 1948.

"A Special Note Concerning the Status of Blessed Constantine XI." The Society of St. John Chrysostom of Ayatriada Rum Katoliki Kilise, http://rumkatkilise.org/statusconstantineXI.htm, archived June 22, 2017, at https://archive.ph/gl9u5.

Tannenbaum, Edward R. *The Fascist Experience*. Basic Books, 1972.

Tawney, R. H. *Religion and the Rise of Capitalism: A Historical Study*. Harcourt, Brace and Company, 1926.

Tolkien, J. R. R. *The Lord of the Rings*. Ballantine Books, 1965.

——. *The Silmarillion*. Edited by Christopher Tolkien. Ballantine Books, 1977.

Villarrubia, Eleonore. "Dios, Patria, Fueros, y Rey: The Story of the Spanish Carlistas." *Catholicism.org*, May 17, 2010, https://catholicism.org/dios-patria-fueros-y-rey-the-story-of-the-spanish-carlistas.html.

——. "The Pope's Legion: The Multinational Fighting Force That Defended the Vatican." *Catholicism.org*, December 23, 2008, https://catholicism.org/the-popes-legion-the-multinational-fighting-force-thatdefended-the-vatican-book-review.html.

Wade, Mason. *The French Canadians 1760–1945*. The Macmillan Company, 1955.

Walsh, Thomas. *The Catholic Anthology*. The Macmillan Company, 1927.

Williams, Charles. *Many Dimensions*. Faber & Faber, 1931.

——. *Shadows of Ecstasy*. Faber & Faber, 1931.

——. *War in Heaven*. Faber & Faber, 1962.

RELEVANT WEBSITES

Christendom Awake • http://www.christendom-awake.org/
Paneuropa Union • https://paneuropa.org/
Identità Europea • http://www.identitaeuropea.org/
Sacrum Imperium • http://www.monarchieliga.de/
Europa Cristiana • http://www.europacristiana.it/
Interlingua • http://www.interlingua.fi/ceiafil/ceia.htm
Alliance Royale • http://www.allianceroyale.fr/
Mouvement pour la France • http://www.pourlafrance.fr/accueil.php
CILANE • http://www.cilane.org/
Europa Nostra • http://www.europanostra.org/
European Landowners' Organisation • http://www.elo.org/
FACE—Europe • http://www.face-europe.org/
Scouts d'Europe • http://www.scouts-europe.org/
Notre-Dame de Chrétienté • http://www.nd-chretiente.com/index-
    site.php
Confraternity of St. James • http://www.csj.org.uk/index.htm
European Institute of Cultural Routes • http://www.culture-routes.
    lu/php/fo_index.php?lng=fr&dest=ac_oo_ooo&lng=en

⊰INDEX OF PROPER NAMES⊱

⊰ABOUT THE AUTHOR⊱

CHARLES A. COULOMBE is a contributing editor at *Crisis Magazine* and its European correspondent. He previously served as a columnist for the *Catholic Herald* of London and a film critic for the *National Catholic Register*. A historian recognized internationally for his in-depth knowledge of Vatican politics and the influence of Catholicism in America and Europe, his books include *Puritan's Empire, Star-Spangled Crown*, and *The Pope's Legion*. His audiences regularly range from graduate students at Oxford University, England to the New Mexico Military Institute, from which he graduated. His work has appeared in *New Oxford Review, National Catholic Register, American Thinker, Los Angeles Catholic Mission, Monarchy Canada, Taki's Magazine, OnePeterFive, The Irish Democrat,* and *The European Conservative*. Mr. Coulombe serves as Western U. S. Delegate of the Grand Council of the U. K.-based International Monarchist League and is a member of the Catholic Writer's Guild of Great Britain (the Keys), the Royal Stuart Society, and the Knights of Peter Claver. He resides in Vienna, Austria and Los Angeles, California.

www.ingramcontent.com/pod-product-compliance
Lightning Source LLC
Chambersburg PA
CBHW032050020426
42335CB00011B/271